the soup bible

the
soup
bible

with more than 300 recipes

MURDOCH BOOKS

contents

Like the cleverest sort of quick-change artist, soup can be many different things depending upon the occasion. Some soups present as light, elegant entrées, raising the curtain on a stylish dinner party. Others are entire filling, meals-in-a-bowl, perfect for a casual family repast. Some soups are purée-smooth and silky, while others are composed of heartier ingredients and are thick, chunky and rustic. Soup can be assembled from no more than the freshest of seasonal vegetables, perfect for those wanting low-fat meal ideas, or made indulgent with generous splashes of cream, coconut milk or the best quality olive oil. A soup can be the sort that takes hours to lovingly construct or the type that is whizzed together in a trice, just the thing for days when time is short. Soup can be summery and refreshing (like yoghurt soup or any tomato-based soup), or as warming and wintry as split pea and ham or roasted pumpkin soup. Soups come from all corners of the globe too so, depending on the mood, they can have the tang and spice of Asian flavours, be mellow with classic Mediterranean ingredients or soothe with the tastes and textures of homey favourites; think of chowder, minestrone or gumbo.

Whatever type of soup you choose to make, and whatever the occasion, one thing is for certain — absolutely nothing goes with soup better than bread. And the best bread for soup is always home-made. This can mean yeasty, slow-rise classics like crusty baguette, chewy ciabatta, golden baps, or more quickly constructed goodies like scones, popovers and muffins. The possibilities are endless! With bowls of steaming soup and morsels of crunchy bread at hand, a superbly delicious (not to mention nutritious and easy) meal, first course or snack is never that far away.

hearty soups

Pumpkin soup with harissa

preparation 10–40 minutes
cooking 20 minutes
serves 6

2.5 kg (5 lb 8 oz) pumpkin (winter squash)
750 ml (26 fl oz/3 cups) vegetable stock
750 ml (26 fl oz/3 cups) milk
sugar, to taste

harissa
250 g (9 oz) fresh or dried red chillies
1 tablespoon caraway seeds
1 tablespoon coriander seeds
2 teaspoons cumin seeds
4–6 garlic cloves
1 tablespoon dried mint
125 ml (4 fl oz/½ cup) extra virgin olive oil

Remove the skin, seeds and fibre from the pumpkin and cut into pieces. Simmer, uncovered, in a large saucepan with the stock and milk for 15–20 minutes, or until tender. Cool slightly before transferring to a food processor, and blending, in batches, until smooth. Season the soup with a little sugar and black pepper. Return to a clean saucepan and gently reheat until ready to serve.

To make the harissa, wearing rubber gloves, remove the stems of the chillies, split in half, remove the seeds and soften the flesh in hot water for 5 minutes (or 30 minutes if using dried). Drain and place in a food processor.

While the chillies are soaking, dry-fry the caraway, coriander and cumin seeds in a frying pan for 1–2 minutes, until they become aromatic.

Add the seeds, garlic, mint and 1 teaspoon salt to the food processor and, slowly adding the olive oil, process until a smooth, thick paste forms. Stir the harissa into individual bowls of soup to suit tastes.

Remove the skin, seeds and fibre from the pumpkin before cutting the flesh into pieces.

Dry-fry the seeds over medium heat until they become aromatic.

hearty soups

Meal-in-a-bowl soup with gorgonzola toasts

preparation 20 minutes
cooking 1 hour 15 minutes
serves 4

2 tablespoons oil
1 onion, cut into 2 cm (¾ inch) chunks
1 leek, white part only, cut into 2 cm (¾ inch) chunks
1 carrot, thickly sliced
1 fresh bay leaf
1.25 litres (44 fl oz/5 cups) vegetable or chicken stock
400 g (15½ oz) tin chopped tomatoes
2 tablespoons tomato paste (concentrated purée)
110 g (3¾ oz/½ cup) pearl barley
¼ white cabbage (about 300 g/10½ oz), core removed,
then cut into 2 cm (¾ inch) chunks
400 g (14 oz) tin borlotti beans, rinsed and drained
1 small handful chopped basil (optional)

gorgonzola toasts
4 slices of ciabatta or other rustic bread
100 g (3½ oz) gorgonzola cheese, crumbled

Heat the oil in a large heavy-based saucepan over medium heat. Sauté the onion, leek and carrot for 5 minutes, or until softened but not browned.

Stir in the bay leaf, stock, tomatoes, tomato paste, barley and cabbage. Bring to the boil, then reduce the heat to medium–low. Cover and simmer the soup for 1 hour, or until the vegetables and barley are tender. Season to taste with sea salt and freshly ground black pepper and stir in the borlotti beans. Return to a simmer, then reduce the heat to low, cover and keep warm.

Meanwhile, to make the gorgonzola toasts, heat the grill (broiler) to medium, then put the bread slices on a baking tray and cook under the grill for 2 minutes on each side, or until golden. Sprinkle the gorgonzola over the toasts and cook until the cheese has melted.

Ladle the hot soup into bowls and sprinkle with the basil, if using. Serve the soup with the hot gorgonzola toasts.

Milanese-style minestrone

preparation 15 minutes + overnight soaking
cooking 2 hours 30 minutes
serves 6

225 g (8 oz) dried borlotti beans
55 g (2 oz) butter
1 onion, finely chopped
1 garlic clove, finely chopped
3 tablespoons parsley, finely chopped
2 sage leaves
100 g (3½ oz) pancetta, cubed
2 celery stalks, halved, then sliced
2 carrots, sliced
3 potatoes, peeled but left whole
1 teaspoon tomato paste (concentrated purée)
400 g (14 oz) tin chopped tomatoes
8 basil leaves
3 litres (104 fl oz/12 cups) chicken or vegetable stock
2 zucchini (courgettes), sliced
225 g (8 oz) shelled peas
125 g (4½ oz) runner beans, cut into 4 cm (1½ inch) lengths
¼ cabbage, shredded
220 g (7¾ oz/1 cup) risotto rice
grated parmesan cheese, to serve

Put the dried beans in a large bowl, cover with cold water and soak overnight. Drain and rinse under cold water.

Melt the butter in a large saucepan. Add the onion, garlic, parsley, sage and pancetta. Cook over low heat, stirring until the onion is soft.

Add the celery, carrot and potatoes, and cook for 5 minutes. Stir in the tomato paste, tomatoes, basil and borlotti beans. Season with pepper. Add the stock and bring slowly to the boil. Cover and simmer for 2 hours, stirring once or twice.

If the potatoes have not broken up, roughly break them up with a fork. Taste for seasoning and add the zucchini, peas, runner beans, cabbage and rice. Simmer until the rice is cooked. Serve with the parmesan cheese.

Soak the borlotti beans in cold water overnight, then drain and rinse them.

Bottom: Milanese-style minestrone. Top: Meal-in-a-bowl soup with gorgonzola toasts.

Peppered vegetable hotpot

preparation 30 minutes
cooking 1 hour 5 minutes
serves 8–10

2 tablespoons olive oil
2 onions, chopped
2 leeks, white part only, chopped
2 garlic cloves, crushed
1.5 litres (52 fl oz/6 cups) chicken stock
2 tablespoons chopped rosemary
1–2 teaspoons green peppercorns
4 large potatoes, cubed
2 large turnips, cubed
200 g (7 oz) broccoli, cut into small florets
200 g (7 oz) cauliflower, cut into small florets
155 g (5½ oz/1 cup) fresh or frozen peas

Heat the oil in a large heavy-based saucepan and cook the onion and leek over medium heat for 10 minutes, or until tender. Add the garlic and cook for 1 minute further.

Add the stock, rosemary, peppercorns and potato to the pan. Bring to the boil and then reduce the heat, cover and leave to simmer for 30 minutes. Add the turnip and allow to simmer for a further 15 minutes.

Add the broccoli, cauliflower and peas. Simmer, uncovered, for 5 minutes. Season with salt and black pepper to taste.

Hint *Serve as a main course with pesto and crusty bread.*

Caribbean black bean soup

preparation 20 minutes + overnight soaking
cooking 1 hour 30 minutes
serves 6

440 g (15½ oz) dried black beans
2 tablespoons oil
1 large onion, sliced
1 teaspoon ground coriander
2 teaspoons ground cumin
½ teaspoon chilli powder
2 garlic cloves, crushed
300 g (10½ oz) bacon bones
2 tablespoons red wine vinegar
1 tablespoon soft brown sugar
3 spring onions (scallions), finely chopped
1 tablespoon chopped parsley
2 hard-boiled eggs, chopped

Put the black beans in a large bowl, cover with cold water and soak overnight. Drain.

Heat the oil in a large saucepan and cook the onion over medium heat for 5 minutes, until softened. Add the coriander, cumin, chilli powder and garlic to the pan and cook for 1 minute.

Add the bacon bones and 1.125 litres (39 fl oz/4½ cups) cold water, stirring well to scrape the spices from the base of the pan. Add the black beans and bring to the boil, then reduce the heat and simmer, partially covered, for 1–1½ hours, or until the beans are very soft.

Remove and discard the bacon bones. Stir in the red wine vinegar and brown sugar. Season. For a thicker soup, mash the beans slightly with a potato masher. Garnish with the spring onions, parsley and hard-boiled egg to serve.

Note *Black beans are also known as turtle beans and are available at good delicatessens. They are not to be confused with Chinese black beans.*

Storage time *The soup will keep, covered, in the refrigerator, for up to 2 days, but will become very thick. Thin it down with chicken stock or water to reheat.*

Add the broccoli, cauliflower and peas for the last 5 minutes of cooking.

Add the garlic and spices to the fried onion and cook for 1 minute.

Bottom: Caribbean black bean soup. Top: Peppered vegetable hotpot.

15

Thai prawn, pumpkin and coconut soup

preparation 20 minutes
cooking 30 minutes
serves 4

250 g (9 oz) small raw prawns (shrimp)
½ teaspoon shrimp paste
2 long red chillies, chopped
¼ teaspoon white peppercorns
2 tablespoons chilli paste
2 garlic cloves
3 teaspoons vegetable oil
5 spring onions (scallions), sliced
125 ml (4 fl oz/½ cup) coconut cream
500 ml (17 fl oz/2 cups) chicken stock
2 lemon grass stems, white part only, bruised
875 ml (30 fl oz/3½ cups) coconut milk
750 g (1 lb 10 oz) pumpkin (winter squash), cut into 2 cm (¾ inch) cubes
1 tablespoon fish sauce
4 tablespoons Thai basil leaves

Peel the prawns and gently pull out the dark vein from each prawn back, starting from the head end.

Wrap the shrimp paste in foil and place it under a hot grill (broiler) for 1 minute. Unwrap the foil and put the shrimp paste in a food processor with the red chilli, peppercorns, chilli paste, garlic and a pinch of salt, and process until smooth. Set aside.

Heat a wok over high heat, add the oil and swirl to coat the side. Cook the spring onion for 1–2 minutes, or until lightly golden, then remove from the wok and set aside. Add the coconut cream and bring to the boil over high heat, then reduce the heat and simmer for 10 minutes, or until the oil starts to separate from the cream — this is called cracking.

Stir in the paste mixture and simmer over medium heat for 1–2 minutes, or until fragrant. Add the stock, lemon grass, coconut milk, pumpkin and spring onion, cover with a lid and simmer for 8–10 minutes, or until the pumpkin is tender. Remove the lid, add the prawns and cook for another 2–3 minutes, or until the prawns are cooked through. Stir in the fish sauce and basil and serve.

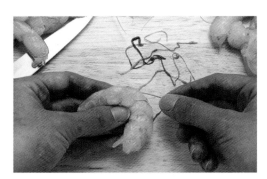

Peel the prawns, discarding the heads and tails, and gently pull out the dark veins.

Spoon the coconut cream out of the tin and measure out the required quantity.

La ribollita
(Tuscan bean soup)

preparation 15 minutes
cooking 1 hour 10 minutes
serves 4

80 ml (2½ fl oz/⅓ cup) olive oil
1 onion, finely chopped
1 large carrot
3 celery stalks
2 garlic cloves, crushed
1 zucchini (courgette), finely chopped
400 g (14 oz) cooked cannellini or borlotti beans
400 g (14 oz) tinned crushed tomatoes
1 whole dried chilli
250 g (9 oz) cavolo nero, leaves chopped
200 ml (7 fl oz) red wine
1 litre (35 fl oz/4 cups) chicken stock
75 g (2½ oz) stale country-style bread,
such as ciabatta or pugliese, crusts removed
extra virgin olive oil, to serve

Pour the oil into a large saucepan and add the onion. Gently cook the onion over low heat. Finely chop the carrot and the celery and add to the pan. Add the garlic, then leave to cook for a few minutes.

Add the zucchini to the pan and cook, stirring occasionally, for about 5 minutes, or until the vegetables are translucent and have soaked up some of the oil. Stir in the beans and cook for 5 minutes, then add the tinned tomatoes and chilli and cook for a further 5 minutes to reduce the liquid.

Add the cavolo nero and stir into the soup until it has just wilted. Add the red wine and stock and gently simmer for about 40 minutes.

Break the bread into 2.5 cm (1 inch) pieces and add to the pan. Mix briefly and remove the pan from the heat. Leave for about 30 minutes to rest the soup. Serve hot with a generous drizzle of extra virgin olive oil.

Heat the oil in a saucepan, add the onion and cook until turning golden.

Barley soup with
golden parsnips

preparation 15 minutes + overnight soaking
cooking 2 hours 30 minutes
serves 6

200 g (7 oz) pearl barley
1 tablespoon oil
2 onions, chopped
2 garlic cloves, finely chopped
2 carrots, chopped
2 potatoes, chopped
2 celery stalks, chopped
2 bay leaves, torn in half
2 litres (70 fl oz/8 cups) chicken stock
125 ml (4 fl oz/½ cup) milk
40 g (1½ oz) butter
3 parsnips, cubed
1 teaspoon soft brown sugar
chopped parsley, to serve

Soak the barley in water overnight. Drain, then place in a saucepan with 2 litres water. Bring to the boil, then reduce the heat and simmer, partially covered, for 1¼ hours, or until tender. Drain the barley.

Heat the oil in a large saucepan and add the onion, garlic, carrot, potato and celery. Cook for 3 minutes. Stir well and cook, covered, for 15 minutes over low heat, stirring often.

Add the drained barley, bay leaves, stock, milk, 2 teaspoons salt and 1 teaspoon black pepper. Bring to the boil, then reduce the heat and simmer the soup, partially covered, for 35 minutes. If the soup is too thick, add about 250 ml (9 fl oz/1 cup) cold water, a little at a time, until the soup reaches your preferred consistency.

While the soup is simmering, melt the butter in a frying pan, add the parsnip and toss in the butter. Sprinkle with the brown sugar and cook until golden brown and tender. Serve the parsnip on top of the soup, sprinkled with the chopped parsley.

Chop the potato, carrot and celery so that they are roughly the same size.

Bottom: Barley soup with golden parsnips. Top: La ribollita.

Fast pasta soup

preparation 10 minutes
cooking 10 minutes
serves 4

1 tablespoon oil
2 spring onions (scallions), chopped
150 g (5½ oz) snow peas (mangetout),
trimmed and cut into pieces
200 g (7 oz) mushrooms, sliced
2 garlic cloves, crushed
1 teaspoon grated fresh ginger
1 litre (35 fl oz/4 cups) vegetable stock
150 g (5½ oz) angel hair pasta

Heat the oil in a saucepan over medium heat and stir-fry the spring onion, snow peas and mushrooms for a few minutes, or until just tender.

Add the garlic and ginger and stir for 1 minute. Add the vegetable stock and bring to the boil. Add the pasta and cook for 3 minutes, or until tender. Serve immediately.

Leek and potato soup

preparation 5 minutes
cooking 45 minutes
serves 6

50 g (1¾ oz) butter
1 onion, finely chopped
3 leeks, white part only, sliced
1 celery stalk, finely chopped
1 garlic clove, finely chopped
200 g (7 oz) potatoes, chopped
750 ml (26 fl oz/3 cups) chicken stock
220 ml (7½ fl oz) cream
2 tablespoons snipped chives

Melt the butter in a large saucepan. Add the onion, leek, celery and garlic. Cover and cook over low heat, stirring occasionally, for 15 minutes, or until the vegetables are softened but not browned. Add the potato and stock and bring to the boil.

Reduce the heat and simmer, covered, for 20 minutes. Allow the soup to cool a little before puréeing in a blender or food processor, then return to the cleaned saucepan.

Gently return the soup to the boil and stir in the cream. Season with salt and white pepper and reheat without boiling. Serve either hot or well chilled. Garnish with the chives.

Carrot soup with caraway butter

preparation 20 minutes
cooking 40 minutes
serves 6

caraway butter
1 tablespoon caraway seeds
125 g (4½ oz) butter, softened

1 onion, chopped
1 garlic clove, crushed
750 g (1 lb 10 oz) carrots, chopped
1 litre (35 fl oz/4 cups) vegetable stock
250 ml (9 fl oz/1 cup) orange juice
rye bread, to serve

To make the caraway butter, dry-fry the caraway seeds in a frying pan over medium heat for 3–4 minutes, or until they start to brown and release their aroma. Leave to cool and then grind in a spice or coffee grinder until fine. Beat the butter and ground caraway seeds until smooth. Place in a small square of foil, roll into a log and refrigerate for 30 minutes, or until firm.

Put the onion, garlic, carrot, stock and orange juice in a pan and bring to the boil. Cover and simmer over low heat for 25 minutes, or until the carrots are cooked. Cool slightly.

Transfer the soup to a blender and blend until smooth. Return to the pan, season to taste and heat through.

Cut the caraway butter into 5 mm (¼ inch) thick slices. Spoon the soup into bowls, top each with two slices of the butter and serve with some rye bread.

Top left: Fast pasta soup. Top right: Leek and potato soup. Bottom left: Carrot soup with caraway butter.

Cannellini bean soup

preparation 20 minutes + overnight soaking
cooking 1 hour 15 minutes
serves 8

500 g (1 lb 2 oz) dried cannellini beans
450 g (1 lb) ripe tomatoes
2 tablespoons olive oil
2 onions, chopped
2 garlic cloves, crushed
60 ml (2 fl oz/¼ cup) tomato passata (puréed tomatoes)
2 large carrots, diced
2 celery stalks, diced
1.7 litres (59 fl oz) vegetable or chicken stock
2 bay leaves
2 tablespoons lemon juice
30 g (1 oz) chopped flat-leaf (Italian) parsley

Put the cannellini beans in a bowl, cover with cold water and leave to soak overnight.

Score a cross in the base of each tomato. Put in a heatproof bowl and cover with boiling water. Leave for 30 seconds and then transfer to cold water. Peel the skin away from the cross and roughly chop the flesh.

Drain the beans and rinse under cold water.

Heat the oil in a large saucepan. Add the onion, reduce the heat and cook gently for 10 minutes, stirring occasionally.

Stir in the garlic and cook for 1 minute. Add the cannellini beans, chopped tomato, tomato passata, carrot, celery and stock. Add the bay leaves and stir. Bring to the boil, then reduce the heat to medium–low and simmer, covered, for 45–60 minutes, or until the beans are tender.

Just before serving, stir in the lemon juice and then season, to taste. Stir in the chopped parsley.

Soak the dried cannellini beans overnight in a bowl of cold water.

Score a cross in the base of the tomatoes, soak in boiling water for 30 seconds, then drain and peel.

Pumpkin, lentil and tomato soup
with cheesy toasts

preparation 20 minutes
cooking 30 minutes
serves 4

2 tablespoons olive oil
1 kg (2 lb 4 oz) pumpkin (winter squash), peeled,
and cut into 2 cm (¾ inch) chunks
2 carrots, finely chopped
2 onions, finely chopped
1 large celery stalk, finely chopped
3 garlic cloves, crushed
1.5 litres (52 fl oz/6 cups) vegetable or chicken stock
125 g (4½ oz/½ cup) red lentils
400 g (14 oz) tin chopped tomatoes
1 tablespoon finely chopped parsley or
coriander (cilantro) leaves

cheesy toasts
8 slices of ciabatta or other rustic bread,
cut about 2 cm (¾ inch) thick
85 g (3 oz/⅔ cup) finely grated cheddar cheese

Heat the oil in a large saucepan over medium heat. Add the vegetables and garlic and sauté for 5 minutes, or until softened but not browned.

Stir in the stock, lentils and tomatoes. Bring to the boil, then reduce the heat to medium–low and simmer for 20 minutes, or until the lentils are tender. Season well with sea salt and freshly ground black pepper.

Meanwhile, to make the cheesy toasts, heat the grill (broiler) to medium, then place the bread on a baking tray and toast under the grill on one side. Turn the toasts over and scatter with the grated cheese. Grill (broil) for 3–4 minutes, or until the cheese has melted and is golden brown.

Ladle the soup into bowls or cups, sprinkle with parsley and serve with the hot cheesy toasts.

Remove the skin and seeds from the pumpkin, then cut the flesh into cubes.

Discard the stems from the flat-leaf parsley, and finely chop the leaves.

Ratatouille and pasta soup

preparation 25 minutes
cooking 40 minutes
serves 6

1 eggplant (aubergine), chopped
2 tablespoons olive oil
1 large onion, chopped
1 large red capsicum (pepper), seeded and chopped
1 large green capsicum (pepper), seeded and chopped
2 garlic cloves, crushed
3 zucchini (courgettes), sliced
800 g (1 lb 12 oz) tinned crushed tomatoes
1 teaspoon dried oregano leaves
½ teaspoon dried thyme leaves
1 litre (35 fl oz/4 cups) vegetable stock
50 g (1¾ oz) fusilli
parmesan cheese shavings, to serve

To remove any bitterness from the eggplant, spread the pieces out in a colander and sprinkle generously with salt. Set aside for 20 minutes, then rinse thoroughly and pat dry with paper towel.

Heat the olive oil in a large heavy-based saucepan and cook the onion over medium heat for 10 minutes, or until soft and lightly golden. Add the capsicum, garlic, zucchini and eggplant and cook, stirring, for 5 minutes. Add the tomato, herbs and vegetable stock. Bring to the boil, then reduce the heat and simmer for 10 minutes, or until the vegetables are tender.

Add the fusilli and cook for a further 15 minutes, or until the fusilli is tender. Serve sprinkled with parmesan shavings.

Rice soup with fish fillet

preparation 20 minutes
cooking 20 minutes
serves 4

2 tablespoons oil
3–4 large garlic cloves, finely chopped
1.25 litres (44 fl oz/5 cups) vegetable, chicken or fish stock
2½ tablespoons light soy sauce
2 teaspoons preserved radish, sliced
245 g (8½ oz/1⅓ cups) cooked jasmine rice
280 g (10 oz) skinless white fish fillets, cut into bite-sized pieces
1 tablespoon finely sliced fresh ginger
1 spring onion (scallion), finely chopped, to garnish
coriander (cilantro) leaves, to garnish

Heat the oil in a small wok or frying pan. Stir-fry the garlic until light golden, then remove from the heat and discard the garlic, retaining the oil.

Pour the stock into a saucepan and heat it to boiling point. Add the soy sauce, preserved radish and rice and cook over medium heat for 2–3 minutes. Add the fish and ginger and cook for another 1–2 minutes, or until the fish is cooked. Season well, to taste.

Garnish with the spring onion and coriander and sprinkle with ground white pepper and the garlic oil.

Minestra di farro (Farro soup)

preparation 25 minutes + overnight soaking
cooking 2 hours 30 minutes
serves 4

200 g (7 oz) dried borlotti beans
2 tablespoons olive oil
1 small onion, thinly sliced
2 garlic cloves, crushed
1.5 litres (52 fl oz/6 cups) chicken stock
8 mint leaves, roughly torn
200 g (7 oz) farro (spelt)
100 g (3½ oz/1 cup) grated parmesan cheese
1 tablespoon finely chopped mint
1 tablespoon extra virgin olive oil

Soak the borlotti beans in water overnight. Drain and place in a large saucepan with plenty of cold water. Bring to the boil and simmer until tender (about 1½ hours, depending on the age of the beans). Drain.

Heat the oil in a large saucepan and cook the onion over low heat for 6 minutes, or until soft. Season. Add the garlic and cook without browning for 20–30 seconds. Add the stock and torn mint and bring to the boil.

Stir in the farro a little at a time so that the stock continues to boil, then reduce the heat and simmer for 15 minutes. Add the borlotti beans and simmer for 30 minutes, or until the farro is tender and the soup thick. Purée half the soup. Return to the pan and stir in the parmesan and chopped mint. Season and stir in 125–250 ml (4–9 fl oz/½–1 cup) hot water to give a spoonable consistency. Serve immediately, with a teaspoon of the extra virgin olive oil stirred through each bowl.

Top left: Ratatouille and pasta soup. Top right: Rice soup with fish fillet. Bottom left: Minestra di farro.

Pie-crust mushroom soup

preparation 25 minutes
cooking 35 minutes
serves 4

400 g (14 oz) large field mushrooms
60 g (2¼ oz) butter
1 onion, finely chopped
1 garlic clove, crushed
30 g (1 oz/¼ cup) plain (all-purpose) flour
750 ml (26 fl oz/3 cups) chicken stock
2 tablespoons thyme leaves
2 tablespoons sherry
250 ml (9 fl oz/1 cup) cream
1 sheet frozen puff pastry, thawed
1 egg, lightly beaten

Preheat the oven to 200°C (400°F/Gas 6). Peel and roughly chop the mushrooms, including the stems.

Melt the butter in a large saucepan, add the onion and cook over medium heat for 3 minutes, or until soft. Add the garlic and cook for 1 minute. Add the mushrooms and cook until soft. Sprinkle with the flour and stir for 1 minute.

Stir in the stock and thyme and bring to the boil. Reduce the heat and simmer, covered, for 10 minutes. Allow the soup to cool slightly before transferring to a food processor and blending, in batches.

Return the soup to the pan and stir in the sherry and cream. Pour the soup into four ovenproof bowls (use small, deep bowls rather than wide shallow ones, or the pastry may sag into the soup).

Cut rounds of pastry slightly larger than the bowl tops and cover each bowl with pastry. Seal the pastry edges and then lightly brush with the egg. Place the bowls on a baking tray and bake for 15 minutes, or until golden and puffed.

Sprinkle the flour over the softened mushrooms and stir for 1 minute.

Fit the pastry over the bowls and then lightly brush with the egg.

Tarragon, blue-eye trevalla and white bean bourride

preparation 30 minutes
cooking 50 minutes
serves 6

2 tablespoons olive oil
1 onion, finely chopped
2 leeks, white part only, thinly sliced
2 garlic cloves, finely chopped
3 large tomatoes (about 350 g/12 oz each), peeled and chopped
1 x 6 cm (2½ inch) strip orange zest
bouquet garni of thyme, parsley, bay leaf and 3 tarragon sprigs
1.5 litres (52 fl oz/6 cups) fish stock or water
2 x 400 g (14 oz) tins white beans, drained and rinsed
750 g (1 lb 10 oz) blue-eye trevalla or other firm white-fleshed fish, cut into 5–8 cm (2–3¼ inches) chunks
1 tablespoon chopped tarragon leaves

aïoli
3 garlic cloves, crushed
2 teaspoons dijon mustard, at room temperature
1 egg yolk, at room temperature
225 ml (7¾ fl oz) olive oil
2 teaspoons lemon juice

Heat the oil in a large saucepan over medium heat, add the onion, leek and garlic and cook for 5 minutes, or until soft. Add the tomato, orange rind, bouquet garni and fish stock. Bring to the boil, then reduce the heat to low and cook for 30 minutes, or until the liquid has reduced by half.

Strain the liquid, discarding the solids, and return the liquid to the cleaned saucepan. Season to taste with sea salt and freshly ground black pepper. Bring back to the boil, add the beans and fish, reduce the heat to medium–low and cook for 5 minutes, or until the fish is just cooked.

Meanwhile to make the aïoli, crush the garlic with a pinch of salt in a mortar and pestle to form a paste. Transfer to a small bowl, add the dijon mustard and egg yolk and whisk to mix well. Then, whisking constantly, add the olive oil in a slow steady stream until the oil is incorporated and the sauce is very thick. Stir in the lemon juice and season with extra salt if required.

Divide the soup among large shallow bowls. Spoon some aïoli over each and sprinkle with the tarragon leaves. Serve immediately with any remaining aïoli passed separately.

Spiced carrot soup with coriander pesto

preparation 20 minutes
cooking 8 hours
serves 6

2 tablespoons olive oil
1 red onion, diced
1 garlic clove, finely chopped
1 teaspoon cumin seeds
1 teaspoon paprika
1 teaspoon garam masala
3 small red chillies, seeded and finely chopped
6 large carrots, peeled and chopped
1 kg (2 lb 4 oz) sweet potatoes, peeled and diced
2 large desiree potatoes, peeled and diced
1.5 litres (52 fl oz/6 cups) chicken stock
300 ml (10½ fl oz) coconut cream
toasted naan bread, to serve

coriander pesto
45 g (1½ oz/¼ cup) cashew nuts
1 large handful coriander (cilantro) leaves
1 small garlic clove, halved
60 ml (2 fl oz/¼ cup) coconut milk
60 ml (2 fl oz/¼ cup) olive oil

Heat the oil in a frying pan over medium–high heat. Add the onion and garlic and cook, stirring often, for 2–3 minutes, or until the onion has softened. Stir in the spices and chilli and cook for a further 1 minute, or until aromatic.

Spoon the onion and garlic mixture into a slow cooker and add the chopped vegetables and stock. Mix together well. Cover and cook on low for 8 hours.

Meanwhile, near serving time, make the coriander pesto. Put the cashews, coriander, garlic and coconut milk in a food processor and process until the cashews are finely chopped. With the motor running, gradually add the olive oil in a thin steady stream until well combined.

Using a stick blender, purée the soup until smooth. Stir the coconut cream through, then season to taste with sea salt and freshly ground black pepper.

Ladle the soup into serving bowls. Swirl some of the pesto over the top, sprinkle with freshly ground black pepper and serve with toasted naan bread.

Bottom: Spiced carrot soup with coriander pesto. Top: Tarragon, blue-eye trevalla and white bean bourride.

Chickpea and herb dumpling soup

preparation 30 minutes
cooking 35 minutes
serves 4

1 tablespoon oil
1 onion, chopped
2 garlic cloves, crushed
2 teaspoons ground cumin
1 teaspoon ground coriander
¼ teaspoon chilli powder
2 x 300 g (10½ oz) tins chickpeas, drained and rinsed
875 ml (30 fl oz/3½ cups) vegetable stock
2 x 425 g (15 oz) tins chopped tomatoes
1 tablespoon chopped fresh coriander (cilantro) leaves
125 g (4½ oz/1 cup) self-raising flour
30 g (1 oz) butter, chopped
2 tablespoons grated parmesan cheese
2 tablespoons mixed chopped herbs (chives, parsley, coriander)
60 ml (2 fl oz/¼ cup) milk

Heat the oil in a large saucepan and cook the onion over medium heat for 2–3 minutes, or until soft. Add the garlic, cumin, ground coriander and chilli and cook for 1 minute, or until fragrant. Add the chickpeas, stock and tomato and bring to the boil. Reduce the heat and simmer, covered, for 10 minutes. Stir in the coriander.

To make the dumplings, sift the flour into a bowl and add the butter. Rub together with your fingertips until the mixture resembles fine breadcrumbs. Stir in the parmesan and the herbs. Make a well in the centre, add the milk and mix with a flat-bladed knife until just combined. Bring together into a rough ball, then divide the dough into eight portions and roll into small balls.

Add the dumplings to the soup, then cover and simmer for 20 minutes, or until a skewer comes out clean when inserted into the centre of a dumpling.

Curried lentil, carrot and cashew soup

preparation 20 minutes
cooking 25 minutes
serves 6

1.5 litres (52 fl oz/6 cups) vegetable or chicken stock
750 g (1 lb 10 oz) carrots, grated
185 g (6½ oz/¾ cup) red lentils, rinsed and drained
1 tablespoon olive oil
1 large onion, chopped
80 g (2¾ oz/½ cup) unsalted cashew nuts
1 tablespoon Madras curry paste
25 g (1 oz/½ cup) chopped coriander (cilantro) leaves and stems
125 g (4½ oz/½ cup) Greek-style yoghurt
coriander (cilantro) leaves, to garnish

Bring the stock to the boil in a large saucepan. Add the carrot and lentils, bring the mixture back to the boil, then simmer over low heat for about 8 minutes, or until the carrot and lentils are soft.

Meanwhile, heat the oil in a pan, add the onion and cashews and cook over medium heat for 2–3 minutes, or until the onion is soft and browned. Add the curry paste and coriander and cook for a further 1 minute, or until fragrant. Stir the paste into the carrot and lentil mixture.

Transfer to a food processor or blender and process in batches until smooth. Return the mixture to the pan and reheat over medium heat until hot. Season to taste with salt and cracked black pepper and serve with a dollop of yoghurt and a sprinkling of coriander.

Note *Garnish the soup with a pinch of chilli flakes to give it an extra kick.*

Cook the dumplings until a skewer comes out clean when inserted into the centre.

Return the puréed soup to the pan and stir until it is heated through.

Bottom: Curried lentil, carrot and cashew soup. Top: Chickpea and herb dumpling soup.

Zuppa di pesce (Italian fish soup)

preparation 40 minutes
cooking 1 hour 30 minutes
serves 4

300 g (10½ oz) firm white fish fillets, such as red mullet or cod
12 raw prawns (shrimp)
1 small onion, roughly chopped
1 carrot, roughly chopped
15 g (½ oz) parsley, roughly chopped, stalks reserved
200 g (7 oz) squid tubes
80 ml (2½ fl oz/⅓ cup) olive oil
1 onion, finely chopped
1 celery stalk, finely chopped
1 carrot, finely chopped
2 garlic cloves, finely chopped
pinch of cayenne pepper
1 fennel bulb, trimmed and chopped
125 ml (4 fl oz/½ cup) dry white wine
400 g (14 oz) tinned chopped tomatoes
250 g (9 oz) scallops, cleaned

crostini
60 ml (2 fl oz/¼ cup) extra virgin olive oil
2 garlic cloves, crushed
4 slices country-style bread

To make the fish stock, skin the fish and cut it into cubes. Rinse the fish bones in water. Peel and devein the prawns. Put the fish bones and prawn shells in a saucepan with just enough water to cover. Slowly bring to a simmer. Add the onion, carrot and the stalks from the parsley, then simmer for 20 minutes. Strain the stock through a colander and measure 1.5 litres (52 fl oz/6 cups) stock.

Lie the squid out flat, skin side up, and score a crisscross pattern into the flesh. Slice diagonally into bite-sized strips.

Heat the oil in a saucepan and cook the onion, celery, carrot, garlic and chopped parsley over low heat for 5–6 minutes. Add the cayenne pepper and season. Stir in the fennel and cook for 2–3 minutes. Add the wine, increase the heat and

cook until it has been absorbed. Stir in the tomato, then add the fish stock and bring to the boil. Reduce the heat and simmer for 20 minutes.

Add the squid and fish pieces to the pan and simmer for 1 minute. Add the scallops and prawns and simmer for a further 2 minutes.

To make the crostini, heat the oil and garlic in a frying pan over low heat. Add the slices of bread and fry on both sides until golden.

Place a slice of bread into each of four warm serving bowls. Ladle the soup on top and serve immediately.

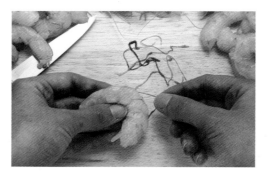

Peel the prawns, reserving the heads and shells, and remove the dark veins.

Trim the top from the fennel bulb, then slice and chop the fennel.

Red lentil, burghul and mint soup

preparation 20 minutes
cooking 45 minutes
serves 4–6

2 tablespoons olive oil
1 large red onion, finely chopped
2 garlic cloves, crushed
2 tablespoons tomato paste (concentrated purée)
2 tomatoes, finely chopped
2 teaspoons paprika
1 teaspoon cayenne pepper
500 g (1 lb 2 oz/2 cups) red lentils
50 g (1¾ oz/¼ cup) long-grain rice
2.125 litres (74 fl oz/8½ cups) chicken stock
45 g (1½ oz/¼ cup) fine burghul (bulgar wheat)
2 tablespoons chopped mint
2 tablespoons chopped flat-leaf (Italian) parsley
90 g (3¼ oz/⅓ cup) plain yoghurt
¼ preserved lemon, pulp removed,
zest washed and julienned

Heat the olive oil in a saucepan over medium heat. Add the onion and garlic and cook for 2–3 minutes, or until soft. Stir in the tomato paste, tomato, paprika and cayenne pepper and cook for 1 minute.

Add the lentils, rice and chicken stock, then cover and bring to the boil over high heat. Reduce the heat and simmer for 30–35 minutes, or until the rice is cooked.

Stir in the burghul and herbs, then season to taste. Divide the soup among serving bowls, garnish with yoghurt and preserved lemon and serve immediately.

Note *This soup will thicken on standing, so if reheating you may need to add more liquid.*

Chestnut, pancetta and cabbage soup

preparation 20 minutes
cooking 45 minutes
serves 4

100 g (3½ oz) cavolo nero or savoy cabbage,
roughly chopped
2 tablespoons olive oil
1 large onion, finely chopped
200 g (7 oz) pancetta, diced
3 garlic cloves, crushed
2 tablespoons chopped rosemary
300 g (10½ oz) cooked peeled chestnuts
170 ml (5½ fl oz/⅔ cup) red wine
extra virgin olive oil, to serve

Cook the cabbage in 1.5 litres (52 fl oz/6 cups) boiling salted water for 10 minutes. Drain, reserving the water. Rinse the cabbage in cold water if it is too hot to handle, then finely chop it.

Heat the oil in a large saucepan. Cook the onion and pancetta over moderately high heat until the onion is soft and the pancetta is lightly browned. Add the garlic and the rosemary and cook for a few minutes.

Break up the chestnuts a little and add to the pan with the cabbage. Stir to infuse the flavours, season with salt and freshly ground black pepper, then add the wine. Bring to the boil and cook for a couple of minutes. Add the cabbage water and simmer for 15 minutes.

Purée half of the soup, leaving the remainder unpuréed to create a little texture. Serve hot with a drizzle of extra virgin olive oil over each bowl.

Bottom: Chestnut, pancetta and cabbage soup. Top: Red lentil, burghul and mint soup.

Sweet potato, chilli and coriander soup

preparation 25 minutes
cooking 40 minutes
serves 4

6 whole coriander (cilantro) plants (roots, stems and leaves)
1 small red chilli, seeded and chopped
2 garlic cloves, chopped
1 tablespoon oil
1 large onion, chopped
1 celery stalk, chopped
650 g (1 lb 7 oz) orange sweet potato,
cut into 5 cm (2 inch) pieces
1 litre (35 fl oz/4 cups) chicken or vegetable stock
145 ml (4¾ fl oz) coconut milk

Remove the leaves from the coriander plants. Reserve a few whole leaves for garnishing and chop the remainder of the leaves. Set aside. Wash the roots and stems and chop roughly. Put in a mini processor and add the chilli and garlic. Add 2 teaspoons of the oil and process for 20 seconds, or until the mixture forms a rough paste.

Heat the remaining oil in a large heavy-based saucepan. Add the paste and stir over low heat for 2 minutes, or until aromatic. Stir in the onion and celery. Cover and cook for 5 minutes, stirring once or twice.

Add the sweet potato and stir to coat. Cook for 2 minutes, then add the stock. Bring to the boil, then reduce the heat, cover and cook for about 20 minutes, or until the sweet potato is tender. Set aside to cool slightly.

Purée the soup, then season well. Stir in the coconut milk and gently reheat the soup. Add the chopped coriander and serve garnished with the reserved coriander leaves.

Smoked fish chowder

preparation 20 minutes
cooking 55 minutes
serves 4–6

500 ml (17 fl oz/2 cups) milk
500 g (1 lb 2 oz) smoked fish, trimmed
and cut into large chunks
50 g (1¾ oz) butter
1 leek, white part only, roughly chopped
2 celery stalks, chopped
1 large carrot, chopped
2 garlic cloves, chopped
400 g (14 oz) potatoes, cut into 5 cm (2 inch) pieces
1 teaspoon freshly grated nutmeg
500 ml (17 fl oz/2 cups) chicken stock or fish stock
125 ml (4 fl oz/½ cup) cream
1 large handful flat-leaf (Italian) parsley, chopped

Heat the milk in a large deep saucepan. Add the smoked fish and simmer for 8 minutes, or until the flesh flakes when tested. Transfer the fish to a plate and set aside to cool. Reserve the milk. Peel and discard the skin from the fish and roughly flake the flesh, removing any bones.

Heat the butter in a large heavy-based saucepan over medium–low heat. Add the leek, celery, carrot and garlic. Stir for 2 minutes to coat the vegetables in the butter. Reduce the heat, cover and sweat, stirring occasionally, for 5 minutes. Do not allow the vegetables to brown.

Add the potato and nutmeg to the saucepan and stir. Cook for 2 minutes, then add the stock. Bring to the boil, then cover and cook for 20 minutes, or until the potato is tender. Set aside to cool slightly.

Roughly purée the soup. Stir in the fish, reserved milk, cream and parsley and gently reheat the soup. Season well with freshly ground black pepper.

Wear gloves to protect your skin when you are chopping the chillies.

Trim the leek, removing the green portion, and roughly chop it.

39

Bottom: Smoked fish chowder. Top: Sweet potato, chilli and coriander soup.

Creamy red lentil soup

preparation 25 minutes
cooking 1 hour
serves 6

croutons
4 thick bread slices, crusts removed
60 g (2¼ oz) butter
1 tablespoon oil

1½ teaspoons cumin seeds
80 g (2¾ oz) butter
1 large onion, diced
185 g (6½ oz/¾ cup) red lentils, rinsed and drained
1.5 litres (52 fl oz/6 cups) vegetable stock
2 tablespoons plain (all-purpose) flour
2 egg yolks
185 ml (6 fl oz/¾ cup) milk

To make the croutons, cut the bread slices into 1 cm (½ inch) cubes. Heat the butter and oil in a frying pan and, when the butter is foaming, add the bread and cook over medium heat until golden and crisp. Drain on crumpled paper towel.

In a small frying pan, dry roast the cumin seeds until they start to pop and become aromatic. Leave to cool, then grind to a fine powder using a mortar and pestle.

Melt half the butter in a heavy-based saucepan and cook the onion over medium heat for 5–6 minutes, until softened. Add the lentils, cumin and stock and bring to the boil. Cover and simmer for 30–35 minutes, until the lentils are very soft. Allow to cool slightly before transferring to a food processor and blending, in batches, until smooth.

Melt the remaining butter in a large heavy-based saucepan, over low heat. Stir in the flour and cook for 2–3 minutes, or until pale and foaming. Stirring constantly, gradually add the lentil purée, then simmer for 4–5 minutes.

In a small bowl, combine the egg yolks and the milk. Whisk a small amount of the soup into the egg mixture and then return it all to the soup, stirring constantly. Be careful not to boil the soup or the egg will curdle. Season to taste. Heat the soup to just under boiling and serve with the croutons.

40

Cook the diced onion, stirring occasionally, until it is soft.

Combine the egg yolks and milk, then whisk in a little of the soup.

Bean and barley soup

preparation 20 minutes + overnight soaking
cooking 2 hours 45 minutes
serves 4

200 g (7 oz) dried borlotti beans
2 tablespoons olive oil
1 small onion, thinly sliced
2 garlic cloves, crushed
1.5 litres (52 fl oz/6 cups) chicken stock
1 tablespoon finely chopped thyme or sage
200 g (7 oz) pearl barley
100 g (3½ oz) parmesan cheese, grated
1 tablespoon finely chopped parsley
1 tablespoon extra virgin olive oil

Soak the borlotti beans in cold water overnight. Drain and put the beans in a large saucepan with plenty of cold water. Bring to the boil and simmer until tender (this will take about 1½ hours, depending on the age of the beans). Drain.

Heat the olive oil in a large saucepan and cook the onion over low heat for 6 minutes, or until soft. Season with salt and pepper. Add the garlic and cook without browning for about 20–30 seconds. Add the stock and thyme or sage and bring to the boil.

Stir in the barley a little at a time so that the stock continues to boil, then lower the heat and simmer for 15 minutes. Add the borlotti beans and simmer for 30 minutes, or until the barley is tender.

Puree one-third of the soup until smooth, leaving the rest unpuréed to give the soup a little texture. Return to the saucepan and stir in the parmesan and chopped parsley. Season to taste and stir in 125–250 ml (4–9 fl oz/½–1 cup) hot water to give the soup a spoonable consistency. Serve immediately, with a teaspoon of the extra virgin olive oil stirred through each bowl.

Green curry vegetable soup

preparation 15 minutes
cooking 25 minutes
serves 6

2 teaspoons peanut oil
1 tablespoon green curry paste
3 makrut (kaffir lime) leaves
1.25 litres (44 fl oz/5 cups) vegetable or chicken stock
670 ml (23 fl oz/2⅔ cups) coconut milk
600 g (1 lb 5 oz) butternut pumpkin (squash),
peeled and cut into 1.5 cm (⅝ inch) cubes
250 g (9 oz) small yellow squash (pattypan squash), sliced
115 g (4 oz) fresh baby corn spears, halved lengthways
2 tablespoons mushroom soy sauce
2 tablespoons lime juice
1 teaspoon sugar
1½ tablespoons Vietnamese mint, finely chopped

Heat the oil in a large saucepan and add the curry paste and makrut leaves. Cook, stirring, over medium heat for 1 minute, or until the mixture is fragrant. Bring the stock to the boil in a separate saucepan.

Gradually add the stock and the coconut milk to the curry mixture and bring to the boil. Add the pumpkin, squash and corn, and simmer over low heat for 12 minutes, or until the pumpkin is tender.

Add the soy sauce and the lime juice, and season to taste with sugar, salt and freshly ground black pepper. Sprinkle the mint over the soup before serving.

Soak the borlotti beans in cold water overnight, then drain and rinse them.

Use fresh baby corn spears, and cut them in half lengthways before cooking.

Bottom: Green curry vegetable soup. Top: Bean and barley soup.

Prawn gumbo

preparation 25 minutes
cooking 1 hour
serves 4

2 tablespoons olive oil
1 large onion, finely chopped
3 garlic cloves, crushed
1 red capsicum (pepper), seeded and chopped
4 slices bacon, chopped
1½ teaspoons dried thyme
2 teaspoons dried oregano
1 teaspoon paprika
½ teaspoon cayenne pepper
60 ml (2 fl oz/¼ cup) sherry
1 litre (35 fl oz/4 cups) fish stock
100 g (3½ oz/½ cup) long-grain rice
2 bay leaves
400 g (14 oz) tin chopped tomatoes
150 g (5½ oz) okra, thinly sliced
850 g (1 lb 14 oz) raw prawns (shrimp),
peeled and deveined
3 tablespoons finely chopped flat-leaf (Italian) parsley

Heat the oil in a large saucepan over low heat. Cook the onion, garlic, capsicum and bacon for 5 minutes, or until soft. Stir in the herbs and spices. Season.

Add the sherry and cook until evaporated, then add the stock and 500 ml (17 fl oz/2 cups) water. Bring to the boil. Add the rice and bay leaves, reduce the heat and simmer, covered, for 20 minutes.

Add the chopped tomato and okra. Simmer, covered, for 20–25 minutes. Stir in the prawns and parsley and simmer for 5 minutes, or until the prawns are cooked through.

Cauliflower, cannellini bean and prosciutto soup

preparation 20 minutes
cooking 40 minutes
serves 4

2 tablespoons olive oil
100 g (3½ oz/about 8 slices) prosciutto, chopped
1 onion, chopped
1 garlic clove, crushed
800 g (1 lb 12 oz) cauliflower, cut into small florets
2 x 400 g (14 oz) tins cannellini beans, drained and rinsed
125 ml (4 fl oz/½ cup) thick (double/heavy) cream
snipped chives, to serve

Heat 1 tablespoon of the oil in a large saucepan over medium–high heat. Fry the prosciutto, stirring often, until crisp. Transfer half the prosciutto to a plate lined with paper towel, leaving the rest in the saucepan.

Reduce the heat to medium. Add the remaining oil and the onion to the pan and fry for 5 minutes, or until softened. Add the garlic and cauliflower and fry for 3 minutes.

Add the cannellini beans and 1 litre (35 fl oz/4 cups) water and season well with salt and freshly ground black pepper. Bring to the boil, then reduce the heat and simmer, covered, for 15 minutes, or until the cauliflower is tender. Set aside to cool for 10 minutes.

Purée the soup until smooth. Season well with salt and freshly ground black pepper. Stir in the cream and gently reheat the soup. Serve immediately, with the reserved crisp prosciutto and the chives sprinkled on top.

Remove the rind from the bacon and then cut it into thin strips.

Cut the cauliflower into small, even-sized florets so they will cook quickly.

Bottom: Cauliflower, cannellini bean and prosciutto soup. Top: Prawn gumbo.

Harira (Moroccan lentil and tomato soup)

preparation 15 minutes
cooking 2 hours 25 minutes
serves 4

2 tablespoons olive oil
2 small onions, chopped
2 large garlic cloves, crushed
500 g (1 lb 2 oz) lamb shoulder steaks, trimmed
and cut into small chunks
1½ teaspoons ground cumin
2 teaspoons paprika
½ teaspoon ground cloves
1 bay leaf
2 tablespoons tomato paste (concentrated purée)
1 litre (35 fl oz/4 cups) beef stock
900 g (2 lb) tinned chickpeas, rinsed and drained
800 g (1 lb 12 oz) tinned chopped tomatoes
30 g (1 oz) finely chopped coriander (cilantro) leaves,
plus extra, to garnish
small black olives, to serve

Heat the oil in a large heavy-based saucepan or stockpot, add the onion and garlic and cook for 5 minutes, or until softened. Add the lamb chunks, in batches, and cook over high heat until browned on all sides. Return all the meat to the pan.

Add the cumin, paprika, cloves and bay leaf to the pan and cook until fragrant. Add the tomato paste and cook for about 2 minutes, stirring constantly.

Add the beef stock, stir well and bring to the boil. Add the chickpeas, tomato and chopped coriander to the pan. Stir, then bring to the boil. Reduce the heat and simmer, stirring occasionally, for 2 hours, or until the lamb is tender. Season to taste.

Serve the soup garnished with coriander leaves and small black olives. This dish can also be served with toasted pitta bread drizzled with a little extra virgin olive oil.

The chickpeas need to be rinsed well and drained before adding to the soup.

Chop the coriander leaves, reserving the root and stems for another use.

Vegetable and lentil soup with spiced yoghurt

preparation 25 minutes
cooking 40 minutes
serves 6

2 tablespoons olive oil
1 small leek, white part only, chopped
2 garlic cloves, crushed
2 teaspoons curry powder
1 teaspoon ground cumin
1 teaspoon garam masala
1 litre (35 fl oz/4 cups) vegetable stock
1 bay leaf
185 g (6½ oz/1 cup) brown lentils
450 g (1 lb) butternut pumpkin (squash), peeled
and cut into 1 cm (½ inch) cubes
2 zucchini (courgettes), cut in half lengthways and sliced
400 g (14 oz) tin chopped tomatoes
200 g (7 oz) broccoli, cut into small florets
1 small carrot, diced
80 g (2¾ oz/½ cup) peas
1 tablespoon chopped mint

spiced yoghurt
250 g (9 oz/1 cup) plain yoghurt
1 tablespoon chopped coriander (cilantro) leaves
1 garlic clove, crushed
3 dashes Tabasco sauce

Heat the oil in a saucepan over medium heat. Add the leek and garlic and cook for 4–5 minutes, or until soft and lightly golden. Add the curry powder, ground cumin and garam masala and cook for 1 minute, or until fragrant.

Add the vegetable stock, bay leaf, lentils and pumpkin. Bring to the boil, then reduce the heat to low and simmer for 10–15 minutes, or until the lentils are tender. Season.

Add the zucchini, tomato, broccoli florets, carrot and 500 ml (17 fl oz/2 cups) water and simmer for 10 minutes, or until the vegetables are tender. Add the peas and simmer for 2–3 minutes.

To make the spiced yoghurt, place the yoghurt, coriander, garlic and Tabasco in a small bowl and stir until combined.

Dollop a spoonful of the yoghurt on each serving of soup and garnish with the chopped mint.

Quinoa and vegetable soup

preparation 20 minutes
cooking 50 minutes
serves 4

2 tablespoons olive oil
1 large onion, finely chopped
2 carrots, finely chopped
2 celery stalks, finely chopped
2 garlic cloves, crushed
2 thyme sprigs
1 tablespoon ground fennel seeds
2 teaspoons ground cumin
1 teaspoon ground turmeric
750 ml (26 fl oz/3 cups) vegetable stock
500 g (1 lb 2 oz/2½ cups) chopped vine-ripened tomatoes
100 g (3½ oz/½ cup) quinoa
400 g (14 oz) tin chickpeas, rinsed and drained
3 tablespoons finely chopped flat-leaf (Italian) parsley
60 g (2 oz/¼ cup) Greek-style yoghurt
lemon or lime wedges, to serve (optional)

Heat the oil in a saucepan over medium–high heat. Add the onion, carrot and celery. Cook, stirring, for 10 minutes, or until the vegetables start to soften. Add the garlic, thyme sprigs, ground fennel, cumin and turmeric. Cook, stirring, for 1 minute, or until aromatic.

Add the stock, tomatoes and 500 ml (17 fl oz/2 cups) water. Bring to the boil, then reduce the heat to low and simmer, uncovered, for 30 minutes.

Meanwhile, cook the quinoa in a small saucepan of boiling water for 10 minutes, or until tender. Drain.

Stir the quinoa, chickpeas and parsley into the soup and heat through. Ladle the soup into serving bowls. Serve with a dollop of yoghurt, and lemon or lime wedges if desired.

Fry the onion, carrot and celery in the olive oil until the vegetables begin to soften.

Bottom: Quinoa and vegetable soup. Top: Vegetable and lentil soup with spiced yoghurt.

light soups

Crab in lime and lemon grass broth with asparagus

preparation 20 minutes
cooking 30 minutes
serves 4 as a starter

1 tablespoon oil
1–2 teaspoons chilli paste in soy bean oil
4 red Asian shallots, finely chopped
1 garlic clove, finely chopped
200 g (7 oz) fresh crab meat
1½ tablespoons fish sauce
1 litre (35 fl oz/4 cups) chicken stock
2 tablespoons lime juice
3 lemon grass stems, white part only, 1 bruised, 2 finely chopped
4 makrut (kaffir lime) leaves, shredded
250 g (9 oz) asparagus, trimmed and cut into 3 cm (1¼ inch) lengths
1 tablespoon chopped coriander (cilantro) leaves,
plus extra sprigs to serve
2 spring onions (scallions), thinly sliced

Heat a wok over medium heat, add the oil and swirl to coat. Stir-fry the chilli paste for 30 seconds, or until fragrant. Add the shallots and garlic and stir-fry for 30 seconds, or until fragrant and just starting to brown. Stir in the crab meat and 3 teaspoons of fish sauce and stir-fry for 1 minute. Remove from the wok.

Put the stock, lime juice, lemon grass, remaining fish sauce and three of the shredded lime leaves into a clean wok and heat until simmering. Simmer for 10 minutes, then strain to remove the lemon grass and makrut leaves.

Return the strained broth to the wok and bring to the boil. Add the asparagus and cook for 2–3 minutes, or until tender but still firm. Add the crab mixture, stirring to combine well, and simmer for 1 minute, or until the crab is heated through.

Remove from the heat and stir in the shredded coriander. Season with ground black pepper and serve topped with the coriander sprigs, spring onion and the remaining shredded makrut leaf.

Finely chop two of the lemon grass stems, and bruise the other one.

Cut the lime leaves into thin shreds, reserving some for garnishing.

Chilled avocado soup with lime-pickled onions

preparation 25 minutes
cooking 10 minutes
serves 4

lime-pickled onions
1 small red onion, halved, very thinly sliced
2 tablespoons lime juice
2 teaspoons caster (superfine) sugar
1 teaspoon sea salt flakes

1½ tablespoons avocado or other vegetable oil
1 onion, chopped
1½ teaspoons ground cumin
1½ teaspoons ground coriander
1 garlic clove, crushed
500 g (1 lb 2 oz) ripe Hass avocados (about 3 small), mashed
1 litre (35 fl oz/4 cups) chicken or vegetable stock, chilled
60 ml (2 fl oz/¼ cup) lime juice, or to taste

To make the lime-pickled onions, put the onion, lime juice, sugar and sea salt in a small bowl and toss to combine well. Cover and stand at room temperature for 30 minutes to allow the onions to 'pickle'.

Meanwhile, heat the oil in a small saucepan, add the onion, cover and cook, stirring occasionally, for 6 minutes, or until soft. Add the cumin and coriander and cook, stirring, for 1 minute or until aromatic. Remove from the heat and cool.

Put the onion mixture, garlic, avocado, stock and lime juice in a food processor or blender and process until a smooth purée forms. Season to taste with salt and freshly ground black pepper, and a little extra lime juice, if necessary. Serve immediately, topped with the lime-pickled onions.

Remove the skin and seeds from the avocados, then use a fork to mash them.

Cook the chopped onion, stirring occasionally, until it is soft.

Spinach, lentil and lemon soup

preparation 20 minutes
cooking 35 minutes
serves 4

chilli oil
1 long red chilli, finely chopped
1½ tablespoons flat-leaf (Italian) parsley, finely chopped
2 tablespoons extra virgin olive oil

1 tablespoon olive oil
1 large onion, finely chopped
2 celery stalks, finely chopped
200 g (7 oz) pancetta, cut into thick strips
2 garlic cloves, crushed
3 lemon thyme sprigs
500 g (1 lb 2 oz) potatoes, peeled and chopped
800 g (1 lb 12 oz) tinned brown lentils, rinsed and drained
1 litre (35 fl oz/4 cups) chicken stock
1 bunch (about 310 g/11 oz) English spinach
80 ml (2½ fl oz/⅓ cup) lemon juice

To make the chilli oil, combine the chilli, parsley and oil in a small bowl. Set aside.

Heat the olive oil in a large saucepan over medium heat. Add the onion, celery and pancetta and cook, stirring, for 10 minutes, or until the vegetables are soft. Add the garlic and thyme and cook for 1 minute, or until aromatic.

Add the potato, lentils, stock and 500 ml (17 fl oz/2 cups) water. Bring to the boil, reduce the heat to low and simmer, uncovered, for 20 minutes, or until the potato is very tender.

Meanwhile, trim and shred the English spinach. Remove the soup from the heat and stir in the spinach and lemon juice. Serve immediately, drizzled with the chilli oil.

Tomato and egg soup

preparation 15 minutes
cooking 15 minutes
serves 4

250 g (9 oz) firm ripe tomatoes
2 eggs
1 spring onion (scallion), finely chopped
1 tablespoon oil
1 litre (35 fl oz/4 cups) vegetable or chicken stock
1 tablespoon light soy sauce
1 tablespoon cornflour (cornstarch)

Score a cross in the bottom of each tomato. Plunge into boiling water for 20 seconds, then drain and peel the skin away from the cross. Cut into slices or thin wedges, trimming off the core. Beat the eggs with a pinch of salt and a few pieces of spring onion.

Heat a wok over high heat, add the oil and heat until very hot. Stir-fry the spring onion for a few seconds to flavour the oil, then pour in the stock and bring to the boil.

Add the tomato and return to the boil. Add the soy sauce and very slowly pour in the beaten eggs, stirring as you pour. Return to the boil.

Combine the cornflour with just enough water to make a paste, add to the soup and simmer until thickened.

Lemon-scented broth with tortellini

preparation 10 minutes
cooking 20 minutes
serves 4–6

1 lemon
125 ml (4 fl oz/½ cup) dry white wine
440 g (15½ oz) tinned chicken consommé
375 g (13 oz) fresh or dried veal or chicken tortellini
4 tablespoons chopped flat-leaf (Italian) parsley
grated parmesan cheese, to garnish

Using a vegetable peeler, peel wide strips from the lemon. Remove the white pith with a small sharp knife. Cut three of the wide pieces into fine strips and set aside for garnishing.

Combine the remaining lemon strips, wine, consommé and 750 ml (26 fl oz/3 cups) water in a large saucepan. Cook for 10 minutes over low heat. Discard the lemon zest and bring to the boil. Add the tortellini and parsley and season with black pepper. Cook for 6–7 minutes, or until the pasta is al dente. Garnish with parmesan and fine strips of lemon zest.

Cantonese corn soup

preparation 20 minutes
cooking 15–20 minutes
serves 6

250 g (9 oz) boneless, skinless chicken breast, minced (ground)
150 ml (5 fl oz) Shaoxing rice wine
400 g (14 oz) tin creamed corn
1.5 litres (52 fl oz/6 cups) chicken stock
1 teaspoon salt
2½ tablespoons cornflour (cornstarch)
2 egg whites, lightly beaten
1 teaspoon roasted sesame oil

Put the chicken and 60 ml (2 fl oz/¼ cup) of the rice wine in a bowl and stir to combine. In a large clay pot or saucepan, combine the creamed corn, stock, remaining rice wine and salt. Bring to the boil, stirring. Add the chicken and stir to separate the meat. Return to the boil and skim any scum from the surface.

Combine the cornflour with enough water to make a paste, add to the soup and simmer until thickened. Remove from the heat.

Mix 2 tablespoons of water into the egg white, then slowly add to the clay pot or saucepan in a thin stream around the edge of the pan. Stir once or twice, then add the sesame oil. Check the seasoning, adding more salt if necessary. Serve the soup immediately.

Top left: Tomato and egg soup. Top right: Lemon-scented broth with tortellini. Bottom left: Cantonese corn soup.

Zucchini pesto soup

preparation 25 minutes
cooking 25 minutes
serves 4

1 tablespoon olive oil
1 large onion, finely chopped
2 garlic cloves, crushed
750 ml (26 fl oz/3 cups) vegetable or chicken stock
750 g (1 lb 10 oz) zucchini (courgettes), thinly sliced
60 ml (2 fl oz/¼ cup) cream
toasted ciabatta bread, to serve

pesto
3 large handfuls basil
25 g (1 oz/¼ cup) finely grated parmesan cheese
2 tablespoons pine nuts, toasted
2 tablespoons extra virgin olive oil

Heat the oil in a large heavy-based saucepan. Add the onion and garlic and cook over medium heat for 5 minutes, or until the onion is soft.

Bring the stock to the boil in a separate saucepan. Add the sliced zucchini and hot stock to the onion mixture. Bring to the boil, then reduce the heat, cover and simmer for about 10 minutes, or until the zucchini is very soft.

To make the pesto, process the basil, parmesan and toasted pine nuts in a food processor for 20 seconds, or until finely chopped. Gradually add the extra virgin olive oil and process until smooth. Spoon into a small bowl.

Transfer the zucchini mixture to a blender or food processor and blend in batches until smooth. Return the mixture to the pan, stir in the cream and 2 tablespoons of the pesto, and reheat over medium heat until hot.

Season the soup with salt and black pepper and serve with toasted ciabatta bread. Serve the remaining pesto in a bowl for diners to help themselves, or cover with olive oil and store in the refrigerator for up to 1 week.

Toast the pine nuts in a dry frying pan, stirring constantly so they don't burn.

Grate the parmesan cheese using the fine side of a grater.

light soups

Clear soup with scallops

preparation 25 minutes
cooking 15 minutes
serves 4 as a starter

8 snow peas (mangetout), very thinly sliced on the diagonal
½ carrot, peeled, very finely julienned
8 large or 12 small scallops, roe removed
1 litre (32 fl oz/4 cups) dashi
1 teaspoon Japanese soy sauce
1 teaspoon mirin
4 thin strips of lemon zest
4 mitsuba leaves or small shiso leaves (optional)

Bring a small saucepan of water to the boil, then reduce to a simmer. Add the snow peas for a few seconds, then remove with a slotted spoon and plunge into iced water. Add the carrot and cook for 30 seconds, then remove with a slotted spoon and plunge into iced water.

Add the scallops to the simmering water and cook for 1 minute, then lift out and drain well. Neatly place a small bundle of the blanched snow pea and carrot into the base of four small soup bowls, then put the scallops on top.

Pour the dashi, soy sauce and mirin into a small saucepan and bring to the boil, then reduce to a simmer.

Tie each lemon strip into a knot and add one to each bowl. Carefully ladle the dashi broth into the soup bowls, then float a mitsuba leaf on top. Serve immediately.

Thai lemon grass broth with mussels

preparation 20 minutes
cooking 25 minutes
serves 4

1.5 kg (3 lb 5 oz) black mussels
1 tablespoon oil
5 spring onions (scallions), thinly sliced
2 garlic cloves, crushed
750 ml (26 fl oz/3 cups) chicken or fish stock
2½ tablespoons sliced fresh galangal or ginger
4 lemon grass stems, white part only, bruised
2 long red chillies, halved lengthways
6 makrut (kaffir lime) leaves, crushed
2 tablespoons roughly chopped coriander (cilantro) leaves

Scrub the mussels with a stiff brush and pull out the hairy beards. Discard any broken mussels, or open ones that don't close when tapped on the bench. Rinse well.

Heat a wok over medium heat, add the oil and swirl to coat the wok. Cook the spring onion and garlic for 1 minute, or until softened. Add the stock, galangal, lemon grass, chilli, makrut leaves and 750 ml (26 fl oz/3 cups) water and rapidly simmer for 15 minutes.

Add the mussels, cover and bring to the boil over high heat, then cook for 7–8 minutes, or until the mussels open, tossing occasionally. Discard any unopened mussels.

Stir in half the coriander, then divide the broth and mussels among four serving bowls. Sprinkle with the rest of the coriander, then serve immediately.

Use a small, sharp knife to remove the roe from the scallops.

Scrub the mussels with a stiff brush, then pull out the hairy beards.

Bottom: Thai lemon grass broth with mussels. Top: Clear soup with scallops.

Winter melon and ham soup

preparation 15 minutes + 1 hour soaking
cooking 10 minutes
serves 4

1 tablespoon dried shrimp
250 g (9 oz) winter melon, rind and seeds removed (see Note)
750 ml (26 fl oz/3 cups) chicken stock
150 g (5½ oz) Chinese ham or prosciutto, chopped

Soak the dried shrimp in boiling water for 1 hour, then drain. Cut the winter melon into small pieces.

Bring the chicken stock to a rolling boil in a large clay pot or saucepan. Add the drained shrimp, winter melon and ham or prosciutto. Return to the boil, then reduce the heat and simmer for 2 minutes. Season the soup with salt and white pepper. Serve hot.

Note Winter melon is a very large dark-green gourd or squash that looks like a watermelon. You can usually buy pieces of it in Asian grocery stores.

Broth with ravioli

preparation 10 minutes
cooking 15 minutes
serves 2

750 ml (26 fl oz/3 cups) vegetable or chicken stock
250 g (9 oz) spinach and ricotta ravioli
85 g (3 oz) snow peas (mangetout), sliced on the diagonal
2 tablespoons chopped flat-leaf (Italian) parsley
2 tablespoons chopped basil
grated parmesan cheese, to garnish

Place the stock in a large heavy-based saucepan and bring to the boil. Add the ravioli and cook for 8–10 minutes, or until the pasta is al dente.

Season to taste with salt and black pepper, and stir in the snow peas, parsley and basil. Pour the soup into two bowls and sprinkle with grated parmesan before serving.

Pancotto (Simple Italian bread soup)

preparation 30 minutes + 1 hour standing
cooking 50 minutes
serves 4

900 g (2 lb) ripe tomatoes
2 tablespoons olive oil
3 garlic cloves, crushed
1 white onion, finely chopped
200 g (7 oz) day-old ciabatta, torn into pieces
875 ml (30 fl oz/3½ cups) chicken stock
20 basil leaves, shredded
parmesan cheese shavings, to garnish

Score a cross in the base of each tomato. Put in a heatproof bowl and cover with boiling water. Leave for 30 seconds, then transfer to cold water and peel the skin away from the cross. Cut in half, remove the seeds and chop the flesh.

Heat the oil in a large saucepan and cook the garlic and onion over low heat until softened but not browned. Add the tomatoes and season well. Cover the pan and simmer for 30 minutes. Add the bread and simmer, stirring once or twice, for 5 minutes.

Slowly stir in the chicken stock and stir until the bread has broken down. Remove the pan from the heat and add the basil. Cover and leave for 1 hour. Serve the soup at room temperature or warm, with parmesan shavings.

Top left: Winter melon and ham soup. Top right: Broth with ravioli. Bottom left: Pancotto.

Red gazpacho

preparation 40 minutes + chilling
cooking nil
serves 4

1 kg (2 lb 4 oz) vine-ripened tomatoes
2 slices day-old white Italian bread, crust removed,
broken into pieces
1 red capsicum (pepper), seeded and roughly chopped
2 garlic cloves, chopped
1 small green chilli, chopped (optional)
1 teaspoon sugar
2 tablespoons red wine vinegar
2 tablespoons extra virgin olive oil
8 ice cubes

garnish
½ Lebanese (short) cucumber, seeded and finely diced
½ red capsicum (pepper), seeded and finely diced
½ green capsicum (pepper), seeded and finely diced
½ red onion, finely diced
½ ripe tomato, diced

Score a cross in the base of each tomato. Put in a heatproof bowl and cover with boiling water. Leave for 30 seconds, then transfer to a bowl of cold water and peel the skin away from the cross. Cut the tomatoes in half, remove the seeds and roughly chop the flesh.

Soak the bread in cold water for 5 minutes, then squeeze out any excess liquid. Put the bread in a food processor with the tomato, capsicum, garlic, chilli, sugar and vinegar, and process until combined and smooth.

With the motor running, add the oil to make a smooth creamy mixture. Season to taste. Chill for at least 2 hours. Add a little extra vinegar, if desired.

To make the garnish, mix all the ingredients in a bowl. Put 2 ice cubes in each bowl of soup and serve the garnish in separate bowls.

Chilled cucumber yoghurt soup

preparation 25 minutes + chilling
cooking nil
serves 4

2 telegraph (long) cucumbers, about 550 g (1 lb 4 oz)
1 large handful mint
2 garlic cloves, chopped
1 teaspoon dried mint
125 ml (4 fl oz/½ cup) milk
500 g (1 lb 2 oz/2 cups) Greek-style yoghurt
2–3 teaspoons lemon juice, to taste
3–4 drops Tabasco sauce, to taste
2 tablespoons snipped chives, to serve

Peel the cucumbers, halve them lengthways and scoop out the seeds. Set aside about one-third of one of the cucumbers for garnishing.

Put the remaining cucumber in a small food processor fitted with the metal blade. Add the mint, garlic, dried mint and milk and process in short bursts for about 20 seconds. Add the yoghurt, lemon juice, and Tabasco sauce to taste. Season well with salt and freshly ground black pepper. Blend until well combined and smooth, then transfer the soup to a bowl, cover and refrigerate for at least 2 hours to allow flavours to develop.

Finely dice the reserved cucumber. Ladle the soup into bowls and top with the diced cucumber and chives.

Note The soup should be eaten within 1 day. It is not suitable for freezing.

Bottom: Chilled cucumber yoghurt soup. Top: Red gazpacho.

Clear soup with salmon quenelles

preparation 20 minutes
cooking 25 minutes
serves 4

400 g (14 oz) salmon cutlets
1 litre (35 fl oz/4 cups) fish stock
125 ml (4 fl oz/½ cup) dry white wine
2 teaspoons lemon juice
1 small carrot, finely chopped
2 spring onions (scallions), sliced
2 dill sprigs
2 parsley sprigs
3 black peppercorns
1 egg white, chilled
125 ml (4 fl oz/½ cup) cream for whipping, chilled
2 tablespoons chervil leaves

Remove the skin and bones from the salmon and set aside. Weigh 150 g (5½ oz) of the fish, chop roughly, cover and chill.

To make the soup, combine the fish skin and bones in a large saucepan with the remaining salmon, stock, wine, lemon juice, carrot, spring onion, dill, parsley and peppercorns. Slowly bring to the boil, then reduce the heat, cover and simmer for 15 minutes. Strain the soup and discard the vegetables. (You won't use the cooked salmon for this recipe, but you can use it as a sandwich filling. When cool, flake the salmon and then mix it with a little mayonnaise.)

Pour the soup into a clean saucepan, bring to the boil, then reduce the heat to just simmering. Season to taste.

To make the quenelles, process the reserved salmon in a food processor until finely chopped. Gradually add the egg white and process until very smooth. Transfer to a chilled bowl and season well with salt and ground white pepper. Whip the cream and quickly fold into the salmon. Shape quenelles using 2 teaspoons dipped in cold water. Add to the soup in two batches and poach for 2 minutes, or until cooked. Transfer the quenelles to warm soup bowls.

Heat the soup until almost boiling and carefully ladle over the quenelles. Sprinkle with chervil leaves and serve.

Notes *Ocean trout can be used instead of salmon.*

To make light fluffy quenelles, the ingredients used should be almost ice cold. The mixture will make about 24 quenelles.

Barley, celery and yoghurt soup

preparation 30 minutes
cooking 55 minutes
serves 6

225 g (8 oz/1 cup) pearl barley
25 g (1 oz) butter
2 onions, finely chopped
2 garlic cloves, crushed
½ head of celery, trimmed and finely chopped
1.5 litres (52 fl oz/6 cups) vegetable stock
1 tablespoon dried mint
3 egg yolks, lightly beaten
60 ml (2 fl oz/¼ cup) lemon juice
1½ teaspoons finely grated lemon rind
625 g (1 lb 6 oz/2½ cups) Greek-style yoghurt
35 g (1¼ oz/¼ cup) plain (all-purpose) flour
shredded mint, to garnish
Turkish bread, to serve

Bring a large saucepan of water to the boil. Add the barley and cook for 35–40 minutes, or until tender. Drain well and set aside.

Heat the butter in a large saucepan over medium heat and cook the onion and garlic, stirring, for 5 minutes, or until the onion is starting to soften. Stir in the celery, then cover and cook, stirring often, for 8 minutes, or until the celery is starting to soften. Add the vegetable stock and mint and bring back to a simmer. Cook for 10 minutes, or until the celery is very tender.

In a bowl, whisk together the egg yolks, lemon juice, lemon rind and yoghurt. Add the flour and whisk until smooth.

Add 500 ml (17 fl oz/2 cups) of the hot soup to the yoghurt mixture and mix until smooth. Pour the mixture back into the soup, add the cooked barley and stir over medium heat until the mixture comes back to a simmer. Cook, stirring, for a further 4–5 minutes, or until the soup thickens slightly. Season to taste with sea salt and black pepper.

Ladle the soup into serving bowls and garnish with the mint. Serve with Turkish bread.

Jungle soup

preparation 10 minutes
cooking 35 minutes
serves 4

2 teaspoons oil
1 onion, finely sliced
225 g (8 oz) butternut pumpkin (squash), peeled and chopped
225 g (8 oz) fresh pineapple or mango, chopped
1 garlic clove, crushed
1 dried red chilli, finely chopped
2 teaspoons grated fresh ginger
1 litre (35 fl oz/4 cups) chicken stock
2 tablespoons lime juice
350 g (12 oz) boneless, skinless chicken breast,
cut diagonally into thin strips

Heat the oil in a large heavy-based saucepan and cook the onion for 5 minutes, or until golden. Add the pumpkin cubes and cook for 5 minutes, or until just brown. Add the pineapple, garlic, chilli and ginger and toss together.

Add the chicken stock and lime juice, bring to the boil and then reduce the heat to a simmer for 20 minutes, or until the pumpkin is nearly tender.

Add the chicken strips and simmer for 5 minutes, or until the chicken is cooked. Serve immediately.

Whole green pea soup

preparation 20 minutes + 1 hour soaking
cooking 40 minutes
serves 6

1 kg (2 lb 4 oz) green peas in the pod
1 litre (35 fl oz/4 cups) vegetable stock
30 g (1 oz) butter
1 small onion, sliced
2 tablespoons finely chopped flat-leaf (Italian) parsley
2 tablespoons olive oil
4 thick slices bread, cut into 1 cm (½ inch) cubes

Shell the peas and set them aside. Cut the stringy tops from the pods and discard them. Wash the pods thoroughly and place in a large bowl. Cover with cold water and soak for 1 hour. Drain the pods well and put them in a large heavy-based saucepan. Add the stock and bring to the boil, then reduce the heat and simmer, covered, for 15 minutes, or until the pods are tender. Leave to cool slightly.

Put the pods and stock in batches into a food processor or blender and process for 30 seconds, or until smooth. Strain the purée, discarding the pods.

Melt the butter in a saucepan, add the onion and cook over medium heat until soft. Add the peas, parsley and 250 ml (9 fl oz/1 cup) water, bring to the boi!, reduce the heat to low and cook, covered, for 15 minutes, or until tender.

Heat the oil in a frying pan, add the bread cubes and cook until lightly brown. Remove them from the pan and leave to drain on paper towel.

Add the purée of pea pods to the simmering peas and stir through. Bring to the boil, then reduce the heat and simmer for 5 minutes to heat through. Season and serve topped with the croutons.

Variation Add 125 ml (4 fl oz/½ cup) of cream at the end and heat through.

Hint If the pea pods seem quite tough, remove the tails as well as the tops.

Toss together the onion, pumpkin, pineapple, garlic, chilli and ginger.

Simmer the empty pea pods in the stock until they are tender.

light soups

Bottom: Whole green pea soup. Top: Jungle soup.

Chilled Moroccan carrot and capsicum soup

preparation 25 minutes + chilling
cooking 50 minutes
serves 4

1 tablespoon olive oil
1 large red onion, chopped
3 large red capsicums (peppers), about 600 g (1 lb 5 oz),
seeded and chopped
2 garlic cloves, sliced
2½ teaspoons ready-made harissa, or to taste
6 carrots (about 1 kg/2 lb 4 oz), chopped
500 ml (17 fl oz/2 cups) vegetable stock
2 tablespoons lemon juice
1 small handful coriander (cilantro) leaves, finely chopped,
plus extra, to garnish
ice cubes, to serve
60 g (2¼ oz/⅔ cup) toasted flaked almonds
Turkish bread, to serve

Heat the oil in a large saucepan over medium heat. Add the onion and capsicum and cook, stirring, for 10 minutes, or until softened. Add the garlic and harissa and cook for 1 minute, or until aromatic.

Add the carrot, stock and 750 ml (26 fl oz/ 3 cups) water. Bring to the boil, then reduce the heat to low and simmer, uncovered, for 30 minutes, or until the carrot is very soft. Remove from the heat and cool for 15 minutes.

Blend or process the soup until smooth. Transfer to a large bowl, then stir in the lemon juice and coriander. Cover and refrigerate for 3 hours, or until well chilled.

Ladle the soup into serving bowls. Add some ice cubes and serve sprinkled with the flaked almonds and coriander leaves, accompanied by Turkish bread.

Green gazpacho with roast almonds

preparation 20 minutes + chilling
cooking nil
serves 6

2–4 garlic cloves, chopped (see Note)
3 spring onions (scallions), chopped
2 Lebanese (short) cucumbers, about 350 g (12 oz),
peeled and chopped
1 green capsicum (pepper), about 250 g (9 oz),
seeded and chopped
80 g (2¾ oz) day-old bread, chopped
½ iceberg lettuce, outer leaves discarded, chopped
2 large handfuls flat-leaf (Italian) parsley, chopped
1 large handful coriander (cilantro) leaves, chopped
310–375 ml (10¾–13 fl oz/1¼–1½ cups) chicken stock
250 ml (9 fl oz/1 cup) extra virgin olive oil
60 ml (2 fl oz/¼ cup) sherry vinegar, or to taste
80 g (2¾ oz/1½ cups) roasted almonds,
coarsely chopped

Combine the garlic, spring onion, cucumber, capsicum, bread, lettuce, parsley and coriander in a large bowl.

Working in batches, process the vegetable mixture in a food processor, adding a little of the stock to each batch, until a purée forms. Transfer the purée to a large bowl, then stir in 185 ml (6 fl oz/¾ cup) of the olive oil and the sherry vinegar. Season to taste with sea salt and freshly ground black pepper.

Cover the bowl tightly, then refrigerate for 2 hours, or until well chilled. Divide the soup among serving bowls and serve sprinkled with the almonds and drizzled with the remaining oil.

Note *The amount of garlic you use will vary according to the size of the cloves. If these are very large, use only two, but if they are small, use four.*

Toast the flaked almonds on a baking tray until golden brown.

Chop the coriander leaves, reserving the root and stems for another use.

Bottom: Green gazpacho with roast almonds. Top: Chilled Moroccan carrot and capsicum soup.

Soupe au pistou

preparation 45 minutes
cooking 35 minutes
serves 8

2 ripe tomatoes
3 flat-leaf (Italian) parsley stalks
1 large rosemary sprig
1 large thyme sprig
1 large marjoram sprig
60 ml (2 fl oz/¼ cup) olive oil
2 onions, thinly sliced
1 leek, white part only, thinly sliced
1 bay leaf
375 g (13 oz) pumpkin (winter squash), cut into small pieces
250 g (9 oz) potatoes, cut into small pieces
1 carrot, halved lengthways and thinly sliced
2 litres (70 fl oz/8 cups) vegetable stock or water
90 g (3¼ oz) fresh or frozen broad (fava) beans
80 g (2¾ oz/½ cup) fresh or frozen peas
2 small zucchini (courgettes), finely chopped
80 g (2¾ oz/½ cup) short macaroni or shell pasta

pistou
1 large handful basil leaves
2 large garlic cloves, crushed
80 ml (2½ fl oz/⅓ cup) olive oil
35 g (1¼ oz/⅓ cup) grated parmesan cheese

Score a cross in the base of each tomato. Put in a heatproof bowl and cover with boiling water. Leave for 30 seconds, then transfer to cold water and peel the skin away from the cross. Chop the flesh.

Tie the parsley, rosemary, thyme and marjoram together with string.

Heat the olive oil in a heavy-based saucepan and add the onion and leek. Cook over low heat for 10 minutes, or until soft. Add the herb bunch, bay leaf, pumpkin, potato, carrot and 1 teaspoon salt. Pour in the stock and simmer, covered, for 10 minutes, or until the vegetables are almost tender.

Add the broad beans, peas, zucchini, chopped tomato and pasta. Cover and cook for 15 minutes, or until the vegetables are very tender and the pasta is al dente. Add more water if necessary. Remove the herbs, including the bay leaf.

To make the pistou, finely chop the basil and garlic in a food processor. Pour in the oil gradually, processing until smooth. Stir in the parmesan and ½ teaspoon freshly ground black pepper and serve spooned over the soup.

Note *The flavour of this soup improves if refrigerated overnight then gently reheated.*

Remove the skin and seeds from the pumpkin, then cut the flesh into small pieces.

Grate the parmesan cheese using the fine side of a grater.

Roasted tomato, almond and basil soup

preparation 25 minutes
cooking 30 minutes
serves 4

60 ml (2 fl oz/¼ cup) olive oil
1 kg (2 lb 4 oz) large, vine-ripened tomatoes
1 large onion, finely chopped
2 garlic cloves, thinly sliced
50 g (1¾ oz/⅓ cup) blanched almonds, roughly chopped
2 handfuls basil, roughly torn
750 ml (26 fl oz/3 cups) chicken stock

Preheat the oven to 180°C (350°F/Gas 4). Grease a baking tray with 1 tablespoon of the oil. Cut the tomatoes in half, scoop out the seeds and arrange, cut side down, on the tray. Roast for 15 minutes, then set aside until the tomatoes are cool enough to handle. Discard the tomato skin and roughly chop the flesh.

Heat the remaining oil in a large saucepan over medium–low heat. Gently sauté the onion and garlic for 5–6 minutes, or until soft and translucent. Add the tomato, almonds and half the basil. Fry, stirring once or twice, for 5 minutes.

Transfer the mixture to a small food processor fitted with a metal blade and process for 20 seconds, or until thick and smooth.

Return the mixture to the saucepan, stir in the chicken stock and bring to the boil over medium–high heat. Stir in the remaining basil, season with salt and black pepper, and serve immediately.

Cream of asparagus soup

preparation 20 minutes
cooking 55 minutes
serves 4–6

1 kg (2 lb 4 oz) asparagus spears
30 g (1 oz) butter
1 onion, finely chopped
1 litre (35 fl oz/4 cups) vegetable stock
1 small handful basil leaves, chopped
1 teaspoon celery salt
250 ml (9 fl oz/1 cup) cream

Break off the woody ends from the asparagus (hold both ends of the spear and bend it gently—the woody end will snap off and can be thrown away) and trim off the tips. Blanch the tips in boiling water for 1–2 minutes, refresh in cold water and set aside. Chop the asparagus stems into large pieces.

Melt the butter in a large saucepan and cook the onion for 3–4 minutes over low–medium heat, or until soft and golden. Add the chopped asparagus stems and cook for 1–2 minutes, stirring continuously.

Add the vegetable stock, basil and celery salt. Bring to the boil, reduce the heat and simmer, covered, for 30 minutes. Check that the asparagus is well cooked and soft. If not, simmer for a further 10 minutes. Set aside and allow to cool slightly.

Pour into a food processor and process in batches until smooth. Then sieve into a clean saucepan. Return to the heat, pour in the cream and gently reheat. Do not allow the soup to boil. Season with salt and white pepper. Serve immediately, topped with the asparagus tips.

Hint If you are not using home-made stock, always taste before adding seasoning to your soup—shop-bought stock can be very salty.

Cut the tomatoes in half and scoop out the seeds before roasting them.

The asparagus needs to be well cooked and soft to produce a very smooth soup.

Bottom: Cream of asparagus soup. Top: Roasted tomato, almond and basil soup.

Tofu and spinach soup

preparation 10 minutes
cooking 10 minutes
serves 4

120 g (4 oz) soft tofu, drained
100 g (3½ oz) baby English spinach leaves
1 litre (35 fl oz/4 cups) chicken stock
1 tablespoon light soy sauce

Cut the tofu into small slices about 5 mm (¼ inch) thick. Roughly chop the baby spinach leaves if they are large.

Bring the stock to a rolling boil in a large saucepan, then add the tofu and soy sauce. Return to the boil, then reduce the heat and simmer gently for 2 minutes. Skim any scum that rises to the surface. Add the baby spinach and cook for 1–2 minutes. Season with salt and white pepper. Serve hot.

Broccoli soup

preparation 15 minutes
cooking 20 minutes
serves 4

2 tablespoons olive oil
1 large onion, thinly sliced
50 g (1¾ oz) diced prosciutto or unsmoked ham
1 garlic clove, crushed
1.25 litres (44 fl oz/5 cups) chicken stock
50 g (1¾ oz) stellini or other small pasta shapes
250 g (9 oz) broccoli, tops cut into small florets and the tender stems cut into thin batons
grated parmesan cheese, to serve

Heat the oil in a large saucepan over low heat, add the onion, prosciutto and garlic and cook for 4–5 minutes. Add the chicken stock, then bring to the boil, reduce the heat slightly and simmer for 10 minutes with the lid three-quarters on.

Add the stellini and broccoli and cook until the pasta is al dente and the broccoli is crisp but tender. Season to taste. Serve in warm bowls with the grated parmesan.

Chilled cucumber soup with curry oil

preparation 20 minutes + chilling
cooking 2 minutes
serves 4–6

3 telegraph (long) cucumbers, peeled, seeded and coarsely chopped
3 spring onions (scallions), thinly sliced
1 garlic clove
125 g (4½ oz/½ cup) Greek-style yoghurt
2 tablespoons lime juice
2 tablespoons sour cream
Tabasco sauce, to taste (optional)
185 ml (6 fl oz/¾ cup) chicken or vegetable stock
1 small handful mint, chopped
290 ml (10 fl oz) oil
½ teaspoon curry powder
4 x 15 cm (6 inch) poppadoms

Combine the cucumber, spring onion, garlic, yoghurt, lime juice, sour cream, Tabasco, stock and chopped mint in a food processor and process until a smooth purée forms. Season to taste with sea salt and freshly ground black pepper, then transfer to a bowl, cover and refrigerate for 2 hours, or until well chilled.

Heat 2 tablespoons of the oil in a small saucepan, add the curry powder and cook over medium heat for 30 seconds, or until fragrant, then cool.

Heat the remaining oil in a small frying pan until almost smoking. Add the poppadoms, in batches, and cook for 4–5 seconds, or until they are puffed and golden. Remove with a slotted spoon and drain on paper towel. When cool enough to handle, roughly break into small pieces.

Serve the soup in bowls, drizzled with the curry oil and topped with the poppadom pieces.

Top left: Tofu and spinach soup. Top right: Broccoli soup. Bottom left: Chilled cucumber soup with curry oil.

Chicken consommé

preparation 40 minutes
cooking 2 hours 40 minutes
serves 4

stock
1 kg (2 lb 4 oz) chicken carcasses, halved
185 g (6½ oz) chicken legs
1 carrot, chopped
1 onion, chopped
1 celery stalk, chopped
2 parsley sprigs
20 black peppercorns
1 bay leaf
1 thyme sprig

clarification mixture
2 chicken legs
1 carrot, finely chopped
1 leek, white part only, finely chopped
1 celery stalk, finely chopped
10 black peppercorns
1 parsley sprig, chopped
2 tomatoes, chopped
2 egg whites, lightly beaten

1 small carrot, julienned
½ small leek, white part only, julienned

To make the stock, remove any skin and fat from the chicken carcasses and legs. Place in a large heavy-based saucepan with 3 litres (102 fl oz/12 cups) cold water. Bring to the boil. Add the remaining ingredients and simmer for 1½ hours, skimming the top occasionally. Strain the stock and return to the saucepan.

To make the clarification mixture, remove the skin and meat from the chicken legs and discard the skin. Finely chop the meat and mix it with the carrot, leek, celery, peppercorns, parsley, tomato and egg white. Add 190 ml (6½ fl oz) of the warm stock.

Add the clarification mixture to the strained stock and whisk in well. Bring to a gentle simmer. Simmer for 1 hour. Ladle out the chicken stock and strain through a fine sieve lined with damp muslin. Place sheets of paper towel over the top and quickly lift away to remove any remaining fat. Season.

Just before serving, reheat the soup. Place the julienned vegetables in a saucepan of boiling water and cook for 2 minutes. Drain, spoon into bowls and pour the soup over the top.

Strain the stock, discarding the solids, and return it to the saucepan.

Add the clarification mixture to the stock and simmer for 1 hour.

meat soups

Spicy Vietnamese beef and pork noodle soup

preparation 20 minutes
cooking 40 minutes
serves 4

300 g (10½ oz) beef fillet steak
¼ cup (60 ml/2 fl oz) oil
300 g (10½ oz) pork leg fillet, cut into
3 cm (1¼ inch) cubes
1 large onion, cut into thin wedges
2 litres (70 fl oz/8 cups) beef stock
2 lemon grass stems
2 tablespoons fish sauce
1 teaspoon ground dried shrimp
1 teaspoon sugar
2 large red chillies, sliced
400 g (14 oz) fresh rice noodles
185 g (6½ oz/2 cups) bean sprouts, trimmed
3 tablespoons mint
1 large handful coriander (cilantro) leaves
thinly sliced chilli, to serve (optional)

Put the beef in the freezer for 20–30 minutes, or until partially frozen, then cut across the grain into paper-thin slices. Set the beef aside.

Heat a wok until hot, add 1 tablespoon of the oil and swirl it around to coat the base and side. Stir-fry the pork in batches for 2–3 minutes, or until browned. Remove from the wok and set aside.

Add another tablespoon of oil and stir-fry the onion wedges for 2–3 minutes, or until softened. Pour in the beef stock and 500 ml (17 fl oz/2 cups) water. Bruise one of the lemon grass stems and add it to the wok. Return the pork to the wok and bring the liquid to the boil, then reduce the heat and simmer for 15 minutes, or until the pork is tender, skimming off any scum that rises to the surface. Meanwhile, thinly slice the white part of the remaining lemon grass stem.

Remove the whole lemon grass stem from the broth and then stir in the fish sauce, dried shrimp and sugar and keep at a simmer.

Heat the remaining oil in a small frying pan over medium heat. Cook the sliced lemon grass and chilli for 2–3 minutes, or until fragrant. Stir into the broth. Just before serving, bring the broth to the boil over medium–high heat.

Meanwhile, put the rice noodles in a large heatproof bowl, cover with boiling water and gently separate the noodles. Drain immediately and rinse. Divide the noodles among four warmed serving bowls. Top with the bean sprouts and cover with the boiling broth. Add the sliced beef to the soup (the heat of the soup will cook it). Sprinkle the soup with the mint, coriander, and chilli, if desired. Serve immediately.

Slice the partially frozen beef across the grain into paper-thin slices.

Using only the white part of the stem, thinly slice the lemon grass.

Oxtail soup with stout and vegetables

preparation 25 minutes
cooking 4 hours 15 minutes
serves 4

2 kg (4 lb 8 oz) oxtails, trimmed
2 tablespoons oil
2 onions, finely chopped
1 leek, white part only, finely chopped
2 carrots, diced
1 celery stalk, diced
2 garlic cloves, crushed
2 bay leaves
2 tablespoons tomato paste (concentrated purée)
1 thyme sprig
2 flat-leaf (Italian) parsley sprigs
3.5 litres (122 fl oz/14 cups) chicken stock
375 ml (13 fl oz/1½ cups) stout
2 tomatoes, seeded and diced
100 g (3½ oz) cauliflower florets
100 g (3½ oz) green beans
100 g (3½ oz) broccoli florets
100 g (3½ oz) asparagus, cut into
3 cm (1¼ inch) lengths

Preheat the oven to 200°C (400°F/Gas 6). Place the oxtails in a baking dish and bake for 1 hour, turning occasionally, or until dark golden. Leave to cool.

Heat the oil in a large saucepan over medium heat. Cook the onion, leek, carrot and celery for 3–4 minutes, or until soft. Stir in the garlic, bay leaves and tomato paste, then add the oxtails, thyme and parsley.

Add the chicken stock and bring to the boil over high heat. Reduce the heat and simmer for 3 hours, or until the oxtails are tender and the meat is falling off the bone. Skim off any scum that rises to the surface. Remove the oxtails and set aside to cool slightly.

Take the meat off the bones and discard any fat or sinew. Roughly chop the meat and add it to the soup along with the stout, diced tomato and 500 ml (17 fl oz/2 cups) water. Add the vegetables and simmer for 5 minutes, or until the vegetables are tender. Season.

Bean soup with sausage

preparation 25 minutes
cooking 40 minutes
serves 4–6

4 Italian sausages
2 teaspoons olive oil
2 leeks, white part only, sliced
1 garlic clove, crushed
1 large carrot, cut into small cubes
2 celery stalks, sliced
2 tablespoons plain (all-purpose) flour
2 beef stock (bouillon) cubes, crumbled
2 litres (70 fl oz/8 cups) boiling water
125 ml (4 fl oz/½ cup) dry white wine
125 g (4½ oz) conchiglie (shell pasta)
440 g (15½ oz) tinned mixed beans, drained and rinsed
chopped parsley, to serve (optional)

Cut the sausages into small pieces. Heat the oil in a large heavy-based saucepan and add the sausage pieces. Cook over medium heat for 5 minutes, or until golden, stirring regularly. Remove from the pan, set aside and drain on paper towel.

Add the leek, garlic, carrot and celery to the pan and cook for 2–3 minutes or until soft, stirring occasionally. Add the flour and stir for 1 minute. Gradually stir in the combined stock cubes, water and the wine. Bring to the boil, reduce the heat and simmer for 10 minutes.

Add the pasta and beans to the pan. Increase the heat and cook for 8–10 minutes, or until the pasta is al dente. Return the sausage to the pan and season to taste. Serve sprinkled with chopped fresh parsley, if desired.

Note *Use dried beans, if preferred. Put them in a bowl, cover with cold water and soak overnight. Drain and add to a large saucepan with enough water to cover the beans well. Bring to the boil, reduce the heat and simmer for 1 hour. Drain well before adding to the soup.*

Bottom: Bean soup with sausage. Top: Oxtail soup with stout and vegetables.

Twelve varieties soup

preparation 45 minutes
cooking 20 minutes
serves 8

300 g (10½ oz) pork liver or lamb liver
30 g (1 oz) dried Chinese mushrooms
60 ml (2 fl oz/¼ cup) oil
3 onions, finely sliced
200 g (7 oz) boneless, skinless chicken breast, thinly sliced
4 garlic cloves, finely chopped
1 teaspoon finely chopped fresh ginger
2 tablespoons fish sauce
40 g (1½ oz/⅓ cup) green beans, sliced
40 g (1½ oz/⅓ cup) small cauliflower florets
30 g (1 oz/⅓ cup) sliced button mushrooms
15 g (½ oz/⅓ cup) shredded Chinese cabbage (wong bok)
20 g (¾ oz/⅓ cup) shredded English spinach
30 g (1 oz/⅓ cup) bean sprouts, trimmed
3 spring onions (scallions), finely sliced
1 tablespoon coriander (cilantro) leaves
3 eggs
1 tablespoon soy sauce
lime wedges, to serve

Cook the liver in simmering water for 5 minutes. Remove from the heat, allow to cool and slice thinly.

Put the Chinese mushrooms in a heatproof bowl, cover with boiling water and soak for 20 minutes. Drain well and slice.

Heat the oil in a wok, add the onion and cook over medium heat for 5 minutes, or until golden. Add the liver and chicken and stir to combine. Add the garlic and ginger and cook for 1 minute, then pour in the fish sauce and cook for 2 minutes.

Put the sliced Chinese mushrooms, beans, cauliflower florets, button mushrooms and onion mixture in a large saucepan. Add 2 litres (70 fl oz/8 cups) water, bring to the boil and cook until the vegetables are just tender. Stir in the shredded cabbage, spinach and bean sprouts and cook for a further 5 minutes, or until just tender. Add the spring onion and coriander leaves.

Break the eggs into the boiling soup and stir immediately. (The eggs will break up and cook.) Add the soy sauce and ¼ teaspoon ground black pepper. Serve immediately with the lime wedges to squeeze into the soup.

Shred the cabbage as finely as possible. This will ensure it wilts quickly in the broth.

The dried Chinese mushrooms need to be soaked in boiling water to soften them.

Meat dumpling soup

preparation 45 minutes
cooking 35 minutes
serves 4–6

1 tablespoon sesame seeds
2 tablespoons oil
2 garlic cloves, finely chopped
150 g (5½ oz) lean minced (ground) pork
200 g (7 oz) lean minced (ground) beef
200 g (7 oz) Chinese cabbage (wong bok), finely shredded
100 g (3½ oz) bean sprouts, trimmed and chopped
100 g (3½ oz) mushrooms, finely chopped
3 spring onions (scallions), finely chopped
150 g (5½ oz) gow gee (egg) dumpling wrappers

soup
2.5 litres (87 fl oz/10 cups) beef stock
2 tablespoons soy sauce
3 cm (1¼ inch) piece fresh ginger, very finely sliced
4 spring onions (scallions), chopped, to serve

To make the filling, toast the sesame seeds in a dry frying pan over medium heat for 3–4 minutes, shaking the pan gently, until the seeds are golden brown. Remove from the pan at once to prevent burning. Crush the seeds in a food mill or using a mortar and pestle.

Heat the oil in a saucepan. Cook the garlic, pork and beef mince over medium heat until the meat changes colour, breaking up any lumps with a fork. Add the cabbage, bean sprouts, mushrooms and 80 ml (2½ fl oz/⅓ cup) water. Cook, stirring occasionally, for 5–6 minutes, or until the water evaporates and the vegetables soften. Add the spring onion and sesame seeds and season to taste. Set aside.

Work with one gow gee wrapper at a time and keep the extra wrappers covered with a damp tea towel (dish towel). Place 1 teaspoon of filling on a wrapper, just off-centre, and gently smooth out the filling a little. Brush the edges of the wrapper with a little water and fold it over the filling to form a semi-circle. Press the edges together to seal. Repeat with the extra wrappers and filling.

To make the soup, combine the stock, soy sauce, ginger and half the spring onion in a large saucepan. Bring to the boil, then reduce the heat and simmer for 15 minutes.

Drop the dumplings into the simmering soup and gently cook for 5 minutes, or until they change colour and look plump. Serve immediately, garnished with the remaining spring onion.

Wipe the mushrooms clean with a soft, damp cloth before chopping them.

Fold over the wrapper to enclose the filling, then press firmly to seal.

Winter lamb shank soup

preparation 25 minutes
cooking 3 hours 45 minutes
serves 4

1 tablespoon olive oil
1.25 kg (2 lb 12 oz) lamb shanks
2 onions, chopped
4 garlic cloves, chopped
250 ml (9 fl oz/1 cup) red wine
2 bay leaves
1 tablespoon chopped rosemary
2.5 litres (87 fl oz/10 cups) beef stock
425 g (15 oz) tin crushed tomatoes
165 g (5¾ oz/¾ cup) pearl barley, rinsed and drained
1 large carrot, diced
1 potato, diced
1 turnip, diced
1 parsnip, diced
2 tablespoons redcurrant jelly (optional)

Heat the oil in a large saucepan over high heat. Cook the lamb shanks for 2–3 minutes, or until brown. Remove.

Add the chopped onion to the saucepan and cook over low heat for 8 minutes, or until soft. Add the garlic and cook for 30 seconds, then add the red wine and simmer for 5 minutes.

Add the lamb shanks, bay leaves, half the rosemary and 1.5 litres (52 fl oz/6 cups) of the beef to the pan. Season. Bring to the boil over high heat, then reduce the heat and simmer, covered, for 2 hours, or until the meat falls off the bone. Remove the shanks and cool slightly.

Take the meat off the bone and roughly chop. Add to the broth with the tomato, barley, remaining rosemary and stock and simmer for 30 minutes. Add the carrot, potato, turnip and parsnip and cook for 1 hour, or until the barley is tender. Remove and discard the bay leaves, then stir in the redcurrant jelly.

Gypsy stew

preparation 15 minutes + 3 hours soaking
cooking 1 hour 45 minutes
serves 4

250 g (9 oz/1¼ cups) dried white haricot beans
(such as navy beans)
80 ml (2½ fl oz/⅓ cup) olive oil
2 garlic cloves, chopped
2 onions, chopped
1 teaspoon sweet paprika
1 teaspoon smoked paprika
2 teaspoons ground cumin
¼ teaspoon ground cinnamon
¼ teaspoon cayenne pepper
1 teaspoon dried rosemary
1 red capsicum (pepper), seeded and diced
750 g (1 lb 10 oz) pork tenderloin, roughly diced
400 g (14 oz) tinned chopped tomatoes
250 ml (9 fl oz/1 cup) chicken stock
300 g (10½ oz) orange sweet potato, peeled and
roughly diced
60 g (2¼ oz) silverbeet (Swiss chard),
washed well and shredded

Cover the haricot beans with cold water and soak for at least 3 hours. Drain well. Preheat the oven to 160°C (315°F/Gas 2–3). Heat 2 tablespoons of the oil in a large saucepan over medium heat, add half the garlic and half the onion and cook for 5 minutes, or until soft. Add the beans and cover with water. Bring to the boil, then reduce the heat and simmer for 45 minutes, or until the beans are soft.

Meanwhile, heat the remaining oil in a large flameproof casserole dish over medium heat. Add the remaining garlic and onion and cook for 5 minutes, or until softened. Stir in the spices, rosemary, capsicum and pork and cook until the pork is evenly pale brown. Add the tomato and stock, bring to the boil, then cover and transfer to the oven for 1 hour. Add the beans, sweet potato and 250 ml (9 fl oz/1 cup) water and return to the oven for 30 minutes, or until the sweet potato is tender.

Stir in the shredded silverbeet and cook for 5 minutes, or until the silverbeet is wilted. Season to taste.

Bottom: Gypsy stew. Top: Winter lamb shank soup.

Sichuan beef noodle soup

preparation 10 minutes
cooking 3 hours
serves 4

1.5 litres (52 fl oz/6 cups) beef stock
1 tablespoon peanut oil
400 g (14 oz) beef chuck steak
½ cinnamon stick
2 star anise
1½ teaspoons Sichuan peppercorns, crushed
1 tablespoon finely sliced fresh ginger
2 tablespoons dark soy sauce
1 tablespoon Chinese rice wine
1 tablespoon brown bean sauce
3 x 5 cm (1¼ x 2 inch) piece dried mandarin peel (see Note)
125 g (4½ oz) fresh thin egg noodles
3 spring onions (scallions), thinly sliced

Pour the beef stock and 2 litres (70 fl oz/8 cups) water into a stockpot and simmer over low heat; keep warm until needed.

Heat a wok over high heat, add the oil and swirl to coat the base and side. Add the steak and sear it for 2–3 minutes on each side. Add the cinnamon stick, star anise, Sichuan peppercorns, ginger, soy sauce, rice wine, bean sauce and mandarin peel. Pour in the hot broth then cover and bring to simmering point over medium heat. Reduce the heat to low and simmer, covered, for 2–2½ hours, or until the steak is tender (you should be able to shred it; if not, return it to the simmer until tender). Remove the steak and discard the mandarin peel.

Meanwhile, cook the egg noodles in a large saucepan of boiling water for 1 minute to separate them. Drain. Just before serving, add the noodles to the broth and let them stand for 1–2 minutes, or until heated through.

Shred the steak into bite-sized pieces and divide evenly among four large serving bowls. Ladle on the broth and noodles, sprinkle with the spring onion and serve.

Note *Dried citrus peel is one of the most important Chinese flavourings and the dried peel of mandarins, tangerines and oranges is sold at many Asian food stores.*

Cut the spring onions into very thin slices to garnish the soup.

Put the Sichuan peppercorns in a mortar and use the pestle to crush them.

Lamb and cucumber soup

preparation 15 minutes + marinating
cooking 10–15 minutes
serves 4

250 g (9 oz) lamb fillet
1 tablespoon Shaoxing rice wine
1 tablespoon light soy sauce
1 teaspoon roasted sesame oil
½ Lebanese (short) cucumber
750 ml (26 fl oz/3 cups) chicken stock
2 teaspoons Chinese black rice vinegar, or to taste
coriander (cilantro) leaves

Cut the lamb fillet into very thin slices and combine with the rice wine, soy sauce and sesame oil. Marinate the lamb in the fridge for at least 15 minutes.

Halve the cucumber lengthways, discarding the seeds, and cut it into thin slices.

Bring the chicken stock to a rolling boil in a large clay pot or saucepan. Add the lamb and stir to separate the meat. Return to the boil, then add the cucumber and rice vinegar, and season with salt and white pepper. Return to the boil. Serve garnished with the coriander leaves.

Lamb, lemon and rice soup

preparation 30 minutes
cooking 35 minutes
serves 4

5 teaspoons olive oil, plus extra, for drizzling
1 small onion, chopped
2 small desiree potatoes, peeled and cut into
1 cm (½ inch) pieces
1 small garlic clove, crushed
100 g (2½ oz/ ½ cup) medium-grain rice
large pinch ground allspice
1 teaspoon dried mint
700 ml (25 fl oz/3 cups) chicken stock
2 large handfuls baby English spinach leaves
300 g (10 oz) lamb fillets (about 4), trimmed and cut
into 1 cm (½ inch) pieces
4 teaspoons lemon juice, or to taste
Greek-style yoghurt and lemon wedges, to serve

Heat the olive oil in a saucepan over medium heat. Add the onion, potato and garlic and cook, stirring, for 5 minutes, or until the vegetables have started to soften. Add the rice, allspice, mint, 750 ml (26 fl oz/3 cups) water and the stock, then bring the mixture to a gentle boil.

Reduce the heat to low, partially cover the pan and cook for 30 minutes, or until the rice and potato are very tender. Stir in the spinach, lamb and lemon juice, season to taste with sea salt and freshly ground black pepper, then cook for 3–4 minutes, or until the lamb is just cooked but still a little pink in the middle.

Serve the soup immediately with a drizzle of the olive oil and lemon wedges, and the yoghurt on the side.

Pork and buttered corn ramen noodle soup

preparation 15 minutes
cooking 30 minutes
serves 4

200 g (7 oz) Chinese barbecued pork fillet, in one piece
2 small fresh corn cobs
200 g (7 oz) dried ramen noodles
2 teaspoons peanut oil
1 teaspoon grated fresh ginger
1.5 litres (52 fl oz/6 cups) chicken stock
2 tablespoons mirin
2 spring onions (scallions), sliced
20 g (¾ oz) unsalted butter
1 spring onion (scallion), sliced, extra, to serve

Cut the pork fillet into thin slices. Cut the kernels from the corn cobs.

Cook the noodles in a large saucepan of boiling water for 4 minutes, or until tender. Drain, rinse in cold water, then drain again. Set aside.

Heat a wok over high heat, add the peanut oil and swirl to coat the base and side. Stir-fry the ginger for 1–2 minutes, then pour in the stock, mirin and 500 ml (17 fl oz/2 cups) water. Bring to the boil, then reduce the heat and simmer for 6–8 minutes. Add the pork and cook for 5 minutes. Add the corn kernels and spring onion and cook for a further 4–5 minutes, or until the kernels are tender.

Separate the noodles by running them under hot water, then divide among four deep bowls, shaping them into mounds. Ladle the liquid over the noodles and top with the pork and corn. Put 1 teaspoon butter on top of each mound and garnish with the extra sliced spring onion. Serve immediately.

Top left: Lamb and cucumber soup. Top right: Lamb, lemon and rice soup. Bottom left: Pork and buttered corn ramen noodle soup.

Lamb and chickpea soup

preparation 20 minutes
cooking 2 hours 25 minutes
serves 4

500 g (1 lb 2 oz) boneless lamb shoulder
2 tablespoons olive oil
2 small onions, chopped
2 large garlic cloves, crushed
1½ teaspoons ground cumin
2 teaspoons paprika
1 bay leaf
2 tablespoons tomato paste (concentrated purée)
1 litre (35 fl oz/4 cups) beef stock
600 g (1 lb 5 oz) tinned chickpeas
800 g (1 lb 12 oz) tinned chopped tomatoes
3 tablespoons finely chopped coriander (cilantro) leaves
3 tablespoons finely chopped flat-leaf (Italian) parsley
coriander (cilantro) leaves, extra, to serve

Trim the lamb of excess fat and sinew. Cut the lamb into small chunks.

Heat the oil in a large heavy-based saucepan or stockpot and cook the onion and garlic over low heat for 5 minutes, or until the onion is soft. Add the lamb chunks, increase the heat to medium and stir until the meat changes colour.

Add the cumin, paprika and bay leaf to the pan and cook until fragrant. Add the tomato paste and cook, stirring constantly, for 2 minutes. Add the beef stock to the pan, stir well and bring to the boil.

Drain and rinse the chickpeas and add to the pan, along with the tomatoes and chopped coriander and parsley. Stir, then bring to the boil. Reduce the heat and simmer for 2 hours, or until the meat is tender. Stir occasionally. Season, to taste. Garnish with the extra coriander.

Remove any excess fat from the lamb, then cut it into chunks.

Beef and beet borscht

preparation 30 minutes
cooking 1 hour 50 minutes
serves 4

2 tablespoons olive oil
1 onion, chopped
2 garlic cloves, crushed
500 g (1 lb 2 oz) beef chuck steak, cut into
2 cm (¾ inch) chunks
1 litre (35 fl oz/4 cups) beef stock
2 small beetroot (beets), scrubbed and trimmed
200 g (7 oz) tinned chopped tomatoes
1 carrot, cut into 1 cm (½ inch) cubes
2 potatoes, peeled and cut into 1 cm (½ inch) cubes
190 g (6¾ oz/2½ cups) finely shredded cabbage
2 teaspoons lemon juice
2 teaspoons sugar
2 tablespoons chopped flat-leaf (Italian) parsley
2 tablespoons chopped dill
80 g (2¾ fl oz/⅓ cup) sour cream
crusty bread, to serve

Preheat the oven to 200°C (400°F/Gas 6). Heat the oil in a large saucepan, add the onion and garlic and sauté over medium heat for 5 minutes. Add the beef, stock and 1 litre (35 fl oz/4 cups) water. Bring to the boil, then reduce the heat and simmer, covered, for 1¼ hours, or until the meat is tender. Remove the meat, reserving the stock mixture.

Meanwhile, wrap each beetroot in foil and then bake for 30–40 minutes, or until tender. Remove the foil and set them aside to cool, then peel and cut into 1 cm (½ inch) pieces (wear rubber gloves to stop the beetroot staining your hands).

Return the stock to the boil. Add the tomato, carrot and potato and season with sea salt. Cook over medium heat for 10 minutes, or until the vegetables are tender. Add the cabbage and cook for 5 minutes.

Return the meat to the pan with the beetroot, lemon juice, sugar and 1½ tablespoons each of the chopped parsley and dill. Cook for 2 minutes, or until heated through. Season to taste and divide the borscht among warm bowls. Top with a little sour cream, sprinkle with the remaining herbs and serve with crusty bread.

Bottom: Beef and beet borscht. Top: Lamb and chickpea soup.

Pork congee

preparation 10 minutes
cooking 1 hour 50 minutes
serves 4–6

300 g (10½ oz/1½ cups) long-grain rice, thoroughly rinsed
½ star anise
2 spring onions (scallions), white part only
4 x 4 cm (1½ x 1½ inch) piece fresh ginger, cut into slices
3.5 litres (122 fl oz/14 cups) chicken stock
1 tablespoon peanut oil
2 garlic cloves, crushed
1 teaspoon grated fresh ginger, extra
400 g (14 oz) minced (ground) pork
60 ml (2 fl oz/¼ cup) light soy sauce
sesame oil, to drizzle
6 fried dough sticks (see Note)

Put the rice in a large saucepan with the star anise, spring onions, sliced ginger and chicken stock. Bring to the boil, then reduce the heat to low and simmer for 1½ hours, stirring occasionally.

Heat the oil in a frying pan over high heat. Cook the garlic and grated ginger for 30 seconds. Add the pork and cook for 5 minutes, or until browned, breaking up any lumps with the back of a spoon.

Remove and discard the star anise, spring onions and sliced ginger. Add the pork mixture, then simmer for 10 minutes. Season with white pepper and stir in the soy sauce. Serve with a drizzle of sesame oil and the dough sticks.

Note Fried dough sticks are available at Chinese bakeries and speciality shops and are best eaten soon after purchasing. If not, reheat in a 200°C (400°F/Gas 6) oven for 5 minutes, then serve.

Place the rice in a colander and thoroughly rinse under cold running water.

Peel the skin off the ginger, then cut it into very thin slices.

Scotch broth

preparation 20 minutes
cooking 2 hours 30 minutes
serves 8–10

750 g (1 lb 10 oz) best neck of lamb chops or lamb shanks
250 g (9 oz) pearl barley or soup mix
1 carrot, diced
1 turnip, diced
1 parsnip, diced
1 onion, finely chopped
1 small leek, white part only, thinly sliced
75 g (2½ oz/1 cup) finely chopped cabbage
30 g (1 oz/½ cup) chopped parsley

Cut away any excess fat from the meat. Place the meat in a large heavy-based saucepan with 2.5 litres (87 fl oz/10 cups) water. Bring to the boil, then reduce the heat and simmer, covered, for 1 hour. Skim off any froth from the surface. Meanwhile, soak the barley or soup mix in cold water for 1 hour.

Add the carrot, turnip, parsnip, onion and leek to the pan. Drain the barley and add to the pan. Stir to combine, cover and simmer for 1½ hours. Stir in the cabbage 10 minutes before the end of cooking time. (Add more water, according to taste.)

Remove the meat from the pan and cool before removing from the bones. Chop the meat finely and return to the soup. Add the parsley and season.

Note *Soup mix is a combination of pearl barley, split peas and lentils. The soup may be covered and refrigerated for up to 3 days. Suitable to freeze up to 1 month.*

Goulash soup

preparation 15 minutes
cooking 1 hour 15 minutes
serves 4–6

650 g (1 lb 7 oz) blade steak
2 tablespoons oil
1 large leek, white part only, sliced
2 garlic cloves, crushed
1 teaspoon paprika
1 teaspoon caraway seeds
400 g (14 oz) tin crushed tomatoes
1 litre (35 fl oz/4 cups) beef stock
2 potatoes, diced
sour cream, to serve

Cut the steak into small cubes. Heat the oil in a large pan, brown the meat in batches and set aside.

Add the leek to the pan and cook for 5 minutes, or until just soft. Add the garlic and paprika and cook for 1 minute. Add the caraway seeds, tomatoes, stock and meat. Bring to the boil, then simmer, partially covered, for 30 minutes.

Add the potatoes and simmer for 30 minutes, or until very tender. Serve with sour cream.

Storage time *The soup will keep for up to 2 days in the refrigerator.*

Skim off any froth that forms on the surface while the meat is cooking.

Quickly brown the beef cubes in small batches in the oil.

Bottom: Goulash soup. Top: Scotch broth.

Pork and chickpea stew

preparation 20 minutes
cooking 1 hour 30 minutes
serves 4

2 teaspoons ground cumin
1 teaspoon ground coriander
½ teaspoon chilli powder
¼ teaspoon ground cinnamon
400 g (14 oz) lean diced pork, trimmed
1 tablespoon plain (all-purpose) flour
1 tablespoon olive oil
1 large onion, finely chopped
3 garlic cloves, finely chopped
2 large unpeeled carrots, chopped
2 celery stalks, sliced
250 ml (9 fl oz/1 cup) chicken stock
2 ripe tomatoes, chopped
310 g (11 oz) tinned chickpeas, drained and rinsed
2 tablespoons chopped parsley

Cook the spices in a dry frying pan over low heat, shaking the pan, for 1 minute, or until fragrant.

Combine the trimmed pork with the spices and flour in a plastic bag and toss well to coat. Remove the pork from the bag and shake off the excess flour.

Heat the olive oil in a large heavy-based saucepan over high heat and cook the pork, tossing regularly, for about 8 minutes, or until lightly browned. Add the onion, garlic, carrot, celery and half the stock to the pan and toss well. Cover and cook for 10 minutes.

Add the remaining stock and tomato and season with salt and freshly ground black pepper. Bring to the boil, reduce the heat and cover with a tight-fitting lid, then simmer over low heat for 1 hour. Gently shake the pan occasionally but don't remove the lid during cooking. Stir in the chickpeas and parsley. Simmer, uncovered, for a further 5 minutes before serving.

Rustic lamb, vegetable and mint soup

preparation 20 minutes
cooking 25 minutes
serves 4

1 tablespoon olive oil
6 (about 1 kg/2 lb 4 oz) lamb loin chops, boned, trimmed and cut into 2 cm (¾ inch) pieces (see Notes)
60 ml (2 fl oz/¼ cup) dry white wine
500 g (1 lb 2 oz) potatoes, cut into 1 cm (½ inch) pieces
2 carrots, sliced
1 red onion, cut into wedges
2 mint sprigs
250 ml (9 fl oz/1 cup) vegetable stock
200 g (7 oz) Italian flat beans (see Notes), trimmed and cut into 3 cm (1¼ inch) lengths
1 large handful mint leaves, finely chopped

Heat the oil in a large saucepan over high heat. Cook the lamb, turning occasionally, for 3 minutes, or until browned. Remove the lamb and set aside. Discard the cooking oil.

Add the wine to the saucepan and scrape the base with a wooden spoon to loosen any stuck-on bits. Cook for 1 minute or until the wine is slightly reduced.

Add the potato, carrot, onion, mint sprigs, stock and 500 ml (17 fl oz/2 cups) water. Bring to the boil over high heat, then reduce the heat and simmer, covered, for 10 minutes. Add the beans and simmer, covered, for 5 minutes or until the vegetables are tender.

Discard the mint sprigs, then stir through the chopped mint and the lamb. Season to taste with salt and freshly ground black pepper and serve immediately.

Notes *You will need about 400 g (14 oz) boneless lamb meat for this recipe.*

Italian flat beans are available from selected greengrocers. If unavailable, you can use green beans instead.

Remove the leaves and tough white ends from the celery before slicing the stalks.

Peel the red onion, then use a sharp knife to cut it into thick wedges.

Bottom: Rustic lamb, vegetable and mint soup. Top: Pork and chickpea stew.

Minestrone with pesto

preparation 25 minutes + overnight soaking
cooking 2 hours
serves 6

125 g (4½ oz) dried borlotti beans
60 ml (2 fl oz/¼ cup) olive oil
1 large onion, finely chopped
2 garlic cloves, crushed
60 g (2¼ oz) pancetta, finely chopped
1 celery stalk, halved lengthways and cut into thin slices
1 carrot, halved lengthways and cut into thin slices
1 potato, diced
2 teaspoons tomato paste (concentrated purée)
400 g (14 oz) tin crushed tomatoes
6 basil leaves, roughly torn
2 litres (70 fl oz/8 cups) chicken or vegetable stock
2 zucchini (courgettes), cut into thin slices
115 g (4 oz/¾ cup) fresh peas, shelled
60 g (2¼ oz) green beans, cut into short lengths
80 g (2¾ oz) silverbeet (Swiss chard) leaves, shredded
3 tablespoons chopped flat-leaf (Italian) parsley
70 g (2½ oz) ditalini or other small pasta

pesto
2 handfuls basil leaves
20 g (¾ oz) lightly toasted pine nuts (see Note)
2 garlic cloves
100 ml (3½ fl oz) olive oil
25 g (1 oz/¼ cup) grated parmesan cheese

Soak the borlotti beans in plenty of cold water overnight. Drain and rinse thoroughly under cold water.

Heat the oil in a large, deep saucepan, add the onion, garlic and pancetta and cook over low heat, stirring occasionally, for 8–10 minutes, or until softened. Add the celery, carrot and potato and cook for 5 minutes. Stir in the tomato paste, tomatoes, basil and drained borlotti beans. Season to taste with freshly ground black pepper. Add the stock and bring slowly to the boil. Cover and simmer, stirring occasionally, for 1½ hours.

Add the zucchini, peas, green beans, silverbeet, parsley and pasta to the soup. Simmer for 8–10 minutes, or until the vegetables and pasta are al dente. Check for seasoning and adjust if necessary.

To make the pesto, combine the basil, pine nuts and garlic with a pinch of salt in a food processor. Process until finely chopped. With the motor running, slowing add the oil. Transfer to a bowl and stir in the parmesan and some ground black pepper to taste. Serve with the soup.

Note Toast the pine nuts in a frying pan over medium heat, stirring constantly, until they are golden brown and fragrant.

Osso buco, barley and vegetable soup

Preparation time 25 minutes
Total cooking time 50 minutes
Serves 6

500 g (1 lb 2 oz) veal shanks with bones (osso buco), cut into 5 cm (2 inch) pieces (ask your butcher to do this)
2 tablespoons olive oil
1 onion, diced
1–2 garlic cloves, crushed
425 g (14 oz) tin chopped tomatoes
1 tablespoon tomato paste (concentrated purée)
½ teaspoon dried oregano
1.5 litres (52 fl oz/6 cups) beef stock
300 g (10 oz) potatoes, cubed
300 g (10 oz) pumpkin (winter squash), cubed
165 g (5¾ oz/¾ cup) pearl barley
200 g (7 oz) zucchini (courgette), sliced

Trim the meat from the bones and cut it into cubes. Scrape out the marrow from the bones, if you want to use it, then discard the bones. Heat the oil in a heavy-based saucepan and brown the meat and marrow, in batches if necessary, until a rich brown. Remove and drain on paper towel. Set the fried marrow aside, to garnish.

Add the onion to the pan and cook for 4–5 minutes over low heat; then add the garlic and cook for 1 minute longer. Add the meat, tomato, tomato paste, oregano, beef stock, potato and pumpkin to the pan.

Wash the barley in a sieve until the water runs clean, then drain and add to the soup. Bring to the boil, then reduce the heat to low, cover and simmer for 20 minutes. Add the zucchini and cook, covered, for 10 minutes, until the barley is cooked. Serve garnished with the fried marrow.

Note Osso buco (or ossobuco) is Italian for marrowbone. It is a stew made with the knuckle of veal, usually served in a tomato sauce.

Ask your butcher to cut the osso buco into pieces, then trim the meat from the bones.

Bottom: Osso buco, barley and vegetable soup. Top: Minestrone with pesto.

Lamb soup with rice noodles

preparation 20 minutes + 2 hours marinating
cooking 2 hours
serves 4

2 garlic cloves, crushed
2 teaspoons grated fresh ginger
1 teaspoon five-spice powder
¼ teaspoon ground white pepper
2 tablespoons Chinese rice wine
1 teaspoon sugar
1 kg (2 lb 4 oz) boneless lamb shoulder, trimmed and cut
into 3 cm (1¼ inch) pieces
30 g (1 oz) dried Chinese mushrooms
1 tablespoon peanut oil
1 large onion, cut into wedges
2 cm (¾ inch) piece fresh ginger, cut into thin strips
1 teaspoon Sichuan peppercorns, crushed
2 tablespoons sweet bean paste
1 teaspoon black peppercorns, ground and toasted
500 ml (17 fl oz/2 cups) chicken stock
60 ml (2 fl oz/¼ cup) oyster sauce
2 star anise
60 ml (2 fl oz/¼ cup) Chinese rice wine, extra
80 g (2¾ oz) tinned sliced bamboo shoots, drained
100 g (3½ oz) tinned water chestnuts,
drained and sliced
400 g (14 oz) fresh rice noodles, cut into
2 cm (¾ inch) wide strips
1 spring onion (scallion), sliced, to serve

Combine the garlic, grated ginger, five-spice, white pepper, rice wine, sugar and 1 teaspoon salt in a large bowl. Add the lamb and toss to coat. Cover and marinate for 2 hours.

Meanwhile, soak the dried mushrooms in boiling water for 30 minutes, then drain and squeeze out any excess water. Remove and discard the stems. Chop the caps.

Heat a wok over high heat, add the oil and swirl to coat the base and side. Stir-fry the onion, ginger strips and Sichuan peppercorns for 2 minutes. Add the lamb in batches and cook for 2–3 minutes, or until it is starting to brown. Return all the lamb to the wok. Stir in the bean paste and ground

peppercorns and cook for 3 minutes. Transfer to a 2 litre (70 fl oz/8 cup) flameproof clay pot or casserole dish. Stir in the stock, oyster sauce, star anise and extra rice wine and simmer, covered, over low heat for 1½ hours, or until the lamb is tender. Stir in the bamboo shoots and water chestnuts and cook for 20 minutes. Add the mushrooms.

Cover the noodles with boiling water and gently separate them. Drain and rinse, then add to the soup, stirring for 1–2 minutes, or until heated through. Sprinkle with spring onion to serve.

Ramen noodles with soy broth

preparation 40 minutes + chilling
cooking 6 hours 15 minutes
serves 4

broth
1 kg (2 lb 4 oz) pork bones
1 kg (2 lb 4 oz) chicken bones
10 spring onions (scallions), bruised
10 cm (4 inch) piece fresh ginger, sliced
1 garlic bulb, cut in half through the centre
2 carrots, chopped
10 cm (4 inch) square piece konbu (kelp),
wiped with a damp cloth
125–185 ml (4–6 fl oz/½–¾ cup) shoyu (Japanese
soy sauce)
80 ml (2½ fl oz/⅓ cup) sake

8 dried shiitake mushrooms
500 g (1 lb 2 oz) fresh ramen noodles
100 g (3½ oz) bamboo shoots, sliced
125 g (4½ oz) Chinese barbecued pork, sliced
200 g (7 oz) bok choy (pak choy), sliced lengthways
into wide strips, blanched
50 g (1¾ oz) bean sprouts, blanched
4 spring onions (scallions), cut into
4 cm (1½ inch) lengths

To make the broth, put the pork and chicken bones in a stockpot and cover with water. Bring to the boil over high heat, then drain. Rinse the bones, then return them to the stockpot. Add the spring onions, ginger, garlic, carrot and konbu and pour in enough cold water to cover the solids by about 5 cm (2 inches). Bring to the boil over high heat, then remove the konbu and reduce to a simmer. Cook for 6 hours, or until the liquid has reduced to about 1.5 litres (52 fl oz/6 cups). Cool slightly, remove the bones, then strain the stock and refrigerate for 6 hours, or until cold.

Soak the shiitake mushrooms in hot water for 30 minutes, then drain. Discard the stems.

Bring a saucepan of salted water to the boil, add the ramen noodles and separate them with a pair of chopsticks. Cook for 1–2 minutes. Drain well, then rinse.

Pour the broth into a saucepan. Add the shoyu and sake, bring to the boil over high heat, then reduce to a simmer. Pour a little broth into four bowls, then divide the noodles among the bowls. Pour in the remaining broth. Arrange piles of the shiitake, bamboo shoots, pork, bok choy, bean sprouts and spring onion on top of the noodles.

Chinese lamb, garlic chive and cellophane noodle soup

preparation 10 minutes + 3 hours marinating
cooking 20 minutes
serves 4

2 tablespoons light soy sauce
1 tablespoon oyster sauce
1 tablespoon Chinese rice wine
1 teaspoon sugar
1¼ teaspoons sesame oil
3 slices fresh ginger
250 g (9 oz) lamb fillet
100 g (3½ oz) cellophane noodles
1 tablespoon vegetable oil
1 tablespoon finely chopped fresh ginger
2 spring onions (scallions), finely chopped,
plus extra, to serve
125 g (4½ oz) chopped garlic chives
1 litre (35 fl oz/4 cups) chicken stock

Combine the soy sauce, oyster sauce, rice wine, sugar, ¼ teaspoon of the sesame oil and the ginger slices in a bowl. Add the lamb and marinate for 3 hours, turning occasionally. Remove the lamb and ginger from the marinade with tongs. Set aside.

Meanwhile, soak the noodles in a bowl of boiling water for 3–4 minutes. Rinse, drain and set aside.

Heat a wok over high heat, add the vegetable oil and the remaining sesame oil and swirl to coat the base and side. Add the chopped ginger, spring onion and garlic chives and cook for 30 seconds, stirring constantly. Slowly pour in the stock and bring to the boil. Add the lamb and the ginger slices, reduce the heat to low, cover with a lid and poach the lamb for 10 minutes.

Remove the lamb from the wok. Bring the soup to the boil over medium heat. Meanwhile, thinly slice the lamb. Return the sliced lamb to the wok and add the noodles at the same time, stirring well until mixed together. Serve hot with the sliced spring onion scattered over the top.

Bottom: Chinese lamb, garlic chive and cellophane noodle soup. Top: Ramen noodles with soy broth.

Lamb and fusilli soup

preparation 25 minutes
cooking 40 minutes
serves 6–8

2 tablespoons oil
500 g (1 lb 2 oz) lean lamb meat, cubed
2 onions, finely chopped
2 carrots, diced
4 celery stalks, diced
425 g (15 oz) tinned crushed tomatoes
2 litres (70 fl oz/8 cups) beef stock
500 g (1 lb 2 oz) fusilli
chopped flat-leaf (Italian) parsley, to serve

Heat the oil in a large saucepan and cook the cubed lamb, in batches, until golden brown. Remove each batch as it is done and drain on paper towel. Set aside.

Add the onion to the pan and cook for 2 minutes, or until softened. Return all of the meat to the pan, add the carrot, celery, tomato and beef stock. Stir to combine and bring to the boil. Reduce the heat to low and simmer, covered, for 15 minutes. Add the fusilli and stir to prevent the pasta from sticking to the pan. Simmer, uncovered, for a further 10 minutes, or until the lamb and pasta are tender. Serve sprinkled with parsley.

West Lake soup

preparation 15 minutes + marinating
cooking 15 minutes
serves 4

150 g (5½ oz) rump or fillet steak
1 teaspoon salt
1 teaspoon sugar
1 tablespoon light soy sauce
1 tablespoon Shaoxing rice wine
2 tablespoons cornflour (cornstarch)
½ teaspoon roasted sesame oil
750 ml (26 fl oz/3 cups) chicken stock
100 g (3½ oz) fresh or frozen peas
1 egg, lightly beaten
1 spring onion (scallion), chopped

Trim the fat off the steak and cut the steak into small pieces, about the size of the peas. Combine the steak with a pinch of the salt, half the sugar, 1 teaspoon each of the soy sauce, rice wine and cornflour, and the sesame oil. Marinate in the fridge for at least 20 minutes.

Bring the stock to a rolling boil in a clay pot or saucepan. Add the beef and stir to separate the meat, then add the peas and the remaining salt, sugar, soy sauce and rice wine. Return to the boil, then stir in the egg. Combine the remaining cornflour with enough water to make a paste, add to the soup and simmer until thickened. Garnish with the spring onion.

Quick pea and ham soup with mint

preparation 10 minutes
cooking 10 minutes
serves 4

50 g (1¾ oz) butter
1 onion, finely chopped
500 g (1 lb 2 oz) frozen peas
375 ml (13 fl oz/1½ cups) chicken stock
3 tablespoons roughly chopped mint leaves, plus extra leaves, to serve
250 g (9 oz) leg ham, cut into strips

Melt the butter in a large saucepan over medium heat and cook the onion, stirring, for 5 minutes, or until soft.

Stir in the peas, stock and 375 ml (13 fl oz/1½ cups) water and bring to the boil over high heat. Reduce the heat and simmer, covered, for 5 minutes.

Cool slightly, then stir in the chopped mint and transfer the soup, in batches, to a food processor or blender and process until smooth. Return the soup to the saucepan and reheat over medium heat. Stir in the ham and season to taste with freshly ground black pepper. Serve scattered with the extra mint leaves.

Top left: Lamb and fusilli soup. Top right: West Lake soup. Bottom left: Quick pea and ham soup with mint.

Mongolian hotpot

preparation 15 minutes
cooking 5 minutes
serves 6

80 ml (2½ fl oz/⅓ cup) light soy sauce
2 tablespoons Chinese sesame paste
1 teaspoon chilli paste
1 teaspoon garlic paste
60 ml (2 fl oz/¼ cup) Chinese rice wine
250 g (9 oz) dried rice vermicelli
600 g (1 lb 5 oz) lamb backstraps or loin fillet, thinly sliced across the grain
4 spring onions (scallions), sliced
1.5 litres (52 fl oz/6 cups) chicken stock
6 thin slices fresh ginger
300 g (10½ oz) silken firm tofu, cut into 1.5 cm (⅝ inch) cubes
300 g (10½ oz) Chinese broccoli (gai larn), cut into 4 cm (1½ inch) lengths
90 g (3¼ oz/2 cups) shredded Chinese cabbage (wong bok)

To make the sauce, combine the soy sauce, sesame paste, chilli paste, garlic paste and 1 tablespoon of the rice wine in a small bowl.

Put the rice vermicelli in a large heatproof bowl, cover with boiling water and soak for 6–7 minutes, then drain well. Divide the vermicelli among six serving bowls. Top with the lamb slices and spring onion.

Put the stock, ginger slices and remaining rice wine in a flameproof hotpot or large saucepan. Cover and bring to the boil over high heat. Add the tofu, Chinese broccoli and

Chinese cabbage and simmer, uncovered, for 1 minute, or until the broccoli has wilted. Divide the tofu, broccoli and cabbage among the serving bowls then ladle on the hot stock — it should be hot enough to cook the lamb. Drizzle a little of the sauce on top and serve the rest on the side.

Note *This recipe traditionally uses a Chinese steamboat, which is an aluminium pot with a steam spout in the middle, placed on a propane burner in the middle of the dining table. You could also use a fondue pot.*

Cover the vermicelli with boiling water in a heatproof bowl and leave to soak.

Wash the Chinese cabbage, then shred it by cutting across the leaves.

Spicy lamb soup

preparation 25 minutes
cooking 1 hour 40 minutes
serves 4–6

2 large onions, roughly chopped
3 red chillies, seeded and chopped (or 2 teaspoons dried chilli)
3–4 garlic cloves
2.5 cm (1 inch) piece fresh ginger, chopped
5 cm (2 inch) lemon grass, white part only, finely chopped
½ teaspoon ground cardamom
2 teaspoons ground cumin
½ teaspoon ground cinnamon
1 teaspoon ground turmeric
1 teaspoon ground black pepper
2 tablespoons peanut oil
1.5 kg (3 lb 5 oz) lamb neck chops
2–3 tablespoons vindaloo paste
600 ml (21 fl oz) coconut cream
45 g (1½ oz/¼ cup) soft brown sugar
2–3 tablespoons lime juice
4 makrut (kaffir lime) leaves

Put the onion, chilli, garlic, ginger, lemon grass, cardamom, cumin, cinnamon, turmeric and pepper in a food processor and process to a paste.

Heat half the oil in a large frying pan and brown the chops in batches. Drain on paper towel.

Add the remaining oil to the pan and cook the spice paste and vindaloo paste for 2–3 minutes. Add the chops and 1.75 litres (61 fl oz/7 cups) water, cover and bring to the boil. Reduce the heat and simmer, covered, for 1 hour. Remove the chops from the pan and stir in the coconut cream.

Remove the lamb meat from the bones, shred and return to the pan.

Add the brown sugar, lime juice and makrut leaves. Simmer, uncovered, over low heat for 20–25 minutes, until the soup is slightly thickened.

Beef ball and white bean soup

preparation 30 minutes
cooking 15 minutes
serves 4

600 g (1 lb 5 oz) minced (ground) beef
2 garlic cloves, crushed
1 tablespoon parsley, finely chopped
large pinch of ground cinnamon
large pinch of freshly grated nutmeg
2 eggs, lightly beaten
1.5 litres (52 fl oz/6 cups) beef stock
2 carrots, thinly sliced
2 x 400 g (14 oz) tins white beans, drained and rinsed
½ savoy cabbage, finely shredded
grated parmesan cheese, to serve

Put the beef in a bowl with the garlic, parsley, cinnamon, nutmeg and half of the egg. Mix everything together well and season with salt and pepper. If the mixture is dry, add the rest of the egg – it should be sticky enough so that forming small balls is easy.

Roll the beef mixture into balls small enough to scoop up on a spoon and eat in one mouthful. Put them on a plate as you make them.

Put the beef stock and carrot in a saucepan and bring to the boil. Add the meatballs, one at a time, and reduce the heat to a simmer. Cook for 3 minutes, or until the balls are cooked through. Add the beans and cabbage and cook for another 4–5 minutes. Season the broth, to taste.

Serve the soup with parmesan stirred in and plenty of bread to dunk into the broth.

Process the onion, chilli, garlic, ginger, lemon grass and spices into a paste.

Grate the parmesan cheese using the fine side of a grater.

Bottom: Beef ball and white bean soup. Top: Spicy lamb soup.

Caldo verde

preparation 15 minutes
cooking 1 hour
serves 6

150 g (5½ oz) chorizo sausage, thinly sliced
2 tablespoons olive oil
1 large onion, thinly sliced
4 garlic cloves, finely chopped
2 teaspoons finely chopped oregano
1 large potato, diced
200 g (7 oz/1 cup) long-grain rice
1 litre (35 fl oz/4 cups) chicken stock
1 small green chilli, split lengthways
270 g (9½ oz) shredded kale, silverbeet (Swiss chard) or English spinach
1 large handful flat-leaf (Italian) parsley, chopped
extra virgin olive oil, for drizzling
lemon wedges, to serve

Fry the sliced chorizo in a dry frying pan over medium heat for 5 minutes, or until slightly crispy. Set aside.

Heat the oil in a large saucepan over medium heat, add the onion, garlic and oregano and cook for 8 minutes, or until the onion is softened but not browned. Add the potato and rice and cook for a further 5 minutes, stirring to make sure it doesn't catch on the bottom of the pan.

Pour in the chicken stock and 1 litre (35 fl oz/4 cups) water, and add the chilli. Increase the heat and bring to the boil, stirring occasionally. Reduce the heat and simmer for about 20 minutes, or until the rice is tender and the potato is just starting to fall apart, skimming as needed. Discard the chilli.

Lightly crush the potato with a vegetable masher, then add the kale and the chorizo. Cook for a further 15 minutes, or until the kale is softened and loses its raw flavour.

Stir in the chopped parsley and season to taste. Ladle into bowls and drizzle with extra virgin olive oil, if desired. Serve with lemon wedges to squeeze over the top.

Note Originating in the northern Portuguese province of Minho, this hearty soup is popular throughout the country. The authentic recipe uses couve tronchuda, a dark green cabbage, and linguica, a spicy Portuguese sausage; however, as they are both difficult to obtain outside the Iberian peninsula, we have used kale and chorizo instead.

Cut the onion in half lengthways, then cut it into thin slices.

Remove the tough ends from the silverbeet, then shred the leaves.

Japanese pork and vegetable soup

preparation 30 minutes
cooking 1 hour 15 minutes
serves 4 as a starter

100 g (3½ oz) yam cake (see Note), cut into
1.5 cm (⅝ inch) dice (optional)
100 g (3½ oz) burdock root
1 teaspoon Japanese rice vinegar
1 litre (35 fl oz/4 cups) dashi
200 g (7 oz) pork belly, cut into small bite-sized pieces
4 large fresh shiitake mushrooms, sliced
100 g (3½ oz) daikon, peeled, cut into quarters lengthways,
then thickly sliced
1 carrot, cut into quarters lengthways,
then thickly sliced
2½ tablespoons red miso
150 g (5½ oz) silken firm tofu, cut into 1.5 cm (⅝ inch) dice
1 spring onion (scallion), thinly sliced

Bring a small saucepan of water to the boil, then add the
yam cake and cook for 1 minute. Drain well.

Roughly scrape the skin of the burdock root with a
sharp knife, then rinse. Starting at the thin end, shave
thinly with a knife, turning as you cut. Put the shavings
in a bowl with 500 ml (17 fl oz/2 cups) water and the rice
vinegar. Leave for 15 minutes to remove some of the
bitterness from the burdock root. Drain well.

Pour the dashi into a large saucepan and bring to the boil.
Add the pork, shiitake, daikon, carrot, burdock root and yam
cake and return to the boil. Reduce to a simmer and cook
for 1 hour, or until the pork is cooked through and tender.

Add the miso and stir until dissolved. Gently stir in the tofu
and divide among four small soup bowls. Sprinkle with the
spring onion and serve immediately.

Note Yam cake (konnyaku) and burdock root (gobo) are available
from Japanese grocery stores.

Hot and sour lime soup with beef

preparation 20 minutes
cooking 30 minutes
serves 4

1 litre (35 fl oz/4 cups) beef stock
2 lemon grass stems, white part only, halved
3 garlic cloves, halved
2.5 cm (1 inch) piece fresh ginger, sliced
3 very large handfuls coriander (cilantro), leaves and
stalks separated
4 spring onions (scallions), thinly sliced
2 strips lime zest
2 star anise
3 small fresh red chillies, seeded and finely chopped
500 g (1 lb 2 oz) fillet steak, trimmed
2 tablespoons fish sauce
1 tablespoon grated palm sugar (jaggery)
2 tablespoons lime juice, or to taste
coriander (cilantro) leaves, extra, to garnish

Put the stock, lemon grass, garlic, ginger, coriander stalks,
half the spring onion, lime zest, star anise, 1 teaspoon of
the chilli and 1 litre (35 fl oz/4 cups) water in a saucepan.
Bring to the boil and simmer, covered, for 25 minutes.
Strain and return the liquid to the pan.

Heat a chargrill pan or barbecue flat plate until it is very hot.
Brush lightly with oil and sear the steak on both sides until
browned but very rare in the centre.

Reheat the soup, adding the fish sauce and palm sugar.
Season with salt and black pepper. Add the lime juice, to
taste, to achieve a hot and sour flavour.

Add the remaining spring onion and the chopped coriander
leaves to the soup. Slice the beef across the grain into thin
strips. Curl the strips into a decorative pattern, then place in
the centre of four deep wide serving bowls. Pour the soup
over the beef and garnish with the remaining chilli and a
few extra coriander leaves.

Shave the burdock root with a sharp knife, as if
sharpening a pencil, turning as you cut.

Slice the seared beef into thin strips, then curl the
strips into a decorative pattern.

meat soups

Bottom: Hot and sour lime soup with beef. Top: Pork and vegetable soup.

Ramen noodle soup with barbecued pork and greens

preparation 15 minutes
cooking 10 minutes
serves 4

15 g (½ oz) dried shiitake mushrooms
350 g (12 oz) Chinese broccoli (gai larn),
cut into 4 cm (1½ inch) lengths
375 g (13 oz) fresh ramen noodles
1.25 litres (44 fl oz/5 cups) chicken stock diluted
with 250 ml (9 fl oz/1 cup) water
60 ml (2 fl oz/¼ cup) soy sauce
1 teaspoon sugar
200 g (7 oz) Chinese barbecued pork, thinly sliced
chilli flakes, to serve (optional)

Soak the mushrooms in 125 ml (4 fl oz/½ cup) boiling water for 20 minutes. Squeeze the mushrooms dry, reserving the liquid. Discard the stalks, then thinly slice the caps. Set aside.

Blanch the Chinese broccoli in a large saucepan of boiling salted water for 3 minutes, or until tender but firm to the bite. Drain, then refresh in cold water. Set aside.

Cook the noodles in a large saucepan of boiling water for 2 minutes, or until just tender. Drain and rinse under cold water, then drain again. Set aside.

Pour the stock and 500 ml (17 fl oz/2 cups) water in a non-stick wok and bring to the boil. Add the sliced mushrooms and the reserved mushroom liquid, soy sauce and sugar. Simmer for 2 minutes, then add the Chinese broccoli.

Divide the noodles among four serving bowls. Ladle on the hot stock and vegetables. Top with the pork and chilli flakes, if desired.

Cut the barbecued pork into thin slices, using a small sharp knife.

Wash and trim the Chinese broccoli, then cut it into short lengths.

meat soups

Spaghetti and meatball soup

preparation 25 minutes
cooking 30 minutes
serves 4

150 g (5½ oz) spaghetti, broken into 8 cm (3 inch) lengths
1.5 litres (52 fl oz/6 cups) beef stock
3 teaspoons tomato paste (concentrated purée)
400 g (14 oz) tin chopped tomatoes
3 tablespoons basil leaves, torn
shaved parmesan cheese, to garnish

meatballs
1 tablespoon oil
1 onion, finely chopped
2 garlic cloves, crushed
500 g (1 lb 2 oz) lean minced (ground) beef
3 tablespoons finely chopped flat-leaf (Italian) parsley
20 g (¾ oz/¼ cup) fresh breadcrumbs
2 tablespoons finely grated parmesan cheese
1 egg, lightly beaten

Cook the spaghetti in a large saucepan of boiling water according to the packet instructions until al dente. Drain.

Put the beef stock and 500 ml (17 fl oz/2 cups) water in a large saucepan and slowly bring to a simmer.

Meanwhile, to make the meatballs, heat the oil in a frying pan and cook the onion over medium heat for 2–3 minutes, or until soft. Add the garlic and cook for 30 seconds. Allow to cool.

Combine the beef, parsley, breadcrumbs, parmesan, egg and onion mixture, and season with salt and pepper. Roll the mixture into 40 balls.

Stir the tomato paste and chopped tomato into the stock and simmer for 2–3 minutes. Add the meatballs, return to a simmer and cook for 10 minutes, or until cooked through. Stir in the spaghetti and basil until heated through. Season, garnish with shaved parmesan and serve immediately.

Remove the stems from the parsley, then finely chop the leaves.

Combine the meatball ingredients, then roll the mixture into balls.

Rainbow congee

preparation 15 minutes
cooking 2 hours 15 minutes
serves 6

200 g (7 oz) short-grain rice
2 dried Chinese mushrooms
2 Chinese sausages (lap cheong)
2 tablespoons oil
¼ red onion, finely diced
1 carrot, cut into 1 cm (½ inch) cubes
3 teaspoons light soy sauce
2 litres (70 fl oz/8 cups) chicken stock
85 g (3 oz) snow peas (mangetout), cut
into 1 cm (½ inch) pieces

Put the rice in a bowl and, using your fingers as a rake, rinse under cold running water to remove any dust. Drain the rice in a colander.

Soak the dried mushrooms in boiling water for 30 minutes, then drain and squeeze out any excess water. Remove and discard the stems. Chop the caps into 5 mm (¼ inch) cubes.

Place the sausages on a plate in a steamer, then cover and steam over simmering water in a wok for 10 minutes. Cut the sausages into 1 cm (½ inch) pieces.

Heat the oil in a wok over medium heat. Stir-fry the sausage until it is brown and the fat has melted out of it. Drain on paper towel. Pour the oil from the wok, leaving 1 tablespoon.

Reheat the oil over high heat until very hot. Stir-fry the red onion until soft and transparent. Add the mushrooms and carrot and stir-fry for 1 minute, or until fragrant.

Put the mushroom mixture in a clay pot, casserole dish or saucepan and stir in the soy sauce, rice, chicken stock and ¼ teaspoon salt. Bring to the boil, then reduce the heat and simmer very gently, stirring occasionally, for 1¾–2 hours, or until it has a porridge-like texture and the rice is breaking up. If it is too thick, add some water and return to the boil. Toss in the snow peas and sausage, cover and stand for 5 minutes before serving.

Chinese combination short soup

preparation 20 minutes + chilling
cooking 2 hours 20 minutes
serves 4–6

stock
1.5 kg (3 lb 5 oz) whole chicken
60 ml (2 fl oz/¼ cup) Chinese rice wine
½ star anise
8 spring onions (scallions), chopped
2 leafy celery tops
½ teaspoon white peppercorns
4 garlic cloves, bruised
2 x 10 cm (¾ x 4 inch) piece fresh ginger,
thinly sliced

12 raw prawns (shrimp)
24 won tons
200 g (7 oz) Chinese barbecued pork, thinly sliced
60 g (2¼ oz) Chinese straw mushrooms
70 g (2½ oz) sliced bamboo shoots
500 g (1 lb 2 oz) baby bok choy (pak choy), thinly sliced
2 spring onions (scallions), cut into
3 cm (1¼ inch) lengths
2½ tablespoons light soy sauce
1 tablespoon oyster sauce
½ teaspoon sesame oil

Put all the stock ingredients in a large stockpot and cover with 4 litres (140 fl oz/16 cups) water. Bring to the boil over high heat and skim off any scum that forms on the surface. Reduce the heat and simmer for 2 hours. Cool slightly, then remove the chicken and strain the stock into a bowl. Cover and refrigerate the meat and stock separately until chilled. Skim off the fat from the top of the stock.

Meanwhile, remove one breast from the chicken, discard the skin and thinly slice the flesh. Peel the prawns and then gently pull out the dark vein from each prawn back, starting from the head end.

Pour 2 litres (70 fl oz/8 cups) of the stock into a large wok and bring to the boil. Add the won tons and cook until they have risen to the surface and are cooked through, about 2–3 minutes. Remove the won tons with a slotted spoon and divide among serving bowls. Reduce the stock to a simmer, add the prawns, pork, mushrooms and bamboo shoots and cook for 30 seconds, or until the prawns have just curled. Add the bok choy, spring onion, sliced chicken and the combined soy sauce, oyster sauce and sesame oil. Cook for 2 minutes, or until the prawns are completely cooked. Ladle the soup over the won tons and serve.

129

Bottom: Chinese combination short soup. Top: Rainbow congee.

Galician-style soup

preparation 20 minutes + 5 hours soaking
cooking 2 hours 40 minutes
serves 4

250 g (9 oz/1¼ cups) dried white haricot beans
(such as navy beans)
500 g (1 lb 2 oz) smoked ham hock
2 tablespoons olive oil
1 leek, white part only, chopped
1 garlic clove, chopped
500 g (1 lb 2 oz) pork baby back or American-style ribs,
separated into 5 cm (2 inch) widths
2 all-purpose potatoes, cubed
1 bay leaf
1 kg (2 lb 4 oz) silverbeet (Swiss chard),
washed well and chopped

Rinse the beans, then soak them in cold water for at least 5 hours.

Put the ham hock in a large heavy-based saucepan and cover with cold water. Bring to the boil, then reduce the heat and simmer for about 1 hour, or until the meat starts to come away from the bone. Remove from the heat. Remove the meat from the bone and cut into 2 cm (¾ inch) cubes. Reserve 625 ml (21½ fl oz/2½ cups) of the liquid.

Meanwhile, put the drained beans in a large saucepan and cover with cold water. Bring to the boil, then reduce the heat and simmer for 30 minutes. Drain, reserving 250 ml (9 fl oz/1 cup) of the cooking liquid.

Heat the oil in a large heavy-based saucepan over medium heat and cook the leek and garlic for 5 minutes, or until translucent. Add the ham, beans, pork or ribs, potato, bay leaf and reserved cooking liquid.

Bring to the boil, then reduce the heat, cover and simmer for about 45 minutes. Stir in the silverbeet and cook for a further 5 minutes. Season before serving.

Moroccan chickpea, lamb and coriander soup

preparation 20 minutes + overnight soaking
cooking 2 hours 20 minutes
serves 4–6

165 g (5¾ oz/¾ cup) dried chickpeas
1 tablespoon olive oil
850 g (1 lb 14 oz) boned lamb leg,
cut into 1 cm (½ inch) cubes
1 onion, chopped
2 garlic cloves, crushed
½ teaspoon ground cinnamon
½ teaspoon ground turmeric
½ teaspoon ground ginger
4 tablespoons chopped coriander (cilantro) leaves
800 g (1 lb 12 oz) tinned chopped tomatoes
1 litre (35 fl oz/4 cups) chicken stock
135 g (4¾ oz/⅔ cup) red lentils
fresh coriander (cilantro) leaves, to garnish
Turkish bread, to serve

Put the chickpeas in a large bowl, cover with water and soak overnight. Drain and rinse under cold water and drain again.

Heat the oil in a large saucepan over high heat. Add the lamb cubes and brown in batches for 2–3 minutes. Reduce the heat to medium, return all the lamb to the pan along with the onion and garlic and cook for 5 minutes. Add the cinnamon, turmeric, ginger, a pinch of salt and 1 teaspoon freshly ground black pepper and cook for 2 minutes. Add the chopped coriander, tomatoes, stock and about 500 ml (17 fl oz/2 cups) water and bring to the boil over high heat.

Rinse the red lentils under cold water and drain. Add the lentils and chickpeas to the pan, then reduce the heat and simmer, covered, for 1½ hours. Uncover and cook for a further 30 minutes, or until the lamb is tender and the soup is thick. Season to taste. Divide the soup among serving bowls and garnish with the coriander. Serve with toasted Turkish bread.

Rinse the dried beans before soaking them in cold water for 5 hours.

Trim any excess fat from the boned lamb, then cut it into cubes.

Bottom: Moroccan chickpea, lamb and coriander soup. Top: Galician-style soup.

Chickpea, chorizo and pork rib soup

preparation 20 minutes + overnight soaking
cooking 40 minutes
serves 6–8

180 g (6 oz) dried chickpeas
300 g (10 oz) smoked bacon ribs (see Note)
2 tablespoons olive oil
1 onion, finely chopped
1 garlic clove, crushed
2 tomatoes, peeled, seeded and finely chopped
1 potato, cubed
1 carrot, sliced
200 g (7 oz) pumpkin (winter squash), chopped
150 g (5½ oz) chorizo or pepperoni sausage, sliced
¼ teaspoon dried oregano
1.5 litres (52 fl oz/6 cups) chicken stock

Soak the chickpeas in cold water overnight. Drain.

Blanch the bacon ribs in boiling water for 30 seconds, then plunge into iced water. Drain and slice into pieces.

Heat the oil in a large, heavy-based saucepan and cook the onion over medium heat for 3–4 minutes, stirring continuously. Add the garlic and tomato and cook for a further 5 minutes.

Add the chickpeas, ribs, potato, carrot, pumpkin, chorizo, oregano and stock. Bring to the boil, then reduce the heat and simmer, covered, for 30 minutes, or until the chickpeas are tender. Season to taste.

Note *If bacon ribs are unavailable, use 150 g (5½ oz) smoked bacon instead.*

Steamed beef balls in long soup

preparation 1 hour
cooking 20 minutes
serves 6

500 g (1 lb 2 oz) lean minced (ground) beef
2 egg whites, lightly beaten
1 tablespoon iced water
2 tablespoons soy sauce
1 teaspoon sesame oil
2 teaspoons cornflour (cornstarch)
2 tablespoons finely chopped fresh coriander (cilantro)
2 spring onions (scallions), finely chopped
¼ teaspoon ground white pepper
¼ teaspoon five-spice powder

long soup

1 litre (35 fl oz/4 cups) beef stock, preferably homemade
2 cups assorted Chinese vegetables, sliced very finely for rapid cooking
375 g (13 oz) fresh thin egg noodles, cooked

Place small batches of the beef in a food processor bowl. Process in short bursts for 30 seconds, or until the mixture is a fine paste. Stir in the remaining ingredients.

Roll level tablespoons of the mixture into balls with wet hands. Half-fill a wok with water, cover and bring to the boil. Place the beef balls in a steamer lined with lightly oiled greaseproof paper over the boiling water. Cover and steam for 20 minutes.

To make the long soup, bring the stock to the boil in a saucepan. Add the vegetables and cook for 2 minutes. Pour the soup into a tureen and add the noodles and beef balls.

Variation *For combination long soup, add 125 g (4½ oz) each of peeled, cooked prawns (shrimp), sliced barbecued pork and cooked chicken.*

Blanch the smoked bacon bones, then cut them into pieces between the bones.

Combine the ingredients for the beef balls and then roll them into balls.

Bottom: Steamed beef balls in long soup. Top: Chickpea, chorizo and pork rib soup.

Clear Chinese pork ball and noodle soup

preparation 20 minutes + chilling
cooking 30 minutes
serves 4–6

1 tablespoon peanut oil
2 teaspoons sesame oil
4 garlic cloves, crushed
2 teaspoons grated fresh ginger
150 g (5½ oz) Chinese cabbage (wong bok), shredded
300 g (10½ oz) minced (ground) pork
1 egg white
1½ tablespoons cornflour (cornstarch)
¼ teaspoon ground white pepper
80 ml (2½ fl oz/⅓ cup) light soy sauce
2 tablespoons Chinese rice wine
6 spring onions (scallions), thinly sliced
1 large handful (cilantro) leaves, finely chopped
1.25 litres (44 fl oz/5 cups) chicken stock, diluted
with 250 ml (9 fl oz/1 cup) water
3 teaspoons grated fresh ginger, extra
200 g (7 oz) fresh thin egg noodles
finely chopped red chilli, to garnish
soy sauce, extra, to serve

Heat a wok over high heat, add the peanut oil and 1 teaspoon of the sesame oil, then swirl to coat the base and side. Add the garlic, ginger and Chinese cabbage. Stir-fry for 1 minute, or until the garlic begins to brown. As soon as this happens, remove the wok from the heat and allow to cool.

Transfer the cooled cabbage mixture to a large bowl and add the pork, egg white, cornflour, white pepper, 2 tablespoons of the soy sauce, 1 tablespoon of the rice wine, half of the spring onion and 3 tablespoons of the coriander. Mix well, then cover and refrigerate for 1 hour. Shape 1 tablespoon of the mixture into a ball using wet hands, then repeat with the remaining mixture.

Pour the stock into a clean wok and bring to the boil, then reduce the heat and simmer for 1–2 minutes. Add the extra ginger, remaining soy sauce and rice wine. Cook, covered, for 5 minutes. Add the pork balls. Cook, uncovered, for a further 8–10 minutes, or until the balls rise to the top and are cooked through.

Meanwhile, cook the noodles in a large saucepan of boiling water for 1 minute, or until they separate. Drain, then rinse well. Divide the noodles among serving bowls, then ladle on the soup. Sprinkle with the remaining spring onion and coriander, then add a couple of drops of the sesame oil. Serve with chilli and extra soy sauce, if desired.

Vietnamese beef pho

preparation 15 minutes
cooking 35 minutes
serves 4

2 litres (70 fl oz/8 cups) beef stock
1 star anise
4 cm (1½ inch) piece fresh ginger, sliced
2 pigs' trotters (cut in half)
½ onion, studded with 2 cloves
2 lemon grass stems, bruised
2 garlic cloves, crushed
¼ teaspoon ground white pepper
1 tablespoon fish sauce, plus extra, to serve
200 g (7 oz) fresh thin rice noodles
300 g (10½ oz) beef fillet, partially frozen, thinly sliced
90 g (3¼ oz/1 cup) bean sprouts, trimmed
2 spring onions (scallions), thinly sliced
2 large handfuls coriander (cilantro) leaves, chopped,
plus extra, to serve
4 tablespoons chopped Vietnamese mint, plus extra, to serve
1 red chilli, thinly sliced, plus extra, to serve
2 limes, quartered

Put the beef stock, star anise, ginger, pigs' trotters, onion, lemon grass, garlic and white pepper in a wok and bring to the boil. Reduce the heat to very low and simmer, covered, for 30 minutes. Strain, return the broth to the wok and stir in the fish sauce.

Meanwhile, put the noodles in a heatproof bowl, cover with boiling water and gently separate. Drain well, then refresh them under cold running water. Divide the noodles among four deep soup bowls, then top with the beef strips, bean sprouts, spring onion, coriander, mint and chilli. Ladle over the broth.

Place the extra sliced chilli, mint, coriander, fish sauce and the lime quarters in small bowls on a platter, serve with the soup and allow your guests to help themselves.

Vermicelli soup with minced pork

preparation 25 minutes
cooking 15 minutes
serves 4

15 pieces of dried black fungus
50 g (1¾ oz) mung bean vermicelli
2 tablespoons oil
3–4 large garlic cloves, finely chopped
450 g (1 lb) minced (ground) pork
20 coriander (cilantro) leaves, finely chopped
¼ teaspoon salt
¼ teaspoon ground white pepper
625 ml (21½ fl oz/2½ cups) vegetable or chicken stock
2 tablespoons light soy sauce
1 tablespoon preserved radish
a few coriander (cilantro) leaves, to garnish

Soak the mushrooms in hot water for 5 minutes or until they are soft, then drain them and cut into smaller pieces if necessary.

Soak the mung bean vermicelli in hot water for 5–7 minutes until soft, then drain it well and cut it into small pieces.

Heat the oil in a small wok or frying pan and stir-fry the garlic until light golden. Remove from the heat, lift out the garlic with a slotted spoon and drain on paper towel.

In a bowl, combine the pork with the coriander leaves, salt and pepper. Use a spoon or your wet hands to shape the mixture into small balls about 1 cm (½ inch) across.

Heat the stock to boiling point in a saucepan. Add the light soy sauce and preserved radish. Lower the pork balls into the stock and cook for 2 minutes over medium heat.

Add the mushrooms and noodles and cook for another 1–2 minutes, stirring frequently. Taste, adjust the seasoning if necessary, and sprinkle with the crispy garlic, garlic oil and coriander leaves.

the **soup** bible

Slice the partially frozen beef across the grain into paper-thin slices.

The dried black fungus needs to be soaked in hot water until it is soft.

Bottom: Vermicelli soup with minced pork. Top: Vietnamese beef pho.

poultry soups

Indonesian spicy chicken soup

preparation 30 minutes + overnight chilling
cooking 2 hours
serves 6

2 teaspoons coriander seeds
2 tablespoons oil
1.4 kg (3 lb 2 oz) whole chicken, jointed into 8 pieces
4 garlic cloves
1 onion, chopped
2 teaspoons finely sliced fresh ginger
1 dried red chilli, halved
2 lemon grass stems, white part only, roughly chopped
50 g (1¾ oz) coriander (cilantro) roots and stems, well rinsed
and roughly chopped
2 teaspoons ground turmeric
1 teaspoon galangal powder
1 teaspoon sugar
1 litre (35 fl oz/4 cups) chicken stock
2 tablespoons lemon juice
120 g (4¼ oz) cellophane noodles
1½ tablespoons fish sauce
90 g (3¼ oz/1 cup) bean sprouts, trimmed
3 tablespoons chopped coriander (cilantro) leaves
4 spring onions (scallions), thinly sliced
20 g (¾ oz/¼ cup) crisp fried onions
1 tablespoon sambal oelek

Dry-fry the coriander seeds in a frying pan over medium heat for 1 minute, or until fragrant. Cool, then finely grind using a mortar and pestle.

Heat a wok to very hot, add 2 teaspoons of the oil and swirl to coat the base and side. Add the chicken pieces and cook in batches for 3–4 minutes, or until they are browned all over. Remove from the wok and set aside.

Heat the remaining oil in the wok, then add the garlic, onion, ginger and chilli and stir-fry for 5 minutes, or until softened. Add the lemon grass, coriander root and stem, turmeric, galangal, sugar and ground coriander seeds and cook for 5 minutes. Return the chicken to the wok and pour in the stock, lemon juice and 500 ml (17 fl oz/2 cups) water to cover the chicken. Cover the wok with a lid and simmer for 20 minutes, skimming the surface periodically to remove any scum that rises to the surface. Remove only the chicken breast pieces, then cover the wok and simmer (skimming the surface occasionally) for 20 minutes. Remove the rest of the chicken pieces, cover and refrigerate the chicken until needed. Return the lid to the wok and simmer the broth over low heat for 1 hour. Strain through a fine sieve, and allow to cool to room temperature before covering with plastic wrap and refrigerating overnight.

Soak the noodles in boiling water for 3–4 minutes, then drain and rinse.

Remove any fat from the top of the cold broth. Remove the flesh from the chicken and shred with a fork. Place the broth and chicken flesh in the wok, and place over medium heat. Bring to the boil, then stir in the fish sauce, bean sprouts, coriander leaves and noodles. Season well, then ladle into large bowls. Sprinkle with spring onion and crisp fried onion, and serve with sambal oelek.

Canja

preparation 15 minutes
cooking 1 hour
serves 6

3 tomatoes
2.5 litres (87 fl oz/10 cups) chicken stock
1 onion, cut into thin wedges
1 celery stalk, finely chopped
1 teaspoon grated lemon zest
1 mint sprig
1 tablespoon olive oil
2 boneless, skinless chicken breasts
200 g (7 oz/1 cup) long-grain rice
2 tablespoons lemon juice
2 tablespoons shredded mint

Score a cross in the base of each tomato. Put them in a heatproof bowl and cover with boiling water. Leave for 30 seconds, then transfer to cold water, drain and peel away the skin from the cross. Cut the tomatoes in half, scoop out the seeds and roughly chop the flesh.

Combine the stock, onion, celery, lemon zest, tomato, mint and olive oil in a large saucepan. Slowly bring to the boil, then reduce the heat, add the chicken and gently simmer for 20–25 minutes, until the chicken is cooked.

Remove the chicken from the saucepan and discard the mint sprig. Allow the chicken to cool, then thinly slice.

Meanwhile, add the rice to the saucepan and simmer for 25–30 minutes, or until the rice is tender. Return the chicken to the pan, add the lemon juice and stir for 1–2 minutes, or until the chicken is warmed through. Season to taste and stir in the shredded mint just before serving.

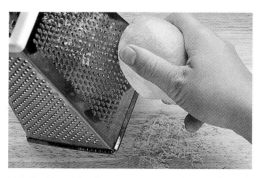

Use the fine side of a grater to grate the zest from the lemon.

Scoop out the seeds from the peeled tomatoes, then roughly chop the flesh.

Creamy spinach and chicken soup

preparation 40 minutes
cooking 55 minutes
serves 6

1 tablespoon oil
1 kg (2 lb/4 oz) chicken pieces
1 carrot, chopped
2 celery stalks, chopped
1 onion, chopped
6 black peppercorns
2 garlic cloves, chopped
bouquet garni
800 g (1 lb 12 oz) sweet potato, chopped
500 g (1 lb/2 oz) English spinach
125 ml (4 fl oz/½ cup) cream

Heat the oil in a large saucepan, add the chicken pieces in batches and brown well. Drain on paper towel. Pour off the excess fat, leaving 1 tablespoon in the pan.

Return the chicken to the pan with the carrot, celery, onion, peppercorns, garlic and bouquet garni, and add 1.5 litres (52 fl oz/6 cups) water. Bring the soup to the boil, then reduce the heat and simmer for 40 minutes.

Strain, the soup, discarding the vegetables, peppercorns and bouquet garni. Return the stock to the pan. Pull the chicken meat from the bones, shred and set aside.

Add the sweet potato to the stock in the pan. Bring to the boil, then reduce the heat and simmer until tender. Add the spinach and cook until wilted. Process the spinach in batches in a food processor until finely chopped.

Return the spinach to the pan, add the shredded chicken and stir in the cream. Season to taste. Reheat gently but do not allow the soup to boil.

Herbed chicken soup

preparation 30 minutes
cooking 30 minutes
serves 6

1 boneless, skinless chicken breast
6 black peppercorns
1 bay leaf
1 clove
4 parsley sprigs
2 tablespoons olive oil
1 onion, finely chopped
1 small carrot, finely chopped
1 celery stalk, finely chopped
1 large potato, finely chopped
1 teaspoon finely chopped rosemary, or ¼ teaspoon dried
1 teaspoon chopped thyme, or ½ teaspoon dried
1 teaspoon chopped marjoram, or ½ teaspoon dried
1 litre (35 fl oz/4 cups) chicken stock
310 g (11 oz) tinned creamed corn
4 tablespoons finely chopped flat-leaf (Italian) parsley

Trim the chicken breast of excess fat and sinew. Put 500 ml (17 fl oz/2 cups) water in a saucepan and bring to a simmer. Add the chicken, peppercorns, bay leaf, clove and parsley. Cook for 8 minutes, or until the chicken is tender and just cooked through. Remove the chicken from the liquid and cool slightly before shredding. Discard the peppercorns, bay leaf, clove and parsley, reserving the cooking liquid.

Heat the oil in a large, heavy-based saucepan. Add the onion, carrot and celery and cook over medium heat for 5 minutes, or until the onion is soft. Add the potato, rosemary, thyme and marjoram and cook, stirring, over medium heat for 1 minute.

Add the chicken stock and reserved cooking liquid. Season to taste with salt and pepper and bring to the boil. Reduce the heat and simmer for 15 minutes, or until the potato and carrot have softened. Add the creamed corn and shredded chicken and stir for 2 minutes, or until heated through. Stir in the parsley.

To make a bouquet garni, tie parsley, thyme and a bay leaf with string.

Simmer the chicken breast with the bay leaf, peppercorns, clove and parsley until cooked.

Bottom: Herbed chicken soup. Top: Creamy spinach and chicken soup.

Chicken and vegetable soup

preparation 1 hour + 30 minutes cooling
cooking 1 hour 25 minutes
serves 6–8

1.5 kg (3 lb 5 oz) chicken
2 carrots, roughly chopped
2 celery stalks, roughly chopped
1 onion, quartered
1 parsley sprig
2 bay leaves
4 black peppercorns
50 g (1¾ oz) butter
2 tablespoons plain (all-purpose) flour
2 potatoes, chopped
250 g (9 oz) butternut pumpkin (squash), peeled and cut into bite-sized pieces
2 carrots, extra, cut into thin matchsticks
1 leek, white part only, cut into short lengths
3 celery stalks, extra, cut into thin matchsticks
100 g (3½ oz) green beans, cut into short lengths, or baby green beans, halved
200 g (7 oz) broccoli, cut into small florets
100 g (3½ oz) sugar snap peas, trimmed
50 g (1¾ oz) English spinach leaves, shredded
125 ml (4 fl oz/½ cup) cream
4 tablespoons chopped flat-leaf (Italian) parsley

Place the chicken in a large saucepan with the carrot, celery, onion, parsley, bay leaves, peppercorns and 2 teaspoons salt. Add 3 litres (105 fl oz/12 cups) water and bring to the boil, then reduce the heat and simmer for 1 hour, skimming the surface as required. Allow to cool for at least 30 minutes. Strain the stock through a sieve, discarding the vegetables.

Remove the chicken and leave until cool enough to handle. Discard the skin, then cut or pull the flesh from the bones and shred it into small pieces. Cover and set the chicken meat aside.

Heat the butter in a large saucepan over medium heat and, when foaming, add the flour. Cook, stirring, for 1 minute. Remove from the heat and gradually stir in the stock. Return the pan to the heat and bring to the boil, stirring constantly.

Add the potato, pumpkin and extra carrot and simmer for 7 minutes. Add the leek, extra celery and beans. Simmer for a further 5 minutes. Finally, add the broccoli and sugar snap peas and cook for a further 3 minutes.

Just before serving, add the chicken, spinach, cream and chopped parsley. Reheat gently without allowing the soup to boil. Keep stirring until the spinach has wilted. Season with salt and black pepper. Serve the soup immediately and sprinkle with chopped parsley.

Roughly chop the carrot and celery to use when making the stock.

Once the chicken is cool enough to handle, remove the skin and shred the flesh.

Shanghai chicken and noodle soup

preparation 10 minutes
cooking 35 minutes
serves 4–6

2 litres (70 fl oz/8 cups) chicken stock diluted
with 500 ml (17 fl oz/2 cups) water
1 star anise
4 thin slices fresh ginger
600 g (1 lb 5 oz) boneless, skinless chicken breasts
375 g (13 oz) Shanghai noodles
200 g (7 oz) asparagus, woody ends trimmed,
cut into 3 cm (1¼ inch) pieces
1 tablespoon finely sliced fresh ginger
1½ tablespoons light soy sauce
1 tablespoon Chinese rice wine
½ teaspoon sugar
4 spring onions (scallions), thinly sliced
on the diagonal
50 g (1¾ oz) watercress tips (optional)
¼ teaspoon sesame oil, to drizzle
soy sauce, extra, to serve (optional)

Pour the stock into a non-stick wok and bring to the boil.
Reduce the heat to medium–low, add the star anise, ginger
slices and chicken and poach for 15–20 minutes, or until
cooked through. Remove the chicken with a slotted spoon
and set aside to cool. Leave the stock in the wok.

Meanwhile, bring 2 litres (70 fl oz/8 cups) water to the boil
in a large saucepan and cook the noodles for 3 minutes.
Drain and refresh under cold water.

Cut the chicken across the breast into 5 mm (¼ inch) slices.
Return the stock to the boil and add the asparagus, ginger,
soy sauce, rice wine, sugar and ½ teaspoon salt. Reduce
the heat, add the noodles and simmer for 2 minutes. Return
all of the chicken to the wok and cook for 1 minute, or until
heated through.

Remove the noodles from the liquid with tongs and divide
among serving bowls. Divide the chicken, asparagus, spring
onion and watercress (if using) among the bowls, then ladle
the broth on top. Drizzle with the sesame oil and serve with
extra soy sauce, if desired.

Baby corn and chicken soup

preparation 15 minutes
cooking 15 minutes
serves 4

150 g (5½ oz) baby corn
1 tablespoon oil
2 lemon grass stems, white part only,
very thinly sliced
2 tablespoons grated fresh ginger
6 spring onions (scallions), chopped
1 red chilli, finely chopped
1 litre (35 fl oz/4 cups) chicken stock
375 ml (13 fl oz/1½ cups) coconut milk
250 g (9 oz) boneless, skinless chicken breasts,
thinly sliced
135 g (4¾ oz) creamed corn
1 tablespoon soy sauce
2 tablespoons finely snipped chives, to serve
1 red chilli, thinly sliced, to serve

Cut the baby corn in half or quarters lengthways.

Heat the oil in a saucepan over medium heat and cook the
lemon grass, ginger, spring onion and chilli for 1 minute,
stirring continuously. Add the stock and coconut milk and
bring to the boil—do not cover the pan or the coconut milk
will curdle.

Add the baby corn, chicken and creamed corn and simmer
for 8 minutes, or until the corn and chicken are just tender.
Add the soy sauce, season well and serve garnished with
the chives and chilli.

Cut the baby corn in half or quarters lengthways,
depending on their size.

Bottom: Baby corn and chicken soup. Top: Shanghai chicken and noodle soup.

Chicken laksa

preparation 30 minutes
cooking 35 minutes
serves 4–6

1½ tablespoons coriander seeds
1 tablespoon cumin seeds
1 teaspoon ground turmeric
1 onion, roughly chopped
1 tablespoon roughly chopped fresh ginger
3 garlic cloves
3 lemon grass stems, white part only, sliced
6 macadamia nuts
4–6 small red chillies
3 teaspoons shrimp paste, roasted (see Note)
1 litre (35 fl oz/4 cups) chicken stock
60 ml (2 fl oz/¼ cup) oil
400 g (14 oz) boneless, skinless chicken thighs, cut
into 2 cm (¾ inch) pieces
750 ml (26 fl oz/3 cups) coconut milk
4 makrut (kaffir lime) leaves
2½ tablespoons lime juice
2 tablespoons fish sauce
2 tablespoons grated palm sugar (jaggery)
or soft brown sugar
250 g (9 oz) dried rice vermicelli
90 g (3¼ oz/1 cup) bean sprouts, trimmed
4 fried tofu puffs, cut into thin batons
3 tablespoons chopped Vietnamese mint
1 handful coriander (cilantro) leaves
lime wedges, to serve

Toast the coriander and cumin seeds in a frying pan over medium heat for 1–2 minutes, or until fragrant, tossing the pan constantly to prevent them from burning. Grind finely using a mortar and pestle or a spice grinder.

Put the spices, onion, ginger, garlic, lemon grass, macadamia nuts, chillies and shrimp paste in a food processor or blender. Add 125 ml (4 fl oz/½ cup) of the stock and blend to a paste.

Heat the oil in a wok or large saucepan over low heat and gently cook the paste for 3–5 minutes, stirring constantly to prevent it burning or sticking to the bottom of the pan. Add the remaining stock and bring to the boil over high heat. Reduce the heat to medium and simmer for 15 minutes, or until reduced slightly.

Add the chicken and simmer for another 4–5 minutes. Add the coconut milk, lime leaves, lime juice, fish sauce and palm sugar and simmer for 5 minutes over medium–low heat. Do not bring to the boil or cover with a lid, as the coconut milk will split.

Meanwhile, put the rice vermicelli in a heatproof bowl, cover with boiling water and soak for 6–7 minutes, or until softened. Drain and divide the noodles among large serving bowls with the bean sprouts. Ladle the hot soup over the top and garnish with some tofu strips, mint and coriander leaves. Serve with a wedge of lime.

Note *To roast the shrimp paste, wrap the paste in foil and put under a hot grill (broiler) for 1 minute.*

Five-spice duck and somen noodle soup

preparation 15 minutes
cooking 20 minutes
serves 4

4 duck breasts, skin on
1 teaspoon Chinese five-spice
1 teaspoon peanut oil
200 g (7 oz) dried somen noodles

star anise broth
1 litre (35 fl oz/4 cups) chicken stock
3 whole star anise
5 spring onions (scallions), chopped
1 large handful coriander (cilantro) leaves, chopped

Preheat the oven to 200°C (400°F/Gas 6). Trim the duck breast of excess fat, then lightly sprinkle both sides with the Chinese five-spice.

Heat the oil in a large frying pan over medium heat. Add the duck, skin side down, and cook for 2–3 minutes, until brown and crisp. Turn and cook for 3 minutes. Transfer to a baking tray and cook, skin side up, for 8–10 minutes, or until cooked to your liking.

Meanwhile, to make the star anise broth, put the chicken stock and star anise in a small saucepan. Bring to the boil, then reduce the heat and simmer for 5 minutes. Add the spring onion and coriander and simmer for 5 minutes.

Cook the somen noodles in a saucepan of boiling water for 2 minutes, or until soft. Drain and divide among four bowls. Ladle the broth on the noodles and top each bowl with one sliced duck breast.

Tamarind and chicken soup

preparation 20 minutes + soaking
cooking 30 minutes
serves 4

30 g (1 oz) tamarind pulp
1½ tablespoons coriander seeds
2 tablespoons cumin seeds
1 tablespoon black peppercorns
1 tablespoon oil
5 garlic cloves, skins on, roughly pounded
1 red onion, thinly sliced
2–3 dried chillies, torn into pieces
2 stalks curry leaves
200 g (7 oz) skinless, boneless chicken thighs, cut into small pieces

Soak the tamarind pulp in 50 ml (1½ fl oz) very hot water for 3 hours, or until soft. Mash the tamarind with a fork, then push the mixture through a sieve. Put the tamarind in the sieve with another 1 tablespoon of hot water and mash again. Strain again, discarding the fibres left in the sieve. Mix the tamarind with 750 ml (26 fl oz/3 cups) water.

Dry-roast the coriander seeds in a small frying pan over low heat until aromatic. Remove, then dry-roast the cumin seeds, followed by the black peppercorns. Grind the spices together using a spice grinder or a mortar and pestle.

Heat the oil in a large, heavy-based saucepan over low heat, add the garlic and onion and fry until golden. Add the chilli and curry leaves and fry for 2 minutes, or until aromatic. Add the tamarind water and ground spices and season with salt. Bring to the boil, then reduce the heat and simmer for 10 minutes.

Add the chicken to the saucepan with 250 ml (9 fl oz/1 cup) water and simmer for 20 minutes, gradually adding another 250 ml (9 fl oz/1 cup) water as the soup reduces. Remove any garlic skin that has floated to the top. Season with salt, to taste.

Bottom: Tamarind and chicken soup. Top: Five-spice duck and somen noodle soup.

Chicken soup with vermicelli and vegetables

preparation 15 minutes
cooking 45 minutes
serves 4

1 kg (2 lb 4 oz) chicken pieces (such as drumsticks
and thighs)
6 spring onions (scallions), chopped
2 cm (¾ inch) piece fresh ginger, very finely sliced
2 bay leaves
2 tablespoons soy sauce
100 g (3½ oz) dried rice vermicelli
50 g (1¾ oz) English spinach leaves, chopped
2 celery stalks, thinly sliced
200 g (7 oz) bean sprouts, trimmed
crisp fried onion, to garnish
chilli sauce, to serve

Combine the chicken and 1.5 litres (52 fl oz/6 cups) water
in a saucepan and bring to the boil. Skim off any scum.
Add the spring onion, ginger, bay leaves, soy sauce and
¼ teaspoon each of salt and pepper, then reduce the heat
and simmer for 30 minutes.

Put the vermicelli in a heatproof bowl. Cover it with boiling
water and leave to soak for 10 minutes, or until soft. Drain.

Arrange the vermicelli, spinach, celery and bean sprouts on
a platter. To serve, each diner places a serving of vermicelli
and a selection of vegetables in a large individual serving
bowl. Pour the soup and chicken into the bowls. Sprinkle
over the fried onion and season with chilli sauce.

Chicken, asparagus and egg noodle soup

preparation 15 minutes
cooking 15 minutes
serves 4

200 g (7 oz) fresh thin egg noodles
200 g (7 oz) asparagus, trimmed
4 spring onions (scallions)
1.5 litres (52 fl oz/6 cups) salt-reduced chicken stock
6 thin slices fresh ginger
1 tablespoon light soy sauce, or to taste
600 g (1 lb 5 oz) boneless, skinless chicken breasts,
thinly sliced
150 g (5½ oz) baby English spinach leaves
lemon cheeks or wedges, to serve

Put the noodles in a colander and place the colander in a
heatproof bowl. Pour over some boiling water. Use a fork
to loosen the noodles, then drain immediately. Set aside.

Remove the top third of the asparagus and cut in half
lengthways. Slice the remaining stalks. Remove the green
tops of the spring onions and thinly slice on the diagonal.
Thinly slice the white part of the spring onion into rounds.

Put the stock, 500 ml (17 fl oz/2 cups) water, ginger and the
white part of the spring onion in a large saucepan over high
heat and bring to the boil. Reduce the heat and simmer for
5 minutes. Add the soy sauce, chicken and asparagus and
simmer for 2 minutes, then stir in the spinach and noodles
and simmer for 2 minutes, until the chicken is just cooked.

Use tongs to divide the noodles and chicken among serving
bowls, then ladle over the broth. Serve immediately, topped
with the spring onion greens and the lemon on the side.

Fragrant corn, coconut and chicken noodle soup

preparation 20 minutes
cooking 20 minutes
serves 4

100 g (3½ oz) dried rice vermicelli
250 ml (9 fl oz/1 cup) coconut cream
500 ml (17 fl oz/2 cups) coconut milk
250 ml (9 fl oz/1 cup) chicken stock
125 g (4½ oz) tinned creamed corn
500 g (1 lb 2 oz) boneless, skinless chicken thighs,
cut into 2 cm (¾ inch) cubes
200 g (7 oz) baby corn, halved lengthways
5 cm (2 inch) piece of galangal, sliced
6 makrut (kaffir lime) leaves, shredded
2 lemon grass stems, white part only, bruised
and cut into 5 cm (2 inch) pieces
2 tablespoons fish sauce
2 tablespoons lime juice
1 tablespoon grated palm sugar (jaggery) or soft brown sugar
1 large handful coriander (cilantro) leaves

Soak the vermicelli in boiling water for 6–7 minutes, or
until soft. Drain and set aside.

Put the coconut cream, coconut milk, stock and creamed
corn in a large saucepan and bring to the boil, then reduce
the heat and simmer for 5 minutes. Add the chicken, baby
corn, galangal, makrut leaves and lemon grass and simmer
for 10 minutes, or until the chicken is tender.

Season with fish sauce, lime juice and palm sugar. Stir
through half the coriander leaves and serve topped with
the remaining leaves.

Top left: Chicken soup with vermicelli and vegetables. Top right: Chicken, asparagus and egg noodle soup. Bottom left: Fragrant corn, coconut and chicken noodle soup.

Curried chicken and peanut soup

preparation 25 minutes
cooking 8 hours 20 minutes
serves 4

2 tablespoons fish sauce
2 garlic cloves, crushed
1 tablespoon lime juice
1 tablespoon soft brown sugar
2 small red chillies, seeded if desired, finely chopped
1.5 kg (3 lb 5 oz) chicken, rinsed
270 ml (9½ fl oz) tin coconut cream
250 g (9 oz) rice vermicelli noodles
chopped salted peanuts, to garnish
coriander (cilantro) sprigs, to garnish

spice paste
1 small handful chopped coriander (cilantro)
½ small onion, chopped
3 spring onions (scallions), chopped
1 teaspoon grated fresh galangal
1 teaspoon ground turmeric
1 teaspoon ground coriander
2 tablespoons salted peanuts

Combine the fish sauce, garlic, lime juice, sugar and chilli in a slow cooker. Pour in 750 ml (26 fl oz/3 cups) water and stir until the sugar has dissolved. Add the chicken, placing it breast side down. Cover and cook on low for 8 hours.

Put the spice paste ingredients in a food processor or blender with 2 tablespoons water and process until they form a smooth paste.

Remove the chicken to a plate. Pour the liquid from the slow cooker through a sieve into the food processor, then blend with the spice paste until smooth. Return the stock to the slow cooker.

Discard the skin and bones of the chicken, then shred the meat using your fingers. Stir the chicken through the soup with the coconut cream. Cover and cook for 20 minutes, or until heated through.

Meanwhile, place the noodles in a large heatproof bowl. Cover with boiling water and leave to soak for 10 minutes, or until softened.

Drain the noodles and divide among serving bowls. Ladle the soup over the top. Serve garnished with the chopped peanuts and coriander sprigs.

Place all the spice paste ingredients in a food processor and process until smooth.

Cover the vermicelli with boiling water in a heatproof bowl and leave to soak.

Spicy chicken broth with coriander pasta

preparation 40 minutes
cooking 50 minutes
serves 4

350 g (12 oz) chicken thighs or wings, skin removed
2 carrots, finely chopped
2 celery stalks, finely chopped
2 small leeks, white part only, finely chopped
3 egg whites
1.5 litres (52 fl oz/6 cups) chicken stock
Tabasco sauce

coriander pasta
60 g (2¼ oz/½ cup) plain (all-purpose) flour
1 egg
½ teaspoon sesame oil
coriander (cilantro) leaves

Put the chicken, carrot, celery and leek in a large heavy-based saucepan. Push the chicken to one side and add the egg whites to the vegetables. Using a wire whisk, beat for a minute or so until frothy.

Warm the chicken stock in another saucepan, then gradually add it to the first pan, whisking continuously to froth the egg whites. Continue whisking while slowly bringing to the boil. Make a hole in the froth on top with a spoon and simmer for 30 minutes without stirring. Line a large strainer with a damp tea towel (dish towel) and strain the broth into a clean bowl (discard the chicken and vegetables). Season with salt, pepper and Tabasco to taste. Set aside.

To make the coriander pasta, sift the flour into a bowl and make a well in the centre. Whisk the egg and oil together and pour into the well. Mix together to make a soft pasta dough and knead on a lightly floured board for 2 minutes, or until smooth.

Divide the dough into four even portions. Roll one portion out very thinly and cover with a layer of evenly spaced coriander leaves. Roll out another portion of pasta and lay on top of the leaves, then gently roll the layers together. Repeat with the remaining pasta and coriander.

Cut out squares of pasta around the coriander leaves. The pasta may then be left to sit and dry out if it is not needed immediately. When you are ready to serve, gently heat the chicken broth in a saucepan. As the broth simmers, add the pasta and cook for 1 minute. Serve immediately.

Note Beg, borrow or steal a pasta machine for making this fine, delicate pasta. A rolling pin will suffice if necessary but try to roll the pasta as thinly as possible.

Lemon chicken soup

preparation 10 minutes
cooking 10 minutes
serves 4

2 boneless, skinless chicken breasts
1 lemon
1 litre (35 fl oz/4 cups) chicken stock
2 lemon thyme sprigs, plus extra, to serve (see Note)

Trim any excess fat from the chicken. Using a vegetable peeler, cut three strips of zest from the lemon and remove the pith.

Place the chicken stock, lemon thyme and two strips of the lemon zest in a shallow saucepan and slowly bring almost to the boil. Reduce the heat to simmering point, add the chicken and cook, covered, for 7 minutes, or until the meat is cooked through. Meanwhile, cut the remaining zest into very fine strips.

Remove the chicken from the pan, transfer to a plate and cover with foil.

Strain the stock into a clean pan through a sieve lined with two layers of damp muslin (cheesecloth). Finely shred the chicken and return it to the soup. Reheat gently and season with salt and black pepper. Serve the soup immediately, garnished with the lemon thyme and lemon zest.

Note Use ordinary thyme if lemon thyme is not available.

Peel three strips of zest from the lemon, then remove the white pith.

Bottom: Lemon chicken soup. Top: Spicy chicken broth with coriander pasta.

Chicken mulligatawny

preparation 25 minutes + overnight refrigeration
cooking 4 hours
serves 6

stock
1.5 kg (3 lb 5 oz) chicken
1 carrot, chopped
2 celery stalks, chopped
4 spring onions (scallions), chopped
2 cm (¾ inch) piece fresh ginger, sliced

2 tomatoes
20 g (¾ oz) ghee
1 large onion, finely chopped
3 garlic cloves, crushed
8 curry leaves
55 g (2 oz/¼ cup) Madras curry paste
250 g (9 oz/1 cup) red lentils, rinsed and drained
70 g (2½ oz/⅓ cup) short-grain rice
250 ml (9 fl oz/1 cup) coconut cream
2 tablespoons chopped coriander (cilantro) leaves
mango chutney, to serve

To make the stock, put the chicken, carrot, celery, spring onion, ginger and 4 litres (140 fl oz/16 cups) cold water in a large stockpot or saucepan. Bring to the boil, removing any scum that rises to the surface. Reduce the heat to low and simmer, partially covered, for 3 hours. Continue to remove any scum from the surface. Carefully remove the chicken and leave to cool. Strain the stock into a bowl and leave to cool. Cover and refrigerate overnight. Discard the skin and bones from the chicken and shred the flesh into small pieces. Cover and refrigerate overnight.

Score a cross in the base of the tomatoes. Put in a heatproof bowl and cover with boiling water. Leave for 30 seconds, then transfer to a bowl of cold water and peel the skin away from the cross. Cut the tomatoes in half, scoop out the seeds and chop the flesh.

Melt the ghee in a large saucepan over medium heat. Cook the onion for 5 minutes, or until softened but not browned. Add the garlic and curry leaves and cook for 1 minute. Add the curry paste and cook for 1 minute, then stir in the lentils. Pour in the stock and then bring to the boil over high heat, removing any scum from the surface. Reduce the heat, add the tomato and simmer for 30 minutes, or until the lentils are soft.

Meanwhile, bring a large saucepan of water to the boil. Add the rice and cook for 12 minutes, stirring once or twice. Drain, then stir the rice into the soup with the chicken and coconut cream until warmed through — don't allow it to boil or it will curdle. Season. Sprinkle with the coriander and serve with the mango chutney.

Score a cross in the base of the tomatoes, soak in boiling water, then cool and peel.

Discard the chicken skin and bones, then shred the flesh into small pieces.

Chicken, mushroom and Madeira soup

preparation 25 minutes + 20 minutes soaking
cooking 1 hour 25 minutes
serves 4

10 g (¼ oz) dried porcini mushrooms
25 g (1 oz) butter
1 leek, white part only, thinly sliced
250 g (9 oz) pancetta or bacon, chopped
200 g (7 oz) Swiss brown mushrooms, roughly chopped
300 g (10½ oz) large field mushrooms, roughly chopped
2 tablespoons plain (all-purpose) flour
125 ml (4 fl oz/½ cup) Madeira
1.25 litres (44 fl oz/5 cups) chicken stock
1 tablespoon olive oil
2 boneless, skinless chicken breasts (200 g/7 oz each)
80 g (2¾ oz/⅓ cup) light sour cream
2 teaspoons chopped marjoram, plus whole leaves,
to garnish

Soak the porcini in 250 ml (9 fl oz/1 cup) boiling water for 20 minutes.

Melt the butter in a large saucepan over medium heat and cook the leek and pancetta for 5 minutes, or until the leek is softened. Add all the mushrooms and the soaking liquid and cook for 10 minutes.

Stir in the flour and cook for 1 minute. Add the Madeira and cook, stirring, for 10 minutes. Stir in the stock, bring to the boil, then reduce the heat and simmer for 45 minutes. Cool slightly.

Heat the oil in a frying pan and cook the chicken fillets for 4–5 minutes on each side, or until cooked through. Remove from the pan and thinly slice.

Blend the soup until smooth. Return to the cleaned pan, add the sour cream and chopped marjoram and stir over medium heat for 1–2 minutes to warm through. Season. Top with the chicken and garnish with the marjoram.

Cover the porcini mushrooms with boiling water and soak until rehydrated.

Vegetable soup with chicken and prawns

preparation 40 minutes
cooking 15 minutes
serves 4

175 g (6 oz) raw prawns (shrimp)
2 coriander (cilantro) roots, washed and finely chopped
2 garlic cloves, roughly chopped
pinch of ground white pepper, plus extra, to sprinkle
150 g (5½ oz) minced (ground) chicken
½ spring onion (scallion), finely chopped
935 ml (32 fl oz/3¾ cups) chicken or vegetable stock
2 tablespoons light soy sauce
2 teaspoons preserved radish
175 g (6 oz) butternut pumpkin (squash), peeled and
cut into 2.5 cm (1 inch) cubes
175 g (6 oz) Chinese cabbage (wong bok), roughly chopped
a few coriander (cilantro) leaves, to garnish

Peel and devein the prawns and cut each prawn along the back so it opens like a butterfly (leave each prawn joined along the base and at the tail, leaving the tail attached).

Using a mortar and pestle or a small blender, pound or blend the coriander roots, garlic, pepper and a pinch of salt into a paste. In a bowl, combine the coriander paste with the chicken and spring onion. Use a spoon or wet hands to shape the chicken mixture into small balls about 1 cm (½ inch) across.

Heat the stock to boiling point in a saucepan. Add the light soy sauce and preserved radish. Lower the chicken balls into the stock and cook over medium heat for 1–2 minutes or until the balls are cooked.

Add the pumpkin to the pan and cook for 2–3 minutes. Add the prawns and the Chinese cabbage and cook for another 1–2 minutes.

Taste, then adjust the seasoning if necessary. Garnish with coriander leaves. Sprinkle with ground white pepper.

Remove the skin and seeds from the pumpkin, then cut it into cubes.

Bottom: Vegetable soup with chicken and prawns. Top: Chicken, mushroom and Madeira soup.

Chicken pho

preparation 25 minutes
cooking 30 minutes
serves 4 as a starter

2.5 litres (87 fl oz/10 cups) chicken stock
8 black peppercorns
2 cm (¾ inch) piece fresh ginger, sliced
1 onion, thinly sliced
20 g (¾ oz/¼ cup) crisp fried shallots
1–1½ tablespoons fish sauce
1 boneless, skinless chicken breast, trimmed
500 g (1 lb 2 oz) fresh round rice noodles
3 tablespoons chopped coriander (cilantro) leaves
90 g (3¼ oz/1 cup) bean sprouts, trimmed
3 tablespoons Vietnamese mint
3 tablespoons Thai basil
2 small red chillies, sliced
lime wedges, to serve

Put the stock in a wok with 125 ml (4 fl oz/½ cup) water, the peppercorns, ginger, onion, crisp fried shallots, fish sauce and ½ teaspoon of salt. Bring to the boil over high heat, then reduce the heat so the stock is just simmering and cook for 5 minutes. Gently poach the chicken in the stock for 12–15 minutes, or until just cooked through and tender. Remove the chicken, shred and set aside. Strain the stock, then return it to a clean wok and bring to a simmer.

Put the noodles in a heatproof bowl and cover with boiling water. Gently separate them, then drain and rinse under cold water and divide among four serving bowls.

Top the noodles with the shredded chicken, then ladle on the stock. Garnish with the coriander, bean sprouts, mint, basil and chilli slices. Serve with lime wedges on the side.

Chicken, tofu and coconut milk soup

preparation 30 minutes
cooking 12 minutes
serves 8

150 g (5½ oz) rice vermicelli
1 lime
4 small fresh red chillies, seeded and chopped
1 onion, chopped
2 garlic cloves, crushed
4 thin slices fresh ginger, finely chopped
2 stalks lemon grass root, roughly chopped
1 tablespoon chopped coriander (cilantro)
1 tablespoon peanut oil
750 ml (26 fl oz/3 cups) chicken stock
685 ml (24 fl oz/2¾ cups) coconut milk
500 g (1 lb 2 oz) chicken tenderloins,
cut into thin strips
4 spring onions (scallions), chopped
150 g (5½ oz) fried bean curd or tofu, sliced
90 g (3¼ oz/1 cup) bean sprouts
3 teaspoons soft brown sugar
thinly sliced red chilli, to serve
coriander (cilantro) leaves, to serve

Cover the rice vermicelli with boiling water and leave for 5 minutes, or until tender. Drain and cut the noodles into shorter lengths with scissors and set aside.

Peel the lime rind and cut into long, thin strips.

Put the red chilli, onion, garlic, ginger, lemon grass and coriander in a food processor or blender. Process in short bursts for 20 seconds, or until the mixture is smooth.

Heat the peanut oil in a large heavy-based saucepan. Add the chilli mixture and cook for 3 minutes, or until the fragrance is released, stirring frequently. Add the stock, coconut milk and lime rind and bring to the boil. Add the chicken and cook, stirring, for 4 minutes, or until tender.

Add the spring onion, bean curd, bean sprouts, sugar and a pinch of salt. Stir over medium heat for 3 minutes, or until the spring onion is tender.

Divide the noodles among serving bowls and pour in the soup. Serve with sliced chillies and coriander leaves.

Bottom: Chicken, tofu and coconut milk soup. Top: Chicken pho.

Japanese udon miso soup with chicken

preparation 35 minutes + soaking
cooking 15 minutes
serves 4–6

8 dried shiitake mushrooms
400 g (14 oz) fresh udon noodles
1 litre (35 fl oz/4 cups) chicken stock
600 g (1 lb 5 oz) boneless, skinless chicken breasts,
cut into 1.5 cm (⅝ inch) thick strips
300 g (10½ oz) baby bok choy (pak choy), halved lengthways
60 g (2¼ oz/¼ cup) white miso paste
2 teaspoons dashi granules
1 tablespoon wakame flakes or other seaweed
150 g (5½ oz) silken firm tofu, cut into 1 cm (½ inch) cubes
3 spring onions (scallions), sliced on the diagonal

Soak the mushrooms in 250 ml (9 fl oz/1 cup) boiling water for 20 minutes. Squeeze dry, reserving the soaking liquid. Discard the woody stalks and thinly slice the caps. Set aside.

Bring 2 litres (70 fl oz/8 cups) water to the boil in a large saucepan and cook the noodles for 1–2 minutes, or until tender. Drain immediately and rinse under cold water. Set aside.

Pour the stock and 1 litre (35 fl oz/4 cups) water into a wok and bring to the boil, then reduce the heat and simmer. Add the chicken and cook for 2–3 minutes, or until almost cooked through.

Add the mushrooms and cook for 1 minute. Add the bok choy halves and simmer for a further 1 minute, or until beginning to wilt, then add the miso paste, dashi granules, wakame and reserved mushroom liquid. Stir to dissolve the dashi and miso paste. Do not allow to boil.

Gently stir in the tofu cubes. Divide the noodles among the serving bowls, then ladle the hot soup over them. Sprinkle with the spring onion.

Trim any excess fat from the chicken breasts, then cut them into strips.

Wash the bok choy well, then trim and cut in half lengthways.

Thai noodle soup with duck

preparation 40 minutes
cooking 25 minutes
serves 4–6

1 whole Chinese roast duck (see Note)
4 coriander (cilantro) roots and stems, well rinsed
50 g (1¾ oz) galangal, sliced
4 spring onions (scallions), sliced
400 g (14 oz) Chinese broccoli (gai larn),
cut into 5 cm (2 inch) lengths
2 garlic cloves, crushed
60 ml (2 fl oz/¼ cup) fish sauce
1 tablespoon hoisin sauce
2 teaspoons grated palm sugar (jaggery)
or soft brown sugar
½ teaspoon ground white pepper
500 g (1 lb 2 oz) fresh rice noodles
crisp fried garlic, to serve
coriander (cilantro) leaves, to serve

To make the stock, cut off the duck's head with a sharp knife and discard. Remove the skin and fat from the duck, leaving the neck intact. Carefully remove the flesh from the bones and set aside. Cut any visible fat from the carcass along with the parson's nose, then discard. Break the carcass into large pieces and put them in a large stockpot with 2 litres (70 fl oz/ 8 cups) water.

Bruise the coriander roots and stems with the back of a knife. Add to the pot with the galangal and bring to the boil. Skim off any scum from the surface. Boil over medium heat for 10 minutes. Strain the stock through a fine sieve, discarding the carcass, and return the stock to a large clean wok.

Slice the duck flesh into strips. Add to the stock with the spring onion, Chinese broccoli, garlic, fish sauce, hoisin sauce, palm sugar and white pepper, and gently bring to the boil.

Put the rice noodles in a heatproof bowl, cover with boiling water and gently separate. Drain well and then refresh under cold water. Divide the noodles among the serving bowls and pour over the soup. Serve immediately, garnished with the fried garlic and coriander leaves.

Note *Whole Chinese roast duck is available from Chinese barbecue shops.*

Trim the ends off the spring onions, then cut them into short lengths.

Grate the block of palm sugar on the large holes of a metal grater.

Curried chicken noodle soup

preparation 15 minutes
cooking 1 hour
serves 4

175 g (6 oz) dried thin egg noodles
2 tablespoons peanut oil
2 boneless, skinless chicken breasts (250 g/9 oz each)
1 onion, sliced
1 small fresh red chilli, seeded and finely chopped
1 tablespoon finely chopped fresh ginger
2 tablespoons Indian curry powder
750 ml (26 fl oz/3 cups) chicken stock
800 ml (28 fl oz) coconut milk
300 g (10½ oz) baby bok choy (pak choy),
cut into long strips
20 g (¾ oz) basil, torn

Cook the noodles in a large saucepan of boiling water for
3–4 minutes, or until soft. Drain well and set aside.

Heat the peanut oil in a large saucepan and add the chicken.
Cook on each side for 5 minutes, or until cooked through.
Remove the chicken and keep warm.

Add the sliced onion to the pan and cook over low heat for
8 minutes, or until softened but not browned. Add the chilli,
ginger and curry powder and cook for a further 2 minutes.
Add the chicken stock and bring to the boil. Reduce the heat
and simmer for 20 minutes.

Meanwhile, thinly slice the chicken on the diagonal.

Pour the coconut milk into the saucepan and simmer for
10 minutes. Add the bok choy and cook for 3 minutes, then
stir in the basil.

Divide the noodles among four deep bowls. Top with slices
of chicken and ladle in the soup. Serve immediately.

Chicken, coconut and galangal soup

preparation 15 minutes
cooking 1 hour 20 minutes
serves 4–6 as a starter

stock
6 red Asian shallots
6 slices galangal
6 coriander (cilantro) roots and stems
500 g (1 lb 2 oz) chicken wings
10 white peppercorns

10 makrut (kaffir lime) leaves, crushed
2 lemon grass stems, bruised
8 slices galangal
1 large red chilli, finely sliced on the diagonal
500 ml (17 fl oz/2 cups) coconut milk
2 large chicken breast fillets, cut into strips
2 tablespoons fish sauce
1 tablespoon lime juice
coriander (cilantro) leaves, to serve

To make the stock, put the shallots, galangal, coriander,
chicken wings, peppercorns and 2.5 litres (87 fl oz/10 cups)
water in a large saucepan and bring to the boil. Reduce the
heat and simmer for 1 hour. Strain.

Put the stock, makrut leaves, lemon grass, galangal, chilli
and coconut milk in a wok and bring to the boil. Reduce the
heat and simmer for 5 minutes. Add the chicken strips and
simmer for 5–6 minutes, or until the chicken is cooked. Stir
in the fish sauce and lime juice and serve garnished with
the coriander leaves.

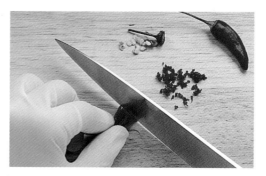

Wear gloves to protect your hands while you are
preparing the chilli.

Trim any excess fat from the chicken breasts, then
cut them into strips.

Bottom: Chicken, coconut and galangal soup. Top: Curried chicken noodle soup.

Rice soup with prawns and chicken

preparation 40 minutes
cooking 15 minutes
serves 4

110 g (3¾ oz) raw prawns (shrimp)
2 tablespoons oil
3–4 large garlic cloves, finely chopped
1 coriander (cilantro) root, finely chopped
1 garlic clove, extra, roughly chopped
pinch of ground white pepper, plus extra, to sprinkle
75 g (2¾ oz) minced (ground) chicken
1 spring onion (scallion), finely chopped
935 ml (32 fl oz/3¾ cups) chicken or vegetable stock
2 tablespoons light soy sauce
2 teaspoons preserved radish
325 g (11½ oz/1¾ cups) cooked jasmine rice
1 tablespoon finely sliced fresh ginger
1 Chinese cabbage (wong bok) leaf, roughly chopped
2 spring onions (scallions), finely chopped, to serve
a few coriander (cilantro) leaves, to serve

Peel and devein the prawns and cut each prawn along the back so it opens like a butterfly (leave each prawn joined along the base and at the tail, leaving the tail attached).

Heat the oil in a small wok or frying pan. Stir-fry the finely chopped garlic until light golden. Remove from the heat and discard the garlic.

Using a mortar and pestle or a small blender, pound or blend the coriander root, roughly chopped garlic, pepper and a pinch of salt into a paste. In a bowl, combine the coriander paste with the chicken and spring onion. Shape the mixture into small balls about 1 cm (½ inch) across.

Heat the stock to boiling point in a saucepan. Add the light soy sauce, preserved radish and rice. Lower the meatballs into the stock over medium heat and cook for 3 minutes, or until the chicken is cooked. Add the prawns, ginger and Chinese cabbage. Cook for another 1–2 minutes, or until the prawns open and turn pink.

Top the soup with the spring onion and coriander. Sprinkle with ground white pepper and the garlic oil.

Greek egg, lemon and chicken soup

preparation 20 minutes
cooking 30 minutes
serves 4

1 onion, halved
2 cloves
1 carrot, cut into chunks
1 bay leaf
500 g (1 lb 2 oz) boneless, skinless chicken breast
70 g (2½ oz/⅓ cup) short-grain rice
3 eggs, separated
60 ml (2 fl oz/¼ cup) lemon juice
2 tablespoons chopped flat-leaf (Italian) parsley
4 thin lemon slices

Stud the onion half with the cloves and place in a large saucepan with 1.5 litres (52 fl oz/6 cups) water. Add the carrot, bay leaf and chicken and season. Slowly bring to the boil, then reduce the heat and simmer for 10 minutes, or until the chicken is cooked.

Strain the stock into a clean pan, reserving the chicken and discarding the vegetables. Add the rice to the stock, bring to the boil, then reduce the heat and simmer for 15 minutes, or until the rice is tender. Meanwhile, tear the chicken into shreds.

Whisk the egg whites in a clean dry bowl until stiff peaks form, then beat in the yolks. Slowly beat in the lemon juice. Gently stir in about 170 ml (5½ fl oz/⅔ cup) of the hot (not boiling) stock and beat thoroughly.

Add the egg mixture to the stock and heat gently, but do not let it boil, otherwise the eggs may scramble. Add the chicken and season to taste.

Set aside for 2–3 minutes to allow the flavours to develop. To serve, spoon the soup into bowls, sprinkle with parsley and top with lemon slices.

173

Bottom: Greek egg, lemon and chicken soup. Top: Rice soup with prawns and chicken.

Chicken noodle and mushroom soup

preparation 10 minutes
cooking 10 minutes
serves 6

cooking oil spray
2 teaspoons grated fresh ginger
4 spring onions (scallions), finely chopped
1 boneless, skinless chicken breast, cut into thin strips
120 g (4¼ oz) button mushrooms, sliced
410 g (14½ oz) tin chicken consommé
60 g (2¼ oz) instant noodles
3 teaspoons kecap manis (see Note)

Heat a little oil in a saucepan, add the ginger, spring onion and chicken, and stir-fry over high heat for 4–5 minutes, or until the chicken changes colour. Add the mushrooms and cook for a further 1 minute.

Add the consommé and 500 ml (17 fl oz/2 cups) water and bring to the boil. Stir in the noodles, then reduce the heat and simmer for 3 minutes, or until the noodles are soft. Stir in the kecap manis and serve.

Note *Kecap manis is a thick, sweet soy sauce available from Asian grocery stores. If you cannot find it, use regular soy sauce with a little soft brown sugar added, as a substitute.*

Cock-a-leekie

preparation 10 minutes + 2 hours refrigeration
cooking 1 hour 40 minutes
serves 4–6

1.5 kg (3 lb 5 oz) chicken
250 g (9 oz) chicken giblets (optional)
1 onion, sliced
2 litres (70 fl oz/8 cups) chicken stock
4 leeks, white part only, thinly sliced
¼ teaspoon ground coriander
pinch of nutmeg
bouquet garni
12 pitted prunes
pinch of cayenne pepper
3 thyme sprigs, plus extra, to serve

Put the chicken in a large saucepan and add the giblets (if using), onion and stock. Bring to the boil, skimming the surface as required. Add the leek, coriander, nutmeg and bouquet garni. Reduce the heat, cover and simmer for 1¼ hours.

Remove the chicken and the bouquet garni from the pan and lift out the giblets with a slotted spoon. Cool the stock, then refrigerate for 2 hours. Spoon the fat from the surface and discard. Remove the chicken meat from the bones and shred. Discard the skin and carcass.

Return the shredded chicken to the soup with the prunes, cayenne pepper and thyme sprigs. Simmer for 20 minutes. Season to taste and garnish with the extra thyme sprigs.

Creamy chicken and paprika soup

preparation 20 minutes
cooking 1 hour
serves 4–6

90 g (3¼ oz) butter
1 onion, finely chopped
1 celery stalk, finely chopped
1 small carrot, finely chopped
2 tablespoons Hungarian sweet paprika
40 g (1½ oz/⅓ cup) plain (all-purpose) flour
2 litres (70 fl oz/8 cups) chicken stock
125 ml (4 fl oz/½ cup) cream
300 g (10½ oz) boneless, skinless cooked
chicken breasts, finely chopped
crusty bread, to serve

Melt the butter over medium–high heat in a large saucepan. Add the chopped onion, celery and carrot. Cook for 5 minutes, or until the vegetables have softened.

Add the paprika and cook for 1 minute, or until the paprika becomes fragrant. Quickly toss in the flour and stir until well combined. Cook for a further 1 minute, then remove from the heat.

Add one-third of the stock to the pan and mix to a thick paste, stirring to remove all the lumps. Return the pan to the heat and add the remaining stock. Stir until the soup boils and thickens slightly. Reduce the heat, cover and simmer for 45–50 minutes.

Remove the soup from the heat and stir in the cream and chicken. Season to taste and serve with crusty bread.

Top left: Chicken noodle and mushroom soup. Top right: Cock-a-leekie. Bottom left: Creamy chicken and paprika soup.

175

Chinese hot and sour noodle soup

preparation 45 minutes
cooking 4 hours
serves 6

stock
1.5 kg (3 lb 5 oz) chicken bones, washed
2 slices fresh ginger
4 spring onions (scallions), white part only, bruised

200 g (7 oz) fresh Shanghai noodles
200 g (7 oz) boneless, skinless chicken breast,
cut into very thin strips
2 tablespoons garlic
2 tablespoons red chilli paste
60 ml (2 fl oz/¼ cup) light soy sauce
¾ teaspoon ground white pepper
4 fresh shiitake mushrooms, stems removed,
caps thinly sliced
100 g (3½ oz) enoki mushrooms, trimmed and separated
115 g (4 oz) fresh baby corn, cut lengthways
60 ml (2 fl oz/¼ cup) Chinese black vinegar
60 g (2¼ oz) black fungus, roughly chopped
200 g (7 oz) firm tofu, cut into 2.5 cm (1 inch) cubes
30 g (1 oz/¼ cup) cornflour (cornstarch)
3 eggs, lightly beaten
1 teaspoon sesame oil
spring onions (scallions), thinly sliced, to serve

To make the stock, put the chicken bones and 3.5 litres (122 fl oz/14 cups) water in a large saucepan and bring to a simmer, but do not boil. Cook for 30 minutes, removing any scum that rises to the surface. Add the ginger and spring onion and simmer gently, partially covered, for 3 hours. Strain through a fine sieve and allow to cool. Cover and refrigerate overnight.

Cook the noodles in a large saucepan of boiling water for 4–5 minutes, then drain, rinse and set aside.

To make the soup, remove the layer of fat from the surface of the stock. Pour 2 litres (70 fl oz/8 cups) of the stock into a non-stick wok and bring to the boil over high heat. Reduce

the heat to medium, add the chicken, garlic, chilli paste, soy sauce and white pepper and stir well. Simmer, covered, for 10 minutes, or until the chicken is cooked through. Add the mushrooms, corn, vinegar, black fungus and tofu. Season with salt, return the lid to the wok and simmer gently for 5 minutes — do not stir.

Mix the cornflour with 60 ml (2 fl oz/¼ cup) water. Add to the soup with the noodles, return to a simmer, then pour the eggs in a very thin stream over the surface. Turn off the heat and stand for 10 minutes before gently stirring in the sesame oil. Divide among the serving bowls and garnish with the spring onion.

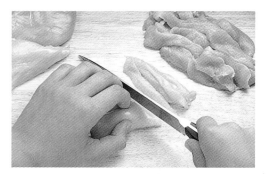

Trim the chicken breast of any excess fat, then cut it into very thin strips.

Cut the ends off the enoki mushrooms, then separate the stems.

Roasted capsicum and smoked chicken soup

preparation 20 minutes
cooking 30 minutes
serves 6–8

4 large red capsicums (peppers)
1 long green chilli
1 tablespoon olive oil
1 large onion, roughly chopped
2 garlic cloves, crushed
½ teaspoon cayenne pepper
1 teaspoon ground coriander
1 teaspoon ground cumin
2 litres (70 fl oz/8 cups) chicken stock
315 g (11 oz) smoked chicken, cubed
1 handful coriander (cilantro) leaves
sour cream and tortilla chips, to serve

Remove the seeds and membrane from the capsicums and the chilli, and cut into large flattish pieces. Cook, skin side up, under a hot grill (broiler) until the skin blackens and blisters. Remove from the heat, place in a plastic bag and leave to cool, then peel away the skin. Roughly chop the capsicum, and finely slice the chilli.

Heat the olive oil in a large saucepan over medium heat. Add the onion and garlic, and fry for 2–3 minutes. Mix in the cayenne pepper, coriander and cumin and cook for a further 1 minute, stirring constantly. Add the chicken stock, roasted capsicum and chilli and bring to the boil. Reduce the heat and simmer gently for 15 minutes.

Remove from the heat, leave to cool slightly, then purée in a blender or food processor in batches until it becomes a smooth soup. Return the soup to the pan.

Reheat the soup over medium heat for 10 minutes. Stir in the chicken and season with pepper. When the soup is hot and ready to serve, add the coriander. Ladle the soup into serving bowls and top each with sour cream. Serve with the tortilla chips.

When the capsicum has cooled, peel away the blackened skin with your fingers.

Transfer the mixture to a food processor in batches and purée until smooth.

Chicken and spinach orzo soup

preparation 15 minutes
cooking 40 minutes
serves 4

1 tablespoon olive oil
1 leek, white part only, trimmed and cut into quarters
lengthways, then rinsed well and thinly sliced
2 garlic cloves, crushed
1 teaspoon ground cumin
1.5 litres (52 fl oz/6 cups) chicken stock
2 boneless, skinless chicken breasts,
about 500 g (1 lb 2 oz) in total
200 g (7 oz/1 cup) orzo (see Note)
150 g (5½ oz/3 cups) baby English spinach leaves,
roughly chopped
1 tablespoon chopped dill
2 teaspoons lemon juice

Heat the oil in a large saucepan over low heat. Add the leek and sauté for 8–10 minutes, or until soft. Add the garlic and cumin and cook for 1 minute.

Pour in the chicken stock, increase the heat to high and bring to the boil. Reduce the heat to low, add the chicken breast, then cover and simmer for 8 minutes. Remove the chicken, reserving the liquid (keep it covered over low heat to keep it hot). When the chicken is cool enough to handle, shred it finely using your fingers.

Stir the orzo into the simmering stock and simmer for 12 minutes, or until al dente.

Return the chicken to the pan and add the spinach and dill. Simmer for 2 minutes, or until the spinach has wilted. Stir in the lemon juice, season to taste with sea salt and freshly ground black pepper and serve.

Note *Orzo is a small rice-shaped pasta.*

Cambodian sour chicken soup

preparation 20 minutes
cooking 40 minutes
serves 4

800 g (1 lb 12 oz) chicken quarters (leg and thigh), skin
removed, cut into 5 cm (2 inch) pieces on the bone
1 tablespoon tamarind pulp, soaked in
60 ml (2 fl oz/¼ cup) boiling water
60 ml (2 fl oz/¼ cup) fish sauce
½ teaspoon sugar
200 g (7 oz) fresh pineapple, cut into
2 cm (¾ inch) cubes
2 small tomatoes, cut into wedges
3 spring onions (scallions), finely chopped
1 teaspoon oil
4 garlic cloves, finely chopped
2 tablespoons chopped coriander (cilantro) leaves
3 tablespoons chopped basil
1 red chilli, thinly sliced
2 tablespoons lime juice
90 g (3¼ oz/1 cup) bean sprouts, trimmed

Pour 1.25 litres (44 fl oz/5 cups) water into a non-stick wok, then bring to the boil over medium heat. Add the chicken pieces and cook for 30 minutes, or until the stock is clear, occasionally skimming any scum from the surface.

Remove the chicken from the wok with a slotted spoon, then take the meat off the bones and discard any fat and bones. Cool the meat slightly, then shred the chicken meat, keeping the stock simmering while you do this.

Strain the tamarind liquid to remove the seeds, then add the liquid to the stock. Return the shredded chicken meat to the wok, add the fish sauce, sugar, pineapple, tomato and spring onion and season to taste with salt, then cook for 1–2 minutes over medium heat, or until the chicken, tomato and pineapple are heated through.

Heat the oil in a small frying pan over medium heat and add the garlic. Cook for 2 minutes, or until golden. Remove the garlic with a slotted spoon and add it to the soup.

Remove the wok from the heat. Stir in the coriander, basil, chilli and lime juice. Divide the bean sprouts among four bowls and ladle the soup over the top. Serve immediately.

Bottom: Cambodian sour chicken soup. Top: Chicken and spinach orzo soup.

Chicken gumbo

preparation 15 minutes
cooking 3 hours 30 minutes
serves 4–6

80 ml (2½ fl oz/⅓ cup) oil
30 g (1 oz/¼ cup) plain (all-purpose) flour
450 g (1 lb) tomatoes
600 g (1 lb 5 oz) boneless, skinless chicken thighs
60 g (2¼ oz) unsalted butter
100 g (3½ oz) smoked ham, diced
150 g (5½ oz) chorizo, thinly sliced
2 onions, chopped
2 garlic cloves, finely chopped
2 celery stalks, thinly sliced
1 red capsicum (pepper), seeded and finely chopped
500 ml (17 fl oz/2 cups) chicken stock
1 bay leaf
2 teaspoons thyme
Tabasco sauce, to taste
350 g (12 oz) okra, cut into 1 cm (½ inch) slices
2 spring onions (scallions), sliced (optional)
2 tablespoons chopped parsley (optional)

Heat 60 ml (2 fl oz/¼ cup) of the oil in a small, heavy-based saucepan, add the flour and stir to make a smooth paste. Stir over very low heat for 1 hour, or until the roux turns very dark brown, but is not burnt. This requires a great deal of patience and stirring, but provides the gumbo with its dark look and rich flavour. When it is done, the roux should be the colour of dark chocolate. Remove from the heat.

Score a cross in the base of each tomato. Put in a heatproof bowl and cover with boiling water. Leave for 30 seconds, then transfer to cold water and peel the skin away from the cross. Cut the tomatoes in half, scoop out the seeds and roughly chop the flesh.

Pat the chicken thighs dry with paper towel, cut them into quarters and lightly season. Heat the remaining oil and half the butter in a heavy-based frying pan over medium heat. Cook the chicken for about 5 minutes, or until golden brown. Remove the chicken with a slotted spoon. Add the ham and chorizo and cook for 4–5 minutes, or until lightly golden. Remove from the pan, leaving as much rendered fat in the pan as possible.

Add the remaining butter to the same pan and cook the onion, garlic, celery and capsicum over medium heat for 5–6 minutes, or until the vegetables have softened but not browned. Transfer the vegetables to a heavy-based, flameproof casserole dish. Add the tomatoes and roux to the vegetables and stir well. Gradually stir the stock into the pan.

Add the herbs and season with the Tabasco. Bring to the boil, stirring constantly. Reduce the heat, add the chicken, ham and chorizo and simmer, uncovered, for 1 hour. Add the okra and cook for a further 1 hour. Skim the surface as the gumbo cooks because a lot of oil will come out of the chorizo. The gumbo should thicken considerably in the last 20 minutes as the okra softens. Remove the bay leaf and serve. Garnish with spring onion and parsley.

Note Gumbo is a speciality of Cajun cuisine and is a cross between a soup and a stew. Traditionally, gumbo is served in deep bowls, each containing a few tablespoons of cooked rice in the bottom.

Cream of chicken soup

preparation 15 minutes
cooking 20 minutes
serves 4–6

60 g (2¼ oz) butter
40 g (1½ oz/⅓ cup) plain (all-purpose) flour
750 ml (26 fl oz/3 cups) chicken stock
2 boneless, skinless chicken breasts, sliced
250 ml (9 fl oz/1 cup) milk
250 ml (9 fl oz/1 cup) cream
1 celery stalk, finely sliced
3 tablespoons lemon thyme leaves
2 spring onions (scallions), finely sliced

Melt the butter in a large saucepan and add the flour. Stir over low heat for 2 minutes, or until lightly golden.

Gradually add the stock, stirring between each addition until smooth. Stir continuously over moderate heat until the mixture boils and thickens.

Reduce the heat and add the chicken, milk, cream and celery. Simmer over low heat for 5 minutes, or until the chicken is cooked but tender. Season, to taste. Sprinkle with the thyme and spring onion before serving.

Chicken and couscous soup

preparation 25 minutes
cooking 30 minutes
serves 6

1 tablespoon olive oil
1 onion, sliced
½ teaspoon ground cumin
½ teaspoon paprika
1 teaspoon grated fresh ginger
1 garlic clove, crushed
2 celery stalks, sliced
2 small carrots, sliced
2 zucchini (courgettes), sliced
1.125 litres (39 fl oz/4½ cups) chicken stock
2 boneless, skinless chicken breasts, sliced
pinch of saffron threads (optional)
95 g (3¼ oz/½ cup) instant couscous
2 tablespoons chopped parsley

Heat the oil in a large saucepan over medium heat and cook the onion for 10 minutes, or until soft, stirring occasionally. Add the spices, ginger and garlic and stir for 1 minute.

Add the celery, carrot and zucchini and stir to coat with the spices. Stir in the chicken stock. Bring to the boil, then reduce the heat and simmer, partially covered, for 15 minutes, or until the vegetables are tender.

Add the chicken and saffron threads to the pan and cook for 5 minutes, or until the chicken is just tender; do not overcook. Stir in the couscous and parsley and serve.

Hint Add the couscous to the soup just before serving: it absorbs liquid quickly and becomes very thick.

Chicken noodle soup

preparation 20 minutes
cooking 20–25 minutes
serves 4–6

2.25 litres (79 fl oz/9 cups) chicken stock
175 g (6 oz) shredded cooked chicken
100 g (3½ oz) broken thin noodles
3 tablespoons snipped chives
3 large handfuls parsley, chopped

Put the chicken stock in a saucepan and bring to the boil. Add the shredded chicken.

Add the noodles, chives and parsley to the pan and simmer over low heat for 15–20 minutes, or until the noodles are tender. Season, then spoon into bowls. Serve immediately.

Notes The noodles must be added immediately before serving, otherwise they will soften too much and become soggy if left to stand.

If you don't have much time, you can use shredded barbecue chicken and broken 2-minute noodles.

Top left: Cream of chicken soup. Top right: Chicken and couscous soup. Bottom left: Chicken noodle soup.

Thai sweet and sour chicken soup

preparation 20 minutes + soaking
cooking 20 minutes
serves 4–6

6 large dried red chillies
4 red Asian shallots, chopped
4 garlic cloves, chopped
2 tablespoons chopped fresh galangal
2 teaspoons chopped fresh turmeric
2 lemon grass stems, white part only, finely chopped
½ teaspoon grated lime zest
1 teaspoon shrimp paste
1 litre (35 fl oz/4 cups) chicken stock
6 makrut (kaffir lime) leaves
2 tablespoons tamarind purée
2 tablespoons fish sauce
30 g (1 oz/¼ cup) grated palm sugar (jaggery)
or soft brown sugar
450 g (1 lb) boneless, skinless chicken breast,
thinly sliced
200 g (7 oz) asparagus, trimmed and cut into thirds
100 g (3½ oz) baby corn, cut in half lengthways
200 g (7 oz) fresh pineapple, cut into 2 cm (¾ inch) cubes

Soak the chillies in 250 ml (9 fl oz/1 cup) boiling water for 20 minutes, then drain and chop them. Put the chilli, shallot, garlic, galangal, turmeric, lemon grass, lime zest and shrimp paste in a food processor or blender and blend to a smooth paste, adding a little water if necessary.

Pour the stock and 250 ml (9 fl oz/1 cup) water into a non-stick wok, add the makrut leaves and bring to the boil over high heat. Stir in the blended chilli paste and simmer for 5 minutes.

Add the tamarind, fish sauce, palm sugar, chicken (using your hands to separate the chicken slices), asparagus and baby corn and stir to prevent the chicken from clumping. Simmer for 10 minutes, or until the chicken is cooked and the vegetables are tender. Stir in the pineapple before serving in individual bowls.

Note *Use a non-stick or stainless steel wok for this recipe as the tamarind purée reacts with a regular wok and will taint the whole dish.*

Duck, shiitake mushroom and rice noodle broth

preparation 20 minutes + soaking
cooking 10 minutes
serves 4–6

3 dried shiitake mushrooms
1 Chinese roast duck (1.5 kg/3 lb 5 oz)
500 ml (17 fl oz/2 cups) chicken stock
2 tablespoons light soy sauce
1 tablespoon Chinese rice wine
2 teaspoons sugar
400 g (14 oz) fresh flat rice noodles
2 tablespoons vegetable oil
3 spring onions (scallions), thinly sliced
1 teaspoon finely chopped fresh ginger
400 g (14 oz) bok choy (pak choy), leaves separated
¼ teaspoon sesame oil

Place the dried mushrooms in a heatproof bowl, cover with 250 ml (9 fl oz/1 cup) boiling water and soak for 20 minutes. Drain, reserving the liquid and squeezing the excess liquid from the mushrooms. Discard the woody stems and thinly slice the caps.

Remove the skin and flesh from the roast duck. Discard the fat and carcass. Finely slice the duck meat and the skin.

Place the chicken stock, soy sauce, rice wine, sugar and the reserved mushroom liquid in a saucepan over medium heat. Bring to a simmer and cook for 5 minutes.

Meanwhile, place the noodles in a heatproof bowl, cover with boiling water and soak briefly. Gently separate the noodles with your hands and drain well. Divide evenly among large soup bowls.

Heat the vegetable oil in a wok over high heat. Add the spring onion, ginger and mushrooms and cook for several seconds. Transfer to the broth with the bok choy and duck and simmer for 1 minute, or until the duck has warmed through and the bok choy has wilted. Ladle the soup over the noodles and drizzle with sesame oil. Serve immediately.

Bottom: Duck, shiitake mushroom and rice noodle broth. Top: Thai sweet and sour chicken soup.

seafood soups

Zarzuela (Spanish seafood soup)

preparation 40 minutes
cooking 1 hour 10 minutes
serves 4

sofrito sauce
2 large tomatoes
1 tablespoon olive oil
2 onions, finely chopped
1 tablespoon tomato paste (concentrated purée)

picada sauce
3 slices white bread, crusts removed
1 tablespoon almonds, toasted
3 garlic cloves
1 tablespoon olive oil

1 raw lobster tail (about 400 g/14 oz)
12–15 black mussels
750 g (1 lb 10 oz) skinless firm white fish fillets, such as flake,
cod or monkfish, cut into bite-sized pieces
plain (all-purpose) flour, seasoned
2–3 tablespoons olive oil
125 g (4½ oz) calamari rings
12 large raw prawns (shrimp), peeled and deveined
125 ml (4 fl oz/½ cup) dry white wine
125 ml (4 fl oz/½ cup) brandy
3 tablespoons chopped parsley, to garnish

To make the sofrito sauce, score a cross in the base of the tomatoes. Put in a heatproof bowl and cover with boiling water. Leave for 30 seconds, then transfer to cold water and peel the skin away from the cross. Cut the tomatoes in half, scoop out the seeds and roughly chop the flesh.

Heat the oil in a saucepan over medium heat. Add the onion and stir for 5 minutes without browning. Add the chopped tomato, tomato paste and 125 ml (4 fl oz/½ cup) water and stir over medium heat for 10 minutes. Stir in 125 ml (4 fl oz/½ cup) water, season and set aside.

To make the picada sauce, chop the bread, almonds and garlic in a food processor. With the motor running, gradually add the oil to form a paste, adding another ½ tablespoon of oil if necessary.

Preheat the oven to 180°C (350°F/Gas 4). Cut the lobster tail into rounds through the membrane that separates the shell segments. Set the rounds aside. Scrub the mussels with a stiff brush and pull out the hairy beards. Discard any broken mussels, or open ones that don't close when tapped on the bench. Rinse well.

Lightly coat the fish in flour. Heat the oil in a large frying pan and fry the fish in batches over medium heat for 2–3 minutes, or until cooked and golden brown all over. Transfer to a large casserole dish. Add a little oil to the pan if necessary, add the calamari and cook, stirring, for 1–2 minutes. Add to the fish. Cook the lobster rounds and prawns for 2–3 minutes, or until the prawns turn pink, then add to the casserole dish.

Add the wine to the pan and bring to the boil. Reduce the heat, add the mussels, cover and steam for 4–5 minutes. Add the mussels to the casserole dish, discarding any that have not opened. Ensuring nothing flammable is nearby, pour the brandy into one side of the pan and, when it has warmed, carefully ignite the brandy. Gently shake the pan until the flames have died down. Pour this mixture over the seafood in the casserole dish. Pour the sofrito sauce over the top. Cover and bake for 20 minutes. Stir in the picada sauce and cook for a further 10 minutes, or until warmed through — do not overcook or the seafood will toughen. Sprinkle with parsley and serve.

Creamy mussel soup

preparation 30 minutes
cooking 40 minutes
serves 4

750 g (1 lb 10 oz) black mussels
1 celery stalk, chopped
1 carrot, chopped
1 onion, chopped
10 black peppercorns
4 flat-leaf (Italian) parsley stalks
100 g (3½ oz) butter, softened
3 spring onions (scallions), chopped
2 garlic cloves, crushed
1 large potato, cut into small cubes
185 ml (6 fl oz/¾ cup) dry white wine
40 g (1½ oz/⅓ cup) plain (all-purpose) flour
250 ml (9 fl oz/1 cup) cream
2 tablespoons chopped flat-leaf (Italian) parsley

Scrub the mussels with a stiff brush and pull out the hairy beards. Discard any broken mussels or any open ones that don't close when tapped on the bench. Rinse well. Put the mussels in a large saucepan with the celery, carrot, onion, peppercorns, parsley and 1.5 litres (52 fl oz/6 cups) water. Bring to the boil, reduce the heat and simmer, covered, for 4–5 minutes.

Strain the stock through a fine sieve, discarding any mussels that have not opened. Remove the meat from the remaining mussels and set it aside. Discard the shells and vegetables. Return the stock to the pan, simmer for 15 minutes, then remove from the heat. Set aside.

Melt half the butter in a large saucepan and stir the spring onion, garlic and potato over medium heat for 3 minutes, or until the onion is soft. Add the wine and bring to the boil. Reduce the heat and simmer for 1 minute.

Blend the flour and the remaining butter in a bowl to form a paste. Pour 875 ml (30 fl oz/3½ cups) of the stock into the saucepan with the potato. Gradually add the butter mixture, whisking until the mixture boils and thickens. Reduce the heat. Simmer for 15 minutes, or until the potato is cooked. Stir in the mussel meat and cream until heated through, then stir in the parsley just before serving.

Moroccan fish stew

preparation 30 minutes
cooking 30 minutes
serves 6

2 red capsicums (peppers), quartered and seeded
1 long red chilli, seeded
2 tablespoons extra virgin olive oil
1 onion, finely chopped
1 tablespoon tomato paste (concentrated purée)
2–3 teaspoons harissa
4 garlic cloves, finely chopped
2 teaspoons ground cumin
750 ml (26 fl oz/3 cups) fish stock
400 g (14 oz) tinned crushed tomatoes
750 g (1 lb 10 oz) skinless firm white fish fillets, such as blue eye or ling, cut into 2 cm (¾ inch) squares
2 bay leaves
2 tablespoons chopped coriander (cilantro) leaves
6 thick slices baguette
1 garlic clove, extra, halved

Grill (broil) the capsicum pieces and chilli until the skin is blackened and blistered. Cool in a plastic bag, then peel and cut into thin strips.

Heat the oil in a large saucepan and cook the onion for 5 minutes, or until softened. Stir in the tomato paste, harissa, garlic, cumin and 125 ml (4 fl oz/½ cup) water. Add the fish stock, tomatoes and 500 ml (17 fl oz/2 cups) water. Bring to the boil, then reduce the heat and add the fish and bay leaves. Simmer for 7–8 minutes, or until the fish is just cooked through.

Remove the fish with a slotted spoon and place on a plate. Discard the bay leaves. When the soup has cooled slightly, add half the chopped coriander and purée in batches, in a food processor, until smooth. Season to taste.

Return the soup and fish to the pan, add the capsicum and chilli and simmer gently while you prepare the toasts.

Toast the bread and, while still warm, rub both sides with the cut garlic. Place one slice of bread in each soup bowl and pile several pieces of fish on top. Ladle the soup over the top, distributing the capsicum evenly. Garnish with the remaining coriander.

193

Bottom: Moroccan fish stew. Top: Creamy mussel soup.

Coconut prawn soup

preparation 20 minutes
cooking 45 minutes
serves 4

curry paste
6 long dried red chillies
2 teaspoons coriander seeds
1 teaspoon cumin seeds
1 teaspoon ground turmeric
½ teaspoon paprika
½ teaspoon black peppercorns
4 red Asian shallots, chopped
4 garlic cloves, roughly chopped
1 tablespoon sliced fresh ginger
4 coriander (cilantro) roots, well rinsed
2 tablespoons chopped coriander (cilantro) stems
1 teaspoon grated lime zest
2 lemon grass stems, white part only, sliced
(reserve the stems for the stock)
2 makrut (kaffir lime) leaves, thinly shredded
1 teaspoon shrimp paste
2 tablespoons oil

stock
700 g (1 lb 9 oz) raw prawns (shrimp)
4 red Asian shallots, chopped
1 garlic clove
6 black peppercorns

2 tablespoons oil
800 ml (28 fl oz) coconut milk
60 ml (2 fl oz/¼ cup) fish sauce
coriander (cilantro) leaves, to garnish
thinly sliced lime zest, to garnish

To make the curry paste, soak the chillies in boiling water for 20 minutes, then drain. Toss the spices and peppercorns in a frying pan over medium heat for 1 minute, or until fragrant. Grind to a powder using a mortar and pestle, then transfer to a food processor and add the remaining paste ingredients and 1 teaspoon salt. Process until smooth. Add a little water, if necessary.

Peel the prawns, leaving the tails intact. Gently pull out the dark vein from each prawn back, starting from the head end. Cover with plastic wrap and refrigerate. Reserve the heads and shells.

To make the stock, dry-fry the prawn heads and shells in a wok over high heat for 5 minutes, or until orange. Add the shallots, garlic, peppercorns and 1.5 litres (52 fl oz/6 cups) water and bring to the boil. Reduce the heat, simmer for 15–20 minutes, then strain into a bowl.

Heat a clean, dry wok over medium heat, add the oil and swirl to coat the side. Add 3 tablespoons of the curry paste and stir over medium heat for 1–2 minutes, or until fragrant. Stir in the stock and coconut milk and bring to the boil, then reduce the heat and simmer for 10 minutes. Add the prawns and cook, stirring, for 2 minutes, or until they are cooked. Stir in the fish sauce and garnish with coriander leaves and lime zest.

Note Freeze the leftover curry paste in an airtight container.

Crab and corn soup

preparation 15 minutes
cooking 10 minutes
serves 4

1½ tablespoons oil
6 garlic cloves, chopped
6 red Asian shallots, chopped
2 lemon grass stems, white part only,
finely chopped
1 tablespoon grated fresh ginger
1 litre (35 fl oz/4 cups) chicken stock
250 ml (9 fl oz/1 cup) coconut milk
375 g (13 oz/2½ cups) frozen corn kernels
2 x 170 g (6 oz) tins crab meat, drained
2 tablespoons fish sauce
2 tablespoons lime juice
1 teaspoon shaved palm sugar (jaggery)
or soft brown sugar

Heat the oil in a large saucepan, add the garlic, shallots, lemon grass and ginger and cook, stirring, over medium heat for 2 minutes.

Pour the chicken stock and coconut milk into the saucepan and bring to the boil, stirring occasionally. Add the corn and cook for 5 minutes.

Add the crab meat, fish sauce, lime juice and sugar and stir until the crab meat is heated through. Season to taste. Ladle into bowls and serve immediately.

Use a sharp knife to shave pieces from the block of palm sugar.

Crab dumpling soup

preparation 25 minutes
cooking 20 minutes
serves 4

170 g (6 oz) tin crab meat, well drained
2 tablespoons finely chopped spring onions (scallions)
2 garlic cloves, finely chopped
2 teaspoons sesame oil
3 teaspoons chopped fresh ginger
12 small round gow gee (egg) or won ton wrappers
3 spring onions (scallions), extra
1.25 litres (44 fl oz/5 cups) chicken stock
1 tablespoon soy sauce
1 tablespoon mirin (see Note)
1 teaspoon sugar

To make the crab filling, mix the crab with the chopped spring onion, half the garlic, 1 teaspoon of the sesame oil and 1 teaspoon of the ginger.

Place 2 teaspoons of the filling on one half of each wrapper. Moisten the edge with some water and fold over to form a crescent. Press the edges together firmly, then place the dumplings on a lightly floured surface.

Cut the extra spring onions into thin strips and set aside. Heat the remaining sesame oil in a saucepan, add the remaining garlic and ginger and cook over medium heat for 3–4 minutes, or until the garlic is lightly golden. Add the chicken stock, soy sauce, mirin and sugar. Bring to the boil, then add the spring onion strips (reserving some for garnish) and simmer for 2–3 minutes.

Bring a large saucepan of water to the boil and cook 3–4 dumplings at a time for 5 minutes, or until just cooked. Place the dumplings in bowls, ladle the stock over them, garnish with the spring onion strips and serve.

Note Mirin is a Japanese sweetened rice wine which is used frequently in cooking.

Form the dumplings into crescent shapes and press the edges together to seal them.

Bottom: Crab dumpling soup. Top: Crab and corn soup.

Bourride (Provencal fish stew)

preparation 25 minutes
cooking 1 hour 10 minutes
serves 8

20 g (¾ oz) butter
1 tablespoon olive oil
4 slices white bread, crusts removed,
cut into 1.5 cm (⅝ inch) cubes
2 kg (4 lb 8 oz) assorted firm white fish fillets,
such as bass, whiting and cod

aïoli
5 egg yolks
3–5 teaspoons lemon juice
4 garlic cloves, crushed
250 ml (9 fl oz/1 cup) olive oil

stock
80 ml (2½ fl oz/⅓ cup) olive oil
1 large onion, chopped
1 carrot, sliced
1 leek, white part only, chopped
420 ml (14½ fl oz/1⅔ cups) dry white wine
1 teaspoon dried fennel seeds
2 garlic cloves, bruised
2 bay leaves
1 large strip orange zest
2 thyme sprigs

Heat the butter and oil in a heavy-based frying saucepan. When the butter begins to foam, add the bread cubes and cook for 5 minutes, or until golden. Drain on crumpled paper towel. Set aside.

Fillet the fish (or ask your fishmonger to do it), reserving the heads and bones for the stock.

To make the aïoli, put 2 of the egg yolks, 3 teaspoons lemon juice and the garlic in a food processor and blend until creamy. With the motor still running, slowly drizzle in the oil. Season and add the remaining lemon juice, to taste. Set aside until needed.

To make the stock, heat the oil in a large saucepan or stockpot and add the onion, carrot and leek. Cook over low heat for 12–15 minutes, or until the vegetables are soft. Add the fish heads and bones, wine, fennel seeds, garlic, bay leaves, orange zest, thyme, black pepper and ½ teaspoon salt. Cover with 2 litres (70 fl oz/8 cups) water. Bring to the boil and skim off the froth. Reduce the heat and simmer for 30 minutes. Strain into a pot, crushing the bones well to release as much flavour as possible. Return to the heat.

Preheat the oven to 120ºC (235ºF/Gas ½). Cut the fish into large pieces about 9 cm (3½ inches) long. Add to the stock and bring to a simmer, putting the heavier pieces in first and adding the more delicate pieces later. Poach for 6–8 minutes, or until the flesh starts to become translucent and begins to flake easily. Transfer the fish pieces to a serving platter and moisten with a little stock. Cover with foil and keep warm in the oven.

Place 8 tablespoons of the aïoli in a large bowl and slowly add the remaining 3 egg yolks, stirring constantly. Ladle a little of the stock into the aïoli mixture, blend well and then return slowly to the rest of the stock. Stir continuously with a wooden spoon for 8–10 minutes over low heat, until the soup has thickened and coats the back of a spoon. Do not boil or the mixture will curdle.

To serve, scatter the croutons and fish into individual bowls and ladle the stock over the top.

Salmon nabe

preparation 20 minutes
cooking 40 minutes
serves 3–4

12 dried shiitake mushrooms
250 g (9 oz) firm tofu
½ Chinese cabbage (wong bok)
4 salmon cutlets
2 x 5 cm (2 inch) pieces tinned bamboo shoots
2 litres (70 fl oz/8 cups) dashi
80 ml (2½ fl oz/⅓ cup) shoyu (Japanese soy sauce)
60 ml (2 fl oz/¼ cup) mirin or sake

sesame seed sauce
100 g (3½ oz) white sesame seeds
2 teaspoons oil
125 ml (4 fl oz/½ cup) shoyu (Japanese soy sauce)
2 tablespoons mirin
3 teaspoons caster (superfine) sugar
½ teaspoon instant dashi granules

Soak the dried mushrooms in warm water for 15 minutes, then drain. Cut the tofu into 12 squares. Coarsely shred the cabbage into 5 cm (2 inch) wide pieces.

Put the mushrooms, tofu, cabbage, salmon, bamboo shoots, dashi, shoyu, mirin and a pinch of salt in a large saucepan. Bring to the boil, then reduce the heat, cover and simmer over medium heat for 15 minutes. Turn the salmon cutlets and simmer for a further 15 minutes, or until tender.

To make the sesame seed sauce, toast the sesame seeds in a frying pan over medium heat for 3–4 minutes, shaking the pan gently, until the seeds are golden brown. Remove from the pan at once to prevent burning. Grind the seeds using

a mortar and pestle until a paste is formed. Add the oil, if necessary, to assist in forming a paste. Mix the paste with the shoyu, mirin, sugar, dashi granules and 125 ml (4 fl oz/½ cup) warm water.

Pour the salmon nabe into warmed serving bowls and serve with the sesame seed sauce.

Note *This dish is traditionally cooked in a clay pot over a burner and served in the same pot. Diners dip the fish and vegetable pieces into the accompanying sauce and the broth is served in small bowls at the end of the meal.*

Drain the block of tofu, then carefully cut it into small cubes.

Dry-fry the sesame seeds in a frying pan until golden brown.

Scallop and eggflower soup

preparation 30 minutes
cooking 45 minutes
serves 4

300 g (10½ oz) scallops
1 tablespoon dry sherry
¼ teaspoon ground white pepper
1 teaspoon grated fresh ginger
2 tablespoons oil
7 spring onions (scallions), thinly sliced,
white and green parts separated
1 tablespoon cornflour (cornstarch)
750 ml (26 fl oz/3 cups) chicken stock
2 tablespoons soy sauce
70 g (2½ oz) tinned straw mushrooms, cut into halves
50 g (1¾ oz/⅓ cup) frozen peas
1 egg, lightly beaten
dry sherry, extra, to taste
2 teaspoons soy sauce, extra

Slice or pull off any vein, membrane or hard white muscle from the scallops, leaving any roe attached. Combine with the sherry, pepper and ginger in a bowl and refrigerate for 10 minutes.

Heat the oil in a wok, swirling gently to coat the base and side. Add the white part of the spring onion and cook for 30 seconds. Add the scallops and marinade and cook over high heat, turning occasionally, until the scallops turn milky white. Remove the scallops from the wok with a slotted spoon and set aside.

Blend the cornflour with a little of the stock until smooth, add to the wok with the remaining stock and soy sauce and bring to the boil, stirring until the mixture boils and thickens.

Add the straw mushrooms and peas and cook for 2 minutes. Return the scallops to the wok, stirring the soup constantly.

Pour in the egg and cook, stirring until it turns opaque. Stir the spring onion greens through and add a little more sherry and soy sauce, to taste.

Note *Drain and rinse straw mushrooms before using. Leftover tinned mushrooms can be kept chilled, covered with water, for up to 3 days. They can be used in dishes such as stir-fries.*

Slice or pull off the vein, membrane or muscle from the scallops, leaving the roe attached.

Peel the ginger, then use the fine side of a grater to grate the flesh.

Lobster bisque

preparation 20 minutes
cooking 1 hour
serves 4–6

1 raw lobster tail, about 400 g (14 oz)
90 g (3¼ oz) butter
1 large onion, chopped
1 large carrot, chopped
1 celery stalk, chopped
60 ml (2 fl oz/¼ cup) brandy
250 ml (9 fl oz/1 cup) dry white wine
6 parsley sprigs
1 thyme sprig
2 bay leaves
1 tablespoon tomato paste (concentrated purée)
1 litre (35 fl oz/4 cups) fish stock
2 tomatoes, chopped
2 tablespoons rice flour or cornflour (cornstarch)
125 ml (4 fl oz/½ cup) cream

Remove the meat from the lobster tail. Wash the shell and crush into large pieces with a mallet or rolling pin, then set aside. Chop the meat into small pieces, cover and chill.

Melt the butter in a large saucepan, add the onion, carrot and celery and cook over low heat for 20 minutes, stirring occasionally, until the vegetables are soft but not brown.

In a small saucepan, heat the brandy, set alight with a long match and carefully pour over the vegetables. Shake the pan until the flame dies down. Add the wine and lobster shell. Increase the heat and boil until the liquid is reduced by half. Add the parsley, thyme, bay leaves, tomato paste, fish stock and tomato. Simmer, uncovered, for 25 minutes, stirring occasionally.

Strain the liquid through a fine sieve or dampened muslin (cheesecloth), pressing gently to extract the liquid. Discard the vegetables and pieces of lobster shell. Return the liquid to a cleaned pan.

Blend the rice flour or cornflour with the cream in a small bowl. Add to the liquid and stir over medium heat until the mixture boils and thickens. Add the lobster meat and season to taste. Cook, without boiling, for 10 minutes, or until the lobster is just cooked. Serve hot.

Note *If you don't dampen the muslin before you strain the mixture, it will soak up too much of the liquid.*

Remove the leaves from the celery stalk, then cut it into pieces.

Remove the lobster meat, then use a mallet to crush the shell into large pieces.

seafood soups

Hot vichyssoise with lemon cream and prawns

preparation 15 minutes
cooking 1 hour
serves 4

60 g (2¼ oz/¼ cup) sour cream
½ teaspoon finely grated lemon rind
½ teaspoon lemon juice, or to taste
55 g (2 oz) butter
2 leeks, white part only, thinly sliced
2 tablespoons dry white wine
500 g (1 lb 2 oz/about 4) boiling potatoes, peeled and chopped
450 ml (16 fl oz) vegetable or chicken stock
250 ml (9 fl oz/1 cup) milk
2 tablespoons cream
8 large cooked king prawns (shrimp), peeled, deveined and chopped
1 tablespoon finely snipped chives

Combine the sour cream, lemon rind and juice in a bowl, season to taste with sea salt and ground white pepper and set aside.

Melt the butter in a saucepan over low heat. Add the sliced leek and cook, stirring often, for 10 minutes or until softened. Add the wine, potato and stock and bring to a simmer. Cook for 40 minutes, or until the potato is very tender. Transfer the mixture to a food processor and process until smooth. Pass the soup through a fine strainer. Return the soup to a clean saucepan, warm through over medium heat, then stir in the milk and cream. Season to taste. Heat for 1–2 minutes more, without allowing the soup to boil.

Divide the soup among four bowls or teacups and top each bowl with a few prawn pieces and a dollop of lemon cream mixture. Scatter over the chives and serve immediately.

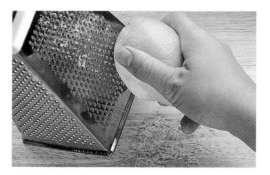

Use the fine side of a grater to grate the lemon rind, avoiding the bitter white pith.

Remove the green part of the leeks, then wash and thinly slice them.

seafood soups

Green tea, rice and salmon soup

preparation 15 minutes
cooking 20 minutes
serves 4

330 g (11½ oz/1½ cups) medium-grain white rice
500 g (1 lb 2 oz) very fresh salmon fillets, skinned, pin-boned
300 g (10½ oz) silken tofu, drained and cut
into 5 mm (¼ inch) cubes
2 spring onions (scallions), very thinly diagonally sliced
1.5 litres (52 fl oz/6 cups) freshly brewed,
very hot Japanese green tea
fine strips of toasted nori, to serve
2 tablespoons toasted sesame seeds, to serve
wasabi and pickled ginger, to serve

Put the rice and 560 ml (16¼ fl oz/2¼ cups) water in a saucepan, cover and bring to a simmer. Reduce the heat to low and cook for 12–15 minutes, or until the water is absorbed.

Remove from the heat and stand, covered, for 5 minutes, or until the rice is tender.

Meanwhile, cut the salmon widthways into 5 mm (¼ inch) thick slices.

Divide the rice among serving bowls and scatter over the tofu and spring onion. Top with the salmon, then pour over the hot green tea. Serve immediately, topped with the nori strips and sesame seeds. Pass the wasabi and the pickled ginger separately.

Thai-style seafood soup

preparation 30 minutes
cooking 40 minutes
serves 6

4 tomatoes
500 g (1 lb 2 oz) raw prawns (shrimp)
1 tablespoon oil
5 cm (2 inch) piece fresh ginger, grated
3 tablespoons finely chopped lemon grass, white part only
3 small red chillies, finely chopped
2 onions, chopped
750 ml (26 fl oz/3 cups) fish stock
4 makrut (kaffir lime) leaves, finely shredded
165 g (5¾ oz/1 cup) chopped pineapple
1 tablespoon tamarind concentrate
1 tablespoon grated palm sugar (jaggery)
or soft brown sugar
2 tablespoons lime juice
1 tablespoon fish sauce
500 g (1 lb 2 oz) skinless firm white fish fillets,
cut into 2 cm (¾ inch cubes)
2 tablespoons chopped coriander (cilantro) leaves

Score a cross in the base of the tomatoes and place in a heatproof bowl. Cover with boiling water and leave for 30 seconds, then transfer to cold water and peel the skin away from the cross. Cut the tomatoes in half, scoop out the seeds and chop the flesh.

Peel the prawns and gently pull out the dark vein from each prawn back, starting from the head end.

Heat the oil in a large saucepan. Add the ginger, lemon grass, chilli and onion and stir over medium heat for 5 minutes, or until the onion is golden.

Add the tomato to the pan and cook for 3 minutes. Stir in the stock, 750 ml (26 fl oz/3 cups) water, the makrut leaves, pineapple, tamarind, palm sugar, lime juice and fish sauce. Cover, bring to the boil, then reduce the heat and simmer for 15 minutes.

Add the fish, prawns and coriander to the pan. Simmer for 10 minutes, or until the seafood is tender. Serve the soup immediately.

Bottom: Thai-style seafood soup. Top: Green tea, rice and salmon soup.

Marmite dieppoise

preparation 45 minutes
cooking 30 minutes
serves 4

500 g (1 lb 2 oz) raw prawns (shrimp)
600 g (1 lb 5 oz) black mussels
350 g (12 oz) scallops
300 g (10½ oz) assorted skinless firm white fish fillets, such as
monkfish, snapper, orange roughy, salmon
½ leek, white part only, sliced
½ small fennel bulb, sliced
375 ml (13 fl oz/1½ cups) dry white wine
2 thyme sprigs
1 bay leaf
150 g (5½ oz) button mushrooms, sliced
250 ml (9 fl oz/1 cup) cream
1 tablespoon chopped flat-leaf (Italian) parsley

Peel the prawns and gently pull out the dark vein from each prawn back, starting at the head end. Scrub the mussels with a stiff brush and pull out the hairy beards. Discard any broken mussels, or open ones that don't close when tapped on the bench. Rinse well. Slice or pull off any vein, membrane or hard muscle from the scallops, leaving any roe attached. Cut the fish fillets into bite-sized cubes.

In a large heavy-based saucepan, combine the leek, fennel, wine, thyme, bay leaf and mussels. Bring to the boil, cover and simmer for 4–5 minutes, stirring occasionally, until the mussels are cooked. Remove the mussels from the pan with tongs, discarding any unopened ones. Remove the mussels from their shells and discard the shells. Set aside.

Bring the cooking liquid to simmering point. Add the prawns and scallops, cover and simmer for 2 minutes, or until just cooked. Remove the prawns and scallops and set aside.

Return the cooking liquid to simmering point, add the fish and poach for 3 minutes, or until cooked. Remove from the pan and set aside.

Line a sieve with a double layer of damp muslin (cheesecloth) and strain the liquid into a clean saucepan. Bring to the boil, add the mushrooms and cook, uncovered, over high heat for 3 minutes. Stir in the cream. Bring to the boil, then reduce the heat and simmer, stirring occasionally, for 5 minutes, or until thick enough to coat the back of a spoon.

Return the mussels, prawns, scallops and fish to the stock and simmer until they are heated through. Season, then stir in the parsley and serve.

Peel the prawns and gently pull out the dark vein from each prawn back.

Scrub the mussels with a stiff brush, then pull out the hairy beards.

Scallops with soba noodles and dashi broth

preparation 10 minutes
cooking 15 minutes
serves 4

250 g (9 oz) dried soba noodles
60 ml (2 fl oz/¼ cup) mirin
60 ml (2 fl oz/¼ cup) light soy sauce
2 teaspoons rice vinegar
1 teaspoon dashi granules
2 spring onions (scallions), sliced
1 teaspoon finely chopped fresh ginger
24 large scallops (without roe)
5 fresh black fungus, chopped (see Note)
1 sheet nori, shredded

Add the noodles to a large saucepan of boiling water. Stir to separate. Return to the boil, adding 250 ml (9 fl oz/1 cup) cold water, and repeat this step three times, as it comes to the boil. Drain and rinse under cold water.

Put the mirin, soy sauce, vinegar, dashi and 875 ml (30 fl oz/ 3½ cups) water in a non-stick wok. Bring to the boil, then reduce the heat and simmer for 3–4 minutes. Add the spring onion and ginger and keep at a gentle simmer.

Heat a chargrill pan or plate until very hot. Sear the scallops in batches for 30 seconds on each side. Remove from the pan. Divide the noodles and black fungus among four deep serving bowls. Pour 185 ml (6 fl oz/¾ cup) of the broth into each bowl and top with six scallops each. Garnish with the shredded nori and serve immediately.

Note If fresh black fungus is not available, use dried and soak it in warm water for 20 minutes.

212

Stuffed squid soup

preparation 30 minutes
cooking 10 minutes
serves 4

280 g (10 oz) small squid
2 coriander (cilantro) roots, washed and finely chopped
3–4 large garlic cloves, roughly chopped
280 g (10 oz) minced (ground) pork or chicken
¼ teaspoon salt
¼ teaspoon ground white pepper
2 litres (70 fl oz/8 cups) vegetable stock
2.5 cm (1 inch) fresh ginger, sliced
80 ml (2½ fl oz/⅓ cup) light soy sauce
1 tablespoon preserved radish, sliced
5 spring onions (scallions), thinly sliced, to garnish
coriander (cilantro) leaves, to garnish
ground white pepper, to sprinkle

To clean each squid, grasp the body in one hand and pull away the head and tentacles from the body. Cut the head off the tentacles just above the eyes. Discard the head and clean out the body. Pull the skin off the squid, then rinse and drain well.

Using a mortar and pestle, pound the coriander roots and garlic into a paste. In a bowl, combine the coriander paste with the pork or chicken and the salt and white pepper. Spoon some mixture into a squid sac until two-thirds full. Squeeze the squid tube closed at the end. With a bamboo stick or sharp toothpick, prick several holes in the body of the squid. Place on a plate and repeat with the remaining squid. Shape the remaining meat mixture into small balls about 1 cm (½ inch) across.

Bring the stock to boiling point in a saucepan. Reduce the heat to low and add the ginger, soy sauce and preserved radish. Lower the meatballs into the stock, then drop in the stuffed squid and cook over low heat for 4–5 minutes or until the meatballs and squid are cooked.

Garnish with spring onions and coriander leaves. Sprinkle with white pepper.

Mediterranean fish soup

preparation 20 minutes
cooking 50 minutes
serves 4

½ teaspoon saffron threads
2 teaspoons olive oil
2 large onions, thinly sliced
1 leek, white part only, chopped
4 garlic cloves, finely chopped
1 bay leaf, torn
½ teaspoon dried marjoram
1 teaspoon grated orange zest
2 tablespoons dry white wine
1 red capsicum (pepper), seeded and cut
into bite-sized pieces
500 g (1 lb 2 oz) ripe tomatoes, chopped
125 ml (4 fl oz/½ cup) tomato passata (puréed tomatoes)
500 ml (17 fl oz/2 cups) fish stock
2 tablespoons tomato paste (concentrated purée)
2 teaspoons soft brown sugar
500 g (1 lb 2 oz) skinless, boneless fish fillets, trimmed and
cut into bite-sized pieces
3 tablespoons chopped parsley
4 slices wholegrain bread

Soak the saffron threads in a bowl with 2 tablespoons of boiling water.

Heat the oil in a large saucepan over low heat. Add the onion, leek, garlic, bay leaf and marjoram. Cook, covered, for 10 minutes, shaking the pan, until the onion is soft. Add the orange zest, wine, capsicum and tomato, cover and cook for 10 minutes.

Add the tomato passata, fish stock, tomato paste, sugar, saffron and soaking liquid to the pan. Stir well and bring to the boil, then reduce the heat to low and simmer, uncovered, for 15 minutes.

Add the fish to the soup, cover and cook for 8 minutes, or until tender. Add half the parsley, then season to taste with salt and freshly ground black pepper. Discard the bay leaf. Sprinkle the soup with the remaining parsley just before serving, accompanied by the bread.

Bottom: Mediterranean fish soup. Top: Stuffed squid soup.

Tom yum goong
(Thai hot and sour soup)

preparation 25 minutes
cooking 45 minutes
serves 4–6

500 g (1 lb 2 oz) raw prawns (shrimp)
1 tablespoon oil
2 tablespoons red curry paste
2 tablespoons tamarind concentrate
2 teaspoons ground turmeric
1 teaspoon chopped red chilli (optional)
4–8 makrut (kaffir lime) leaves, shredded
2 tablespoons fish sauce
2 tablespoons lime juice
2 teaspoons soft brown sugar
10 g (¼ oz) coriander (cilantro) leaves

Peel the prawns, leaving the tails intact and reserving the shells and heads. Gently pull out the dark vein from each prawn back, starting at the head end.

Heat the oil in a large saucepan, add the prawn shells and heads to the pan and cook for 10 minutes over high heat, tossing frequently, until the shells and heads are deep orange in colour.

Have 2 litres (70 fl oz/8 cups) water ready. Add 250 ml (9 fl oz/1 cup) of the water and the curry paste to the pan.

Boil for 5 minutes, until the liquid is reduced slightly. Add the remaining water and simmer for 20 minutes. Drain the stock, discarding the prawn heads and shells.

Return the stock to the pan. Add the tamarind concentrate, turmeric, red chilli and makrut leaves, bring to the boil and cook for 2 minutes. Add the prawns and cook for 5 minutes, or until they turn pink. Stir in the fish sauce, lime juice and sugar. Serve immediately, sprinkled with coriander leaves.

Add the tamarind, turmeric, chilli and shredded makrut leaves to the stock in the pan.

Add the prawns to the boiling stock and cook until they turn pink.

Seafood ravioli in gingery soup

preparation 30 minutes
cooking 20 minutes
serves 4

8 raw prawns (shrimp), about 250 g (9 oz)
1 carrot, chopped
1 onion, chopped
1 celery stalk, chopped
3 spring onions (scallions), thinly sliced
6 cm (2½ inch) fresh ginger, finely shredded
1 tablespoon mirin
1 teaspoon kecap manis
1 tablespoon soy sauce
4 large scallops
100 g (3½ oz) boneless white fish fillet
1 egg white
200 g (7 oz) gow gee wrappers
1 handful coriander (cilantro) leaves

To make the soup, peel and devein the prawns, reserve four for the ravioli filling and chop the rest into small pieces and reserve. Put the prawn heads and shells in a large frying pan, cook over high heat until starting to brown, then cover with 1 litre (35 fl oz/4 cups) water. Add the carrot, onion and celery and bring to the boil. Reduce the heat and simmer for 10 minutes. Strain and discard the prawn heads, shells and vegetables. Return the stock to a clean saucepan and add the spring onion, ginger, mirin, kecap manis and soy sauce. Set aside until needed.

To make the ravioli, chop the whole reserved prawns with the scallops and fish in a food processor until smooth. Add enough egg white to bind. Lay half the round wrappers on a work surface and place a rounded teaspoon of filling in the centre of each. Brush the edges with water and top each with another wrapper. Press the edges to seal, eliminating any air bubbles as you go. Trim the ravioli with a fluted cutter. Cover with plastic wrap.

Bring a large saucepan of water to the boil. Meanwhile, heat the stock and leave simmering. Just prior to serving, drop a few ravioli at a time into the boiling water and cook them for 2 minutes. Remove with a slotted spoon and divide among heated bowls. Cook the chopped prawns in the same water for 2 minutes; drain. Pour the hot stock over the ravioli and serve immediately, sprinkled with the prawns and some coriander leaves.

Place a teaspoon of filling on a gow gee wrapper, top with another wrapper and press to seal.

Cook a few ravioli at a time in a pan of boiling water, then remove with a slotted spoon.

Fennel and oyster soup with sesame pittas

preparation 25 minutes
cooking 40 minutes
serves 4–6

40 g (1½ oz) butter
1 onion, chopped
2 fennel bulbs (600 g/1 lb 5 oz), chopped
500 ml (16 fl oz/2 cups) fish stock
125 ml (4 fl oz/½ cup) dry white wine
125 ml (4 fl oz/½ cup) cream
½ teaspoon freshly grated nutmeg
24 oysters, opened
1 teaspoon lemon juice
salt and ground white pepper
2 tablespoons chopped parsley

sesame pittas
2 small pitta breads
60 g (2¼ oz) butter, melted
2 teaspoons sesame seeds

Melt the butter in a large heavy-based saucepan and cook the onion over medium heat for 5 minutes, or until soft but not brown. Add the fennel and cook, covered, for 5 minutes. Add the stock, wine and 125 ml (4 fl oz/½ cup) water, bring to the boil, reduce the heat to simmer, partially covered, for 30 minutes, or until the fennel is very soft.

Meanwhile, to make the sesame pittas, preheat the oven to 200°C (400°F/Gas 6). Split the breads in half and brush both sides with melted butter. Place on a baking tray, sprinkle with sesame seeds and bake for 10 minutes, or until golden.

Allow the soup to cool before processing in batches until smooth. Return to the pan and reheat gently. Stir in the cream, nutmeg and oysters (and any liquid in the shells). Simmer until the oysters just begin to curl at the edges (about 2 minutes). Do not overcook or they will be tough. Stir in the lemon juice and add salt and pepper to taste. Garnish with chopped parsley.

Norwegian fish soup

preparation 20 minutes
cooking 25 minutes
serves 4–6

30 g (1 oz) butter
2 carrots, diced
1 parsnip, peeled and diced
1 leek, white part only, sliced
1 teaspoon celery seeds
500 g (1 lb 2 oz) skinless, boneless white fish fillets
500 ml (17 fl oz/2 cups) milk
185 ml (6 fl oz/¾ cup) dry white wine
2 teaspoons cornflour (cornstarch)
1 tablespoon milk, extra
2 egg yolks
125 g (4½ oz/½ cup) sour cream
1 large handful chopped parsley

Melt the butter in a large heavy-based saucepan, add the carrot, parsnip, leek and celery seeds and stir over medium heat for 3 minutes, without allowing the vegetables to brown. Cut the fish into bite-sized pieces and add to the pan.

Stir in the milk and wine. Bring to the boil, then reduce the heat and simmer for 15 minutes. Remove from the heat.

Blend the cornflour and extra milk and mix together with the egg yolks and sour cream. Add to the pan, reduce the heat and stir continuously for 3–5 minutes, until the soup thickens a little, but doesn't boil. Stir in the parsley and season to taste. Serve immediately.

Note If you prefer a less chunky soup, you can finely chop the vegetables in a food processor.

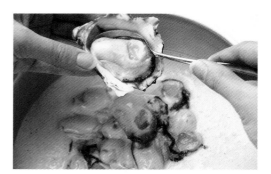

Spoon the oysters out of their shells, and add them to the soup, along with any liquid.

Blend the cornflour mixture with the egg yolks and sour cream.

Bottom: Norwegian fish soup. Top: Fennel and oyster soup with sesame pittas.

Shark's fin soup

preparation 10 minutes + overnight soaking
cooking 3 hours 45 minutes
serves 6

300 g (10½ oz) ready-prepared shark's fin
400 g (14 oz) bacon or ham bones
500 g (1 lb 2 oz) chicken bones
500 g (1 lb 2 oz) beef bones
4 slices fresh ginger
300 g (10½ oz) boneless, skinless chicken breast, minced (ground)
1 egg white, lightly beaten
40 g (1½ oz/⅓ cup) cornflour (cornstarch)
1 tablespoon light soy sauce
red rice vinegar

Put the shark's fin in a large bowl and cover with cold water. Leave to soak overnight. Strain the shark's fin and rinse gently to remove any remaining sand and sediment. Bring a stockpot of water to the boil. Add the shark's fin, reduce the heat and simmer, covered, for 1 hour. Strain and set aside.

Put the bacon or ham bones, chicken bones and beef bones in a large stockpot with the ginger slices and 2 litres (70 fl oz/ 8 cups) water. Bring to the boil, reduce the heat and simmer, covered, for 2 hours. Skim off any scum and fat that rises to the surface. Strain the stock, discarding the bones. You will need 1.5–1.75 litres (52–60 fl oz/6–7 cups). If you have more, return the stock to the pan and reduce it further until you have the correct amount.

Combine the chicken, egg white and 1 tablespoon of the cornflour. Set aside in the fridge.

Put the prepared shark's fin and stock in a large clay pot or saucepan and simmer, covered, for 30 minutes. Add the chicken mixture and stir to separate the meat. Simmer for 10 minutes, or until the chicken is cooked.

Season the soup with the soy sauce and some salt and ground white pepper. Combine the remaining cornflour with 125 ml (4 fl oz/½ cup) water, add to the soup and simmer until thickened.

Serve the soup with some red rice vinegar, which can be added to the soup to taste.

Cioppino
(San Franciscan fish stew)

preparation 30 minutes
cooking 55 minutes
serves 4

2 dried Chinese mushrooms
1 kg (2 lb 4 oz) firm white fish fillets, such as hake,
cod, snapper, ocean perch
375 g (13 oz) large raw prawns (shrimp)
1 raw lobster tail (about 400 g/14 oz)
12–15 black mussels
60 ml (2 fl oz/¼ cup) olive oil
1 large onion, finely chopped
1 green capsicum (pepper), seeded and
finely chopped
2–3 garlic cloves, crushed
400 g (14 oz) tin chopped tomatoes
250 ml (9 fl oz/1 cup) dry white wine
250 ml (9 fl oz/1 cup) tomato juice
250 ml (9 fl oz/1 cup) fish stock
1 bay leaf
2 parsley sprigs
2 teaspoons chopped basil
1 tablespoon chopped parsley

Place the mushrooms in a small bowl, cover with boiling water and soak for 20 minutes. Cut the fish into bite-sized pieces, removing the bones.

Peel the prawns, leaving the tails intact. Gently pull out the dark vein from each prawn back, starting at the head end.

Starting at the end where the head was, cut down the sides of the lobster shell on the underside with kitchen scissors. Pull back the flap, remove the meat and then cut it into small pieces.

Scrub the mussels with a stiff brush and pull out the hairy beards. Discard any broken mussels, or open ones that don't close when tapped on the work surface. Rinse well.

Drain the mushrooms, squeeze dry and chop finely. Heat the oil in a heavy-based saucepan, add the onion, capsicum and garlic and stir over medium heat for about 5 minutes, or until the onion is soft. Add the mushrooms, tomato, wine, tomato juice, stock, bay leaf, parsley sprigs and basil. Bring to the boil, reduce the heat, then cover and simmer for 30 minutes.

Layer the fish and prawns in a large saucepan. Add the sauce, then cover and leave on low heat for 10 minutes, or until the prawns are pink and the fish is cooked. Add the lobster and mussels and simmer for another 4–5 minutes. Season with salt and pepper. Discard any unopened mussels. Sprinkle with parsley before serving.

Lobster soup with
zucchini and avocado

preparation 15 minutes
cooking 20 minutes
serves 4

50 g (1¾ oz) butter
1 garlic clove, crushed
2 French shallots, finely chopped
1 onion, chopped
1 zucchini (courgette), diced
2½ tablespoons dry white wine
400 ml (14 fl oz) fish stock
250 g (9 oz) cooked lobster meat, chopped
250 ml (9 fl oz/1 cup) thick (double/heavy) cream
1 avocado, diced
1 tablespoon coriander (cilantro) leaves, chopped
1 tablespoon parsley, chopped
lemon juice, to serve

Melt the butter in a large saucepan. Add the garlic, chopped shallots, onion and zucchini and cook over medium heat for 8–10 minutes, or until the vegetables are just soft.

Add the wine and bring to the boil, keeping it on the boil for 3 minutes. Pour in the stock and bring to the boil again. Reduce the heat to low, add the lobster meat and simmer for 1–2 minutes, until warmed through. Gently stir in the cream. Season with salt and freshly ground black pepper.

Ladle the soup into four bowls and stir a little avocado, coriander and parsley into each one. Squeeze a little lemon juice over the soup to serve.

Chop the coriander leaves, reserving the root and stems for another use.

Bottom: Lobster soup with zucchini and avocado. Top: Cioppino.

Pumpkin, prawn and coconut soup

preparation 15 minutes
cooking 20 minutes
serves 4–6

500 g (1 lb 2 oz) pumpkin (winter squash), cubed
80 ml (2½ fl oz/⅓ cup) lime juice
1 kg (2 lb 4 oz) large raw prawns (shrimp)
2 onions, chopped
1 small red chilli, finely chopped
1 lemon grass stem, white part only, chopped
1 teaspoon shrimp paste
1 teaspoon sugar
375 ml (13 fl oz/1½ cups) coconut milk
1 teaspoon tamarind purée
125 ml (4 fl oz/½ cup) coconut cream
1 tablespoon fish sauce
2 tablespoons Thai basil leaves, plus extra, to serve

Combine the pumpkin with half the lime juice in a bowl.

Peel the prawns and gently pull out the dark vein from each prawn back, starting at the head end.

Process the onion, chilli, lemon grass, shrimp paste, sugar and 60 ml (2 fl oz/¼ cup) of the coconut milk in a food processor until a paste forms. Combine the paste with the remaining coconut milk, tamarind purée and 250 ml (9 fl oz/ 1 cup) water in a large saucepan and stir until smooth.

Add the pumpkin and lime juice to the pan and bring to the boil. Reduce the heat and simmer, covered, for 10 minutes, or until the pumpkin is just tender.

Add the prawns and the coconut cream, then simmer for 3 minutes, or until the prawns are just pink and cooked through. Stir in the fish sauce, the remaining lime juice and the Thai basil leaves.

To serve, pour the soup into warmed bowls and garnish with basil leaves.

Remove the skin and seeds from the pumpkin, then dice the flesh.

Wear gloves to protect your skin when you are chopping the chillies.

Sour fish soup with water spinach

preparation 15 minutes
cooking 10 minutes
serves 4

sour curry paste
3 garlic cloves, roughly chopped
3 bird's eye chillies, stems removed
1 Asian shallot, chopped
1 teaspoon grated galangal
1 teaspoon grated turmeric (or a pinch of dried)
1 teaspoon shrimp paste

175 g (6 oz) skinless white fish fillets
3 tablespoons tamarind purée
175 g (6 oz) water spinach, cut into pieces, leaves separated
1 tablespoon fish sauce
1 tablespoon sugar

To make the sour curry paste, use a mortar and pestle or food processor to pound or blend all the ingredients together until smooth.

Remove any remaining bones from the fish using tweezers, then cut the fish fillets into 5 cm (2 inch) pieces.

In a saucepan, bring 625 ml (21½ fl oz/2½ cups) water to the boil. Stir in the sour curry paste, then reduce the heat to medium. Add the tamarind purée, water spinach stems, fish sauce and sugar and cook for 2–3 minutes.

Add the fish fillets and cook for another 1–2 minutes. Add the water spinach leaves and gently stir to combine. Taste, then adjust the seasoning if necessary. Spoon into serving bowls and serve hot with rice.

Garlic, pasta and fish soup

preparation 30 minutes
cooking 40 minutes
serves 4–6

80 ml (2½ fl oz/⅓ cup) olive oil
1 leek, white part only, trimmed and sliced
20–30 garlic cloves, thinly sliced
2 potatoes, chopped
2 litres (70 fl oz/8 cups) fish stock
70 g (2½ oz/½ cup) small pasta shapes
10 baby (pattypan) squash, halved
2 zucchini (courgettes), cut into thick slices
300 g (10½ oz) ling fillets, cut into large pieces
1–2 tablespoons lemon juice
2 tablespoons shredded basil

Heat the oil in a large saucepan, add the leek, garlic and potato and cook over medium heat for 10 minutes. Add 500 ml (17 fl oz/2 cups) of the stock and cook for 10 minutes. Allow the soup to cool slightly before transferring to a food processor or blender. Blend, in batches, until smooth.

Pour the remaining stock into the pan and bring to the boil. Add the pasta, squash and zucchini. Add the purée, and simmer for 15 minutes. When the pasta is soft, add the fish pieces and cook for 5 minutes, or until tender. Stir in the lemon juice and basil, and season to taste.

Bottom: Garlic, pasta and fish soup. Top: Sour fish soup with water spinach.

Manhattan-style seafood chowder

preparation 30 minutes
cooking 30 minutes
serves 4–6

12 large raw prawns (shrimp)
60 g (2¼ oz) butter
3 bacon slices, chopped
2 onions, chopped
2 garlic cloves, finely chopped
2 celery stalks, sliced
3 potatoes, diced
1.25 litres (44 fl oz/5 cups) fish or chicken stock
3 teaspoons chopped thyme
1 tablespoon tomato paste (concentrated purée)
425 g (15 oz) tinned chopped tomatoes
375 g (13 oz) skinless firm white fish fillets, such as ling, cod,
flake or hake, cut into bite-sized pieces
310 g (11 oz) tinned baby clams (vongole), with liquid
2 tablespoons chopped parsley
grated orange zest, to garnish

Peel the prawns and gently pull out the dark vein from each prawn back, starting at the head end.

Melt the butter in a large saucepan and cook the bacon, onion, garlic and celery over low heat, stirring occasionally, for 5 minutes, or until soft but not brown. Add the potato, stock and chopped thyme and bring to the boil. Reduce the heat and simmer, covered, for 15 minutes. Add the tomato paste and tomato to the pan, stir through and return to the boil. Add the fish pieces, prawns and clams with the juice and simmer over low heat for 3 minutes.

Just before serving, season to taste and stir in the parsley. Garnish with grated orange zest.

Cook the bacon, onion, garlic and celery until soft but not brown.

Add the potato, stock and chopped thyme to the bacon mixture.

Penang fish laksa

preparation 20 minutes
cooking 40 minutes
serves 4

1 whole snapper (750 g/1 lb 10 oz), scaled and cleaned
750 ml (26 fl oz/3 cups) chicken stock
6 Vietnamese mint stalks
4 dried red chillies
3 cm (1¼ inch) piece of galangal, finely chopped
4 red Asian shallots, finely chopped
2 lemon grass stems, white part only, finely chopped
1 teaspoon ground turmeric
1 teaspoon shrimp paste
4 tablespoons tamarind purée
1 tablespoon sugar
500 g (1 lb 2 oz) fresh rice noodles
1 small Lebanese (short) cucumber, seeded and cut into strips
3 tablespoons Vietnamese mint
1 large green chilli, sliced

Trim the fins and tail off the fish with kitchen scissors. Make several deep cuts through the thickest part of the fish on both sides.

Pour the stock and 750 ml (26 fl oz/3 cups) water into a non-stick wok. Add the mint stalks and bring to the boil over high heat. Add the fish to the wok and simmer for 10 minutes, or until cooked through. The fish should remain submerged during cooking — you might need to add some more boiling water. Lift the fish out of the wok and allow to cool.

Soak the chillies in 250 ml (9 fl oz/1 cup) boiling water for 20 minutes. Drain and chop. To make the laksa paste, put the chilli, galangal, shallots, lemon grass, turmeric and shrimp paste in a food processor or blender and blend to a smooth paste, adding a little water if needed.

Flake the fish flesh and remove all the bones, reserving both. Add the bones and tamarind purée to the stock in the wok and bring to the boil. Simmer for 10 minutes, then strain and return the liquid to a clean wok — make sure no bones slip through. Stir the laksa paste into the liquid and simmer over medium heat for 10 minutes. Stir in the sugar, add the fish and simmer for 1–2 minutes, until the fish is heated through.

Put the noodles in a heatproof bowl and cover with boiling water, then gently separate. Drain immediately and refresh under cold water. Divide the noodles among four serving bowls. Ladle on the fish pieces and broth, then sprinkle with the cucumber, mint and chilli and serve.

Chunky fish soup with bacon and dumplings

preparation 30 minutes
cooking 40 minutes
serves 6

2 tablespoons olive oil
1 onion, chopped
1 small red capsicum (pepper), seeded and chopped
1 small zucchini (courgette), diced
150 g (5½ oz) smoked bacon, chopped
1 garlic clove, crushed
2 tablespoons paprika
400 g (14 oz) tinned chopped tomatoes
400 g (14 oz) tinned chickpeas, drained and rinsed
450 g (1 lb) skinless pike fillet, cut into large pieces
2 tablespoons chopped flat-leaf (Italian) parsley

dumplings
75 g (2½ oz) self-raising flour
1 egg, lightly beaten
1½ tablespoons milk
2 teaspoons finely chopped marjoram

Heat the oil in a saucepan over low heat and cook the onion for 8 minutes, or until softened. Add the capsicum, zucchini, bacon and garlic and cook over medium heat for 5 minutes, stirring occasionally.

Meanwhile, to make the dumplings, combine the flour, egg, milk and marjoram in a bowl and mix with a wooden spoon.

Add the paprika, tomato, chickpeas and 800 ml (28 fl oz) water to the vegetables. Bring the liquid to the boil, then reduce the heat to low and simmer for 10 minutes, or until thickened slightly. Using two tablespoons to help you form the dumplings, lower six rounds of the dumpling mixture into the soup. Poach for 2 minutes, then slide the pieces of fish into the liquid. Poach for a further 2–3 minutes, until the fish is cooked through. Season to taste and sprinkle with the parsley.

Tunisian fish soup

preparation 15 minutes
cooking 40 minutes
serves 6

60 ml (2 fl oz/¼ cup) olive oil
1 onion, chopped
1 celery stalk, chopped
4 garlic cloves, crushed
2 tablespoons tomato paste (concentrated purée)
1½ teaspoons ground turmeric
1½ teaspoons ground cumin
2 teaspoons harissa
1 litre (35 fl oz/4 cups) fish stock
2 bay leaves
200 g (7 oz/1 cup) orzo or other small pasta
500 g (1 lb 2 oz) mixed skinless snapper and sea bass fillets, cut into bite-sized chunks
2 tablespoons chopped mint, plus some extra leaves, to garnish
2 tablespoons lemon juice
pitta bread, to serve (optional)

Heat the oil in a large saucepan over medium heat. Add the onion and celery and cook for 8–10 minutes, or until softened. Add the garlic and cook for a further 1 minute. Stir in the tomato paste, turmeric, cumin and harissa and cook, stirring constantly, for an extra 30 seconds.

Pour the fish stock into the saucepan and add the bay leaves. Bring the liquid to the boil, then reduce the heat to low and simmer gently for 15 minutes.

Add the orzo to the liquid and cook for 2–3 minutes, until al dente. Add the fish to the liquid and poach gently for 3–4 minutes, until the fish is opaque. Stir in the mint and lemon juice and season to taste. Serve with warm pitta bread, if desired. Garnish with mint leaves.

Bottom: Tunisian fish soup. Top: Chunky fish soup with bacon and dumplings.

Mexican soup with salsa

preparation 30 minutes
cooking 40 minutes
serves 4

60 ml (2 fl oz/¼ cup) olive oil
1 large onion, chopped
1 large celery stalk, chopped
3 garlic cloves, crushed
2 thin red chillies, chopped
200 ml (7 fl oz) fish stock
800 g (1 lb 12 oz) tinned chopped tomatoes
2 bay leaves
1 teaspoon dried oregano
1 teaspoon caster (superfine) sugar
2 corn cobs, kernels removed
500 g (1 lb 2 oz) halibut fillets
2 tablespoons chopped coriander (cilantro) leaves
juice of 2 limes
12 prawns (shrimp), peeled and deveined, tails intact
8 scallops, cleaned
12 clams, cleaned
125 ml (4 fl oz/½ cup) thick (double/heavy) cream

salsa
½ small avocado
1 tablespoon coriander (cilantro) leaves
grated zest and juice of 1 lime
½ red onion, finely chopped

Heat the oil in a saucepan and cook the onion and celery over medium heat for 10 minutes. Add the garlic and chilli and cook for 1 minute, stirring. Stir in the fish stock and tomato. Add the bay leaves, oregano and sugar and bring to the boil. Reduce the heat to low and simmer for 10 minutes. Remove the bay leaves, then tip the slightly cooled tomato mixture into a food processor and whiz until smooth. Return the tomato sauce to the pan and season. Add the corn kernels and bring back to the boil. Reduce the heat and simmer for 3 minutes. Cut the fish into chunks.

Stir the coriander and the lime juice into the sauce, add the fish, then simmer for 1 minute. Add the prawns, scallops and clams. Cover with a lid and cook for a further 2–3 minutes, or until the seafood is cooked through.

To make the salsa, chop the avocado into cubes and mix with the coriander, the lime zest and juice, and red onion.

Stir the cream into the soup and top with the salsa.

Stuffed tofu soup with prawns

preparation 30 minutes
cooking 15 minutes
serves 4

275 g (10 oz) raw prawns (shrimp)
2–3 coriander (cilantro) roots, roughly chopped
2 garlic cloves, roughly chopped
¼ teaspoon salt
1 tablespoon cornflour (cornstarch)
¼ teaspoon ground white pepper
320 g (11 oz) firm tofu (bean curd)
1.5 litres (52 fl oz/6 cups) vegetable stock
2.5 cm (1 inch) fresh ginger, sliced
80 ml (2½ fl oz/⅓ cup) light soy sauce
1 tablespoon preserved radish
5 spring onions (scallions), thinly sliced, for garnish

Peel and devein the prawns. Set aside about 80 g (2¾ oz) of the prawns and cut the rest of them along their backs so that they open like a butterfly (leave each prawn joined along the base and at the tail).

Using a food processor or blender, whiz the coriander roots and garlic until as smooth as possible. Add the prawns that are not butterflied, along with the salt, cornflour and white pepper, then blend until as smooth as possible. (You can use a mortar and pestle to pound the coriander roots and garlic into a paste before processing with the prawns. This gives a slightly better flavour.)

Drain the tofu and cut it into 16 triangles. Cut a pocket into the long side of each piece of tofu with a knife. Spoon some prawn mixture into each pocket and gently press down on top. Repeat until you have used all the tofu and the mixture.

Heat the vegetable stock to boiling point in a saucepan. Reduce the heat to low and add the ginger, soy sauce and preserved radish. Lower the tofu envelopes into the stock and cook for 4–5 minutes, until cooked. Add the butterflied prawns and cook for another 1–2 minutes, until the prawns open and turn pink. Taste, then adjust the seasoning if necessary. Serve garnished with spring onions.

Cut a pocket in each tofu triangle, then carefully spoon the prawn mixture into the pockets.

Lower the tofu envelopes into the simmering stock and cook for 4–5 minutes.

Poached seafood broth with soba noodles

preparation 25 minutes
cooking 20 minutes
serves 4

250 g (9 oz) dried soba noodles
8 raw prawns (shrimp)
1½ tablespoons finely chopped fresh ginger
4 spring onions (scallions), diagonally sliced
100 ml (3½ fl oz) light soy sauce
60 ml (2 fl oz/¼ cup) mirin
1 teaspoon grated palm sugar (jaggery) or soft brown sugar
300 g (10½ oz) boneless salmon fillet, skinned and cut into 5 cm (2 inch) strips
300 g (10½ oz) boneless white fish fillet, skinned and cut into 5 cm (2 inch) strips
150 g (5½ oz) cleaned calamari hood, scored and cut into 3 cm (1¼ inch) cubes
50 g (1¾ oz) mizuna, roughly chopped (see Note)

Cook the noodles in a large saucepan of boiling water for 5 minutes, or until they are tender. Drain and rinse under cold water.

Peel and devein the prawns, reserving the shells and leaving the tails intact. Put the heads and shells in a large saucepan with the ginger, half the spring onion and 1.5 litres (52 fl oz/ 6 cups) water. Bring slowly to the boil and boil for 5 minutes. Strain and discard the prawn heads, shells and spring onion. Return the stock to the saucepan. Add the light soy sauce, mirin and palm sugar to the stock. Heat and stir to dissolve the sugar.

Add the fish and calamari to the saucepan and poach over low heat for 2–3 minutes, until it is just cooked through. Add the remaining spring onion.

Divide the noodles evenly among four large bowls. Add the seafood, pour on the stock and scatter with the mizuna.

Note *Mizuna is a salad leaf with dark green, feathery and glossy leaves. It has a mild peppery flavour. Young leaves are often used in salads or as a garnish, while older leaves are used in stir-fries or in Japanese cooking.*

Peel the prawns, leaving the tails intact and keeping the heads and shells for the stock.

Peel off the papery skin, then use a sharp knife to finely chop the ginger.

Cullen skink

preparation 10 minutes
cooking 45 minutes
serves 4

600 g (1 lb 5 oz) smoked haddock,
(preferably Finnan haddock)
1.3 litres (45 fl oz) milk
25 g (1 oz) butter
100 g (3½ oz) smoked streaky bacon, diced
1 large onion, chopped
500 g (1 lb 2 oz) waxy potatoes, peeled and
cut into small chunks
60 ml (2 fl oz/¼ cup) cream
3 tablespoons snipped chives

Put the smoked haddock in a sauté pan or deep frying pan and pour the milk over the top. Bring the liquid to the boil, then reduce to a simmer, cover and gently poach the fish for 10 minutes. When ready, the fish should be flaky when tested with the point of a knife.

Drain, reserving the milk. Flake the haddock into small pieces, discarding any skin and bones. Set aside.

Meanwhile, melt the butter in a large saucepan and when foaming, add the bacon and onion. Cook on a medium–low heat for 10 minutes, or until the onion has softened.

Add the potato and the reserved milk. Bring to the boil and simmer, covered, for 15–20 minutes, or until the potato is cooked. Stir in the haddock and cream, season to taste with salt and pepper, and bring back to a gentle simmer. Sprinkle the chopped chives over the top.

Prawn and udon noodle soup

preparation 20 minutes
cooking 30 minutes
serves 6

500 g (1 lb 2 oz) raw prawns (shrimp)
1½ tablespoons oil
1 lemon grass stem, white part only, chopped
2 garlic cloves, chopped
2 small red chillies, cut in half
2 makrut (kaffir lime) leaves
1 lime, quartered
4 spring onions (scallions), sliced
500 g (1 lb 2 oz) dried udon noodles
2 tablespoons soy sauce
100 g (3½ oz) shiitake mushrooms, halved
1 tablespoon coriander (cilantro) leaves
500 g (1 lb 2 oz) baby bok choy (pak choy),
trimmed, leaves separated
lime wedges, extra, to serve

Peel the prawns, reserving the heads and shells. Gently pull out the dark vein from each prawn back, starting at the head end.

Heat the oil in a large saucepan, add the prawn heads and shells and cook over high heat until pink. Add the lemon grass, garlic, red chillies, makrut leaves, lime quarters, half the spring onion and 2 litres (70 fl oz/8 cups) water. Bring to the boil, reduce the heat and simmer for 20 minutes. Pour the stock into a bowl through a strainer and discard the solids. Rinse the pan and return the stock to the pan.

Add the noodles to a large saucepan of boiling salted water and cook for 5 minutes, or until tender. Drain well.

Bring the stock to the boil. Add the soy sauce and prawns to the pan and cook for 5 minutes, or until the prawns turn pink and are cooked through. Add the remaining ingredients and season to taste.

Divide the cooked noodles among six soup bowls. Ladle the soup over the noodles. The soup can be served garnished with extra lime wedges, if desired.

Remove the rind from the bacon, then cut it into strips and dice it.

Wash the bok choy well, then trim and cut in half lengthways.

Bottom: Prawn and udon noodle soup. Top: Cullen skink.

Spicy seafood and roasted corn soup

preparation 20 minutes
cooking 2 hours 10 minutes
serves 4

2 corn cobs (700 g/1 lb 9 oz)
1 tablespoon olive oil
1 red onion, finely chopped
1 small red chilli, finely chopped
½ teaspoon ground allspice
4 vine-ripened tomatoes, peeled and finely diced
1.5 litres (52 fl oz/6 cups) fish stock or light chicken stock
300 g (10½ oz) boneless firm white fish fillets (such as ling or perch), diced
200 g (7 oz) fresh crab meat
200 g (7 oz) peeled raw prawns (shrimp), roughly chopped
1 tablespoon lime juice

quesadillas
4 flour tortillas (19 cm/7½ inches)
85 g (3 oz/⅔ cup) grated cheddar cheese
4 tablespoons coriander (cilantro) leaves
2 tablespoons olive oil

Preheat the oven to 200°C (400°F/Gas 6). Peel back the husks on the corn cobs (making sure they stay intact at the base) and remove the silks. Fold the husks back over the corn, place in a small baking dish and bake for 1 hour, or until the corn is tender.

Heat the oil in a large saucepan over medium heat. Add the onion and cook until soft. Add the chilli and allspice and cook for 1 minute, then add the tomato and stock and bring to the boil. Reduce the heat and simmer, covered, for 45 minutes.

Slice off the kernels from the corn cobs with a sharp knife, add to the soup and simmer, uncovered, for 15 minutes.

Add the fish, crab and prawn meat to the soup and simmer for 5 minutes, or until the seafood is cooked. Stir in the lime juice and serve with the quesadillas, if desired.

To make the quesadillas, top one tortilla with half the cheese and half the coriander. Season, then top with another tortilla. Heat 1 tablespoon of the oil in a frying pan. Cook the quesadilla for 30 seconds on each side, or until the cheese just begins to melt. Repeat to make the other quesadilla. Cut into wedges.

Wear gloves to protect your skin when you are chopping the chillies.

Score a cross in the base of the tomatoes, soak in boiling water for 30 seconds, then drain and peel.

Fish soup with tomato and olives

preparation 25 minutes
cooking 25 minutes
serves 6–8

1 kg (2 lb 4 oz) white fish fillets
60 ml (2 fl oz/¼ cup) olive oil
2 large onions, chopped
1–2 garlic cloves, crushed
4 large tomatoes, peeled, seeded and chopped
2 tablespoons tomato paste (concentrated purée)
6 tablespoons chopped gherkins
1 tablespoon chopped capers
1 tablespoon pitted and chopped green olives
1 tablespoon pitted and chopped black olives
750 ml (26 fl oz/3 cups) fish stock
250 ml (9 fl oz/1 cup) dry white wine
1 bay leaf
3 tablespoons chopped basil
2 large handfuls chopped parsley

Remove the skin and bones from the fish and chop into bite-sized pieces. Heat the oil in a large heavy-based saucepan and cook the onion and garlic for 8 minutes, or until soft.

Stir in the tomato and tomato paste. Stir for 2–3 minutes, or until the tomato is soft. Stir in the gherkins and half the capers and olives.

Add the fish, stock, wine and bay leaf and season. Bring slowly to the boil, then reduce the heat and simmer for 10–12 minutes, or until the fish is just cooked. Stir in the herbs. Add the remaining capers and olives. Serve.

Remove the skin and bones from the fish before chopping it into pieces.

Bouillabaisse

preparation 40 minutes
cooking 1 hour 30 minutes
serves 4–6

500 g (1 lb 2 oz) raw king prawns (shrimp)
1 lobster tail
1–2 fish heads
250 ml (9 fl oz/1 cup) red wine
1 small and 2 medium red onions, finely chopped
6 garlic cloves, crushed
3 bay leaves
60 ml (2 fl oz/¼ cup) olive oil
1 small leek, white part only, finely sliced
4–6 ripe tomatoes, peeled and chopped
60 g (2¼ oz/¼ cup) tomato paste (concentrated purée)
5 cm (2 inch) piece orange zest
500 g (1 lb 2 oz) white fish, skinned and boned,
cut into 3 cm (1¼ inch) pieces
12 mussels, beards removed
200 g (7 oz) scallops with roe
30 g (1 oz/½ cup) chopped parsley
3 tablespoons basil leaves

Peel and devein the prawns, reserving the heads and tails. Shell the lobster tail, keeping the shell and chopping the meat. Put the fish heads, prawn shells, heads and tails and the lobster shell in a large saucepan. Add the wine, small onion, 2 garlic cloves, 1 bay leaf and 500 ml (17 fl oz/2 cups) water. Bring to the boil, then reduce the heat and simmer for 20 minutes. Strain, reserving the liquid.

Heat the oil in a large heavy-based pan. Add the leek and the remaining onion and garlic. Cover and simmer, stirring occasionally, over low heat for 20 minutes, or until browned. Add the tomato, tomato paste, remaining bay leaves and orange zest, stir well and season. Uncover and cook for 10 minutes, stirring often. Add the reserved stock and bring to the boil, then boil for 10 minutes, stirring often.

Reduce the heat, add the seafood and simmer, covered, for 4–5 minutes. Discard any mussels which haven't opened. Remove the zest and the bay leaves. Sprinkle with the herbs to serve.

Bottom: Bouillabaisse. Top: Fish soup with tomato and olives.

Prawn laksa

preparation 30 minutes
cooking 35 minutes
serves 4–6

750 g (1 lb 10 oz) raw prawns (shrimp)
1½ tablespoons coriander seeds
1 tablespoon cumin seeds
1 teaspoon ground turmeric
1 onion, roughly chopped
2 teaspoons roughly chopped fresh ginger
3 garlic cloves
3 lemon grass stems, white part only, sliced
6 candlenuts or macadamia nuts, roughly chopped
4–6 small red chillies, roughly chopped
2–3 teaspoons shrimp paste
1 litre (35 fl oz/4 cups) chicken stock
60 ml (2 fl oz/¼ cup) vegetable oil
750 ml (26 fl oz/3 cups) coconut milk
4 makrut (kaffir lime) leaves
2½ tablespoons lime juice
2 tablespoons fish sauce
2 tablespoons grated palm sugar (jaggery) or soft brown sugar
250 g (9 oz) dried rice vermicelli
90 g (3¼ oz/1 cup) bean sprouts, trimmed
4 fried tofu puffs, cut into thin strips
3 tablespoons chopped Vietnamese mint
1 small handful coriander (cilantro) leaves
lime wedges, to serve

Peel the prawns, leaving the tails intact. Gently pull out the dark vein from each prawn back, starting from the head end.

Dry-fry the coriander seeds in a frying pan over medium heat for 1–2 minutes, or until fragrant, tossing constantly. Grind finely using a mortar and pestle or spice grinder. Repeat the process with the cumin seeds.

Put the ground coriander and cumin, turmeric, onion, ginger, garlic, lemon grass, candlenuts, chilli and shrimp paste in a food processor or blender. Add about 125 ml (4 fl oz/½ cup) of the stock and blend to a fine paste.

Heat a wok over low heat, add the oil and swirl to coat the base and side. Cook the laksa paste for 3–5 minutes, stirring constantly. Pour in the remaining stock and bring to the boil, then reduce the heat and simmer for 15 minutes, or until reduced slightly. Add the coconut milk, makrut leaves, lime juice, fish sauce and sugar and simmer for 5 minutes. Add the prawns and simmer for 2 minutes, or until pink and cooked through. Do not boil or cover.

Meanwhile, soak the dried rice vermicelli in boiling water for 6–7 minutes, or until soft. Drain and divide among serving bowls along with most of the bean sprouts. Ladle on the hot soup and then top with the tofu strips, mint, coriander and the remaining sprouts. Serve with lime wedges.

Fish soup with noodles

preparation 40 minutes
cooking 25 minutes
serves 8

750 g (1 lb 10 oz) skinless firm white fish fillets,
cut into 3 cm (1¼ inch) pieces
2 teaspoons ground turmeric
3 lemon grass stems
80 ml (2½ fl oz/⅓ cup) peanut oil
2 onions, finely sliced
6 garlic cloves, crushed
2 teaspoons finely chopped fresh ginger
2 teaspoons paprika
1 tablespoon rice flour
500 ml (17 fl oz/2 cups) coconut milk
125 ml (4 fl oz/½ cup) fish sauce
500 g (1 lb 2 oz) somen noodles

garnishes

4 hard-boiled eggs, quartered
chopped coriander (cilantro) leaves
finely sliced spring onion (scallion)
4 limes, quartered
fish sauce, to taste
4 tablespoons chilli flakes
80 g (2¾ oz/½ cup) unsalted roasted peanuts,
roughly chopped

Place the fish on a plate and sprinkle with the turmeric and 1½ teaspoons salt. Set aside for 10 minutes.

Trim the lemon grass stems to about 18 cm (7 inches) long. Bruise the white fleshy ends so that the fragrance will be released during cooking, and tie the stems into loops.

Heat the peanut oil in a large saucepan and cook the onion over medium heat for 10 minutes, or until soft and lightly golden. Add the garlic and ginger and cook for 1 minute. Add the fish, paprika and rice flour and combine well. Pour in 1.5 litres (52 fl oz/6 cups) water, the coconut milk and fish sauce, and stir. Add the loops of lemon grass and simmer for 10 minutes, or until the fish is cooked.

Meanwhile, cook the noodles in a large saucepan of boiling water for 8–10 minutes, or until tender. Drain.

Place a mound of noodles in eight warm individual serving bowls and ladle over the fish soup. Offer the garnishes in separate small bowls so the diners can add them to their own taste.

Vietnamese combination seafood soup

preparation 30 minutes
cooking 30 minutes
serves 4

400 g (14 oz) black mussels
500 g (1 lb 2 oz) raw prawns (shrimp)
1 tablespoon oil
1 lemon grass stem, white part only, finely chopped
1 red chilli, finely chopped
2 garlic cloves, finely chopped
1.5 litres (52 fl oz/6 cups) chicken stock, diluted
with 500 ml (17 fl oz/2 cups) water
1 tablespoon tamarind purée
1 tablespoon fish sauce
500 g (1 lb 2 oz) firm white fish fillets, such as ling,
blue eye or snapper, cut into 2.5 cm (1 inch) pieces
1 ripe tomato, cut into thin wedges
3 tablespoons coriander (cilantro) leaves
1 tablespoon Vietnamese mint
90 g (3 oz/1 cup) bean sprouts, trimmed

Scrub the mussels with a stiff brush and pull out the hairy beards. Discard any broken mussels, or open ones that don't close when tapped on the bench. Rinse well. Peel the prawns, leaving the tails intact. Gently pull out the dark vein from each prawn back, starting from the head end.

Heat a non-stick wok over high heat, add the oil and swirl to coat the base and side. Add the lemon grass, chilli and garlic and cook for 2 minutes, or until softened and fragrant. Add the stock, tamarind and fish sauce, bring to the boil, then reduce the heat to low and simmer for 15 minutes.

Increase the heat to medium–high, add the mussels, cover with a lid and cook for 2–3 minutes, tossing occasionally. Remove the lid and add the prawns, fish pieces and tomato wedges. Cook for a further 3 minutes, or until the seafood is completely cooked. Discard any unopened mussels. Stir in the coriander leaves and mint.

Divide the bean sprouts among four soup bowls, ladle in the soup and serve immediately.

Note It is important to use a non-stick or stainless steel wok for this recipe, as the tamarind purée reacts with a regular wok and will taint the whole dish.

Bottom: Vietnamese combination seafood soup. Top: Fish soup with noodles.

Potato and anchovy chowder with garlic prawns

preparation 25 minutes + marinating
cooking 35 minutes
serves 4

garlic prawns
2 garlic cloves, chopped
1 small red chilli, seeded and chopped
2 tablespoons chopped flat-leaf (Italian) parsley
1 tablespoon olive oil
16 raw prawns (shrimp), peeled and deveined

1 tablespoon olive oil
3 bacon slices, fat trimmed, chopped
1 onion, chopped
2 celery stalks, chopped
2 garlic cloves, chopped
80 g (2¾ oz) tinned anchovies, drained
1 carrot, chopped
3 potatoes, roughly chopped
375 ml (13 fl oz/1½ cups) chicken stock or fish stock
250 ml (9 fl oz/1 cup) milk
125 ml (4 fl oz/½ cup) cream
3 tablespoons finely chopped flat-leaf (Italian) parsley

To make the garlic prawns, put the garlic, chilli and parsley in a food processor and process for 15–20 seconds. With the motor running, add the oil and process to form a rough paste. Transfer to a bowl, add the prawns and toss to coat. Marinate for 30 minutes.

Heat the oil in a large heavy-based saucepan over medium–low heat. Add the bacon, onion, celery and garlic and cook, stirring, for 2 minutes. Reduce the heat, cover and simmer for 5 minutes.

Drain the anchovies on paper towel and pat dry. Roughly chop and add to the bacon mixture. Add the carrot and potato and stir to combine. Cook for 2 minutes, then add the stock and milk. Bring to the boil, then cover and cook for 15 minutes, or until the vegetables are tender.

Remove the saucepan from the heat. Using an immersion blender fitted with the chopping blade, blend the soup until smooth. Add the cream and most of the parsley, reserving some for garnishing. Season and keep warm.

Heat a frying pan over high heat and add the prawns and marinade. Cook, turning, for 2 minutes, or until the prawns are just cooked through.

Place a pile of prawns in the centre of four bowls and ladle the soup around the prawns. Sprinkle with the parsley.

Process the garlic, chilli, parsley and oil to make a rough paste.

Remove the stems from the parsley, then finely chop the leaves.

Sliced fish and coriander soup

preparation 10 minutes
cooking 10 minutes
serves 4

250 g (9 oz) firm white fish fillets, such as cod,
halibut or monkfish, skin removed
2 teaspoons egg white, beaten
1 teaspoon Shaoxing rice wine
2 teaspoons cornflour (cornstarch)
750 ml (26 fl oz/3 cups) chicken stock
1 tablespoon light soy sauce
40 g (1½ oz) coriander (cilantro) leaves

Cut the fish into 2 x 3 cm (¾ x 1¼ inch) slices. Blend the egg white, rice wine and cornflour to make a smooth paste, and use it to coat each fish slice.

Bring the chicken stock to a rolling boil in a large clay pot or saucepan. Add the fish slices one by one, stir gently and return to the boil. Reduce the heat and simmer for 1 minute, then add the soy sauce and coriander leaves. Return the soup to the boil, season with salt and ground white pepper and serve immediately.

Creamy fish soup

preparation 10 minutes
cooking 35 minutes
serves 4–6

¼ teaspoon saffron threads
2 tablespoons boiling water
1 litre (35 fl oz/4 cups) fish stock
125 ml (4 fl oz/½ cup) dry white wine
1 onion, finely chopped
1 small carrot, finely chopped
1 celery stalk, chopped
1 bay leaf
50 g (1¾ oz) butter
2 tablespoons plain (all-purpose) flour
300 g (10½ oz) skinless firm white fish fillets, such as snapper, orange roughy, bream, cut into bite-sized pieces
250 ml (9 fl oz/1 cup) cream
2 teaspoons snipped chives, to garnish

In a small bowl, soak the saffron threads in the boiling water while you prepare the stock.

Put the fish stock, wine, onion, carrot, celery and bay leaf in a large saucepan and slowly bring to the boil. Cover and simmer for 20 minutes. Strain and discard the vegetables.

Stir the saffron and soaking liquid into the hot stock.

In a clean saucepan, melt the butter and stir in the flour for 2 minutes, or until pale and foaming. Remove from the heat and gradually stir in the stock. Return to the heat and stir until the mixture boils and thickens. Add the fish and then simmer for 2 minutes, or until the fish is cooked. Stir in the cream and heat through without boiling. Season to taste. Serve garnished with the chives.

Crab and corn eggflower noodle broth

preparation 15 minutes
cooking 15 minutes
serves 4

70 g (2½ oz) dried thin egg noodles
1 tablespoon peanut oil
1 teaspoon finely chopped fresh ginger
3 spring onions (scallions), thinly sliced,
white and green parts separated
1.5 litres (52 fl oz/6 cups) chicken stock
80 ml (2½ fl oz/⅓ cup) mirin
250 g (9 oz) fresh baby corn, sliced on the diagonal
into 1 cm (½ inch) slices
175 g (6 oz) fresh crab meat
1 tablespoon cornflour (cornstarch) mixed
with 1 tablespoon water
2 eggs, lightly beaten
2 teaspoons lime juice
1 tablespoon soy sauce
3 tablespoons chopped coriander (cilantro) leaves

Cook the noodles in a large saucepan of boiling salted water for 3 minutes, or until just tender. Drain, then rinse under cold water. Set aside.

Heat a non-stick wok over high heat, add the peanut oil and swirl to coat the side of the wok. Add the ginger and white part of the spring onion and cook over medium heat for 1–2 minutes. Add the stock, mirin and corn and bring to the boil, then simmer for 3 minutes. Stir in the noodles, crab meat and cornflour mixture. Return to a simmer and stir constantly until it thickens. Reduce the heat and pour in the egg in a thin stream, stirring constantly — do not boil. Gently stir in the lime juice, soy sauce and half the coriander leaves.

Divide the noodles among four bowls and ladle on the soup. Top with the green spring onion and the remaining coriander leaves.

Top left: Sliced fish and coriander soup. Top right: Creamy fish soup. Bottom left: Crab and corn eggflower noodle broth.

Spanish-style rice, mussel, prawn and chorizo soup

preparation 45 minutes
cooking 45 minutes
serves 4

500 g (1 lb 2 oz) raw prawns (shrimp)
1 kg (2 lb 4 oz) black mussels
250 ml (9 fl oz/1 cup) dry sherry
1 tablespoon olive oil
1 red onion, chopped
200 g (7 oz) chorizo sausage, thinly sliced
4 garlic cloves, crushed
100 g (3½ oz/½ cup) long-grain rice
400 g (14 oz) tinned chopped tomatoes
2 litres (70 fl oz/8 cups) chicken stock
½ teaspoon saffron threads
2 bay leaves
1 tablespoon chopped oregano
3 tablespoons chopped flat-leaf (Italian) parsley

Peel the prawns, leaving the tails intact. Gently pull out the dark vein from each prawn back, starting from the head end. Scrub the mussels with a stiff brush and pull out the hairy beards. Discard any broken mussels or open ones that don't close when tapped on the bench. Rinse well.

Put the mussels in a saucepan with the sherry, cover and cook over high heat for 3 minutes, or until the mussels have opened. Strain the liquid into a bowl. Discard any unopened mussels. Remove all but eight mussels from their shells and discard the empty shells.

Heat the oil in a large saucepan over medium heat and cook the onion for 5 minutes, or until softened but not browned. Add the chorizo and cook for another 3–5 minutes, or until browned, then add the garlic and cook for a further 1 minute.

Add the rice and stir to coat with the chorizo mixture. Add the reserved cooking liquid and cook for 1 minute before adding the chopped tomatoes, stock, saffron, bay leaves and oregano. Bring to the boil, then reduce the heat and simmer, covered, for 25 minutes.

Add the prawns and the mussels (except the ones in their shells) to the soup, cover and cook for 3 minutes, then stir in the parsley. Ladle into four serving bowls, then top each bowl with two mussels still in their shells.

Scrub the mussels to remove any grit, then pull out the hairy beards.

Peel the prawns, keeping the tails intact, and pull out the dark intestinal vein.

Corn and lemon grass soup with yabbies

preparation 25 minutes
cooking 2 hours
serves 4

4 corn cobs
1 tablespoon oil
1 leek, white part only, chopped
1 celery stalk, chopped
3 lemon grass stems, white part only, bruised
5 garlic cloves, crushed
1 teaspoon ground cumin
1 teaspoon ground coriander
¾ teaspoon ground white pepper
3 makrut (kaffir lime) leaves
750 ml (26 fl oz/3 cups) chicken stock
800 ml (28 fl oz) coconut milk
125 ml (4 fl oz/½ cup) cream
2 teaspoons butter
½ teaspoon sambal oelek
1.25 kg (2 lb 12 oz) cooked yabbies or crayfish, shredded
1 tablespoon finely chopped coriander (cilantro) leaves

Trim the kernels from the corn. Heat the oil in a saucepan over medium heat. Add the leek, celery and lemon grass. Stir for 10 minutes, or until the leek is soft. Add half the garlic, and the cumin, coriander and ½ teaspoon of the pepper. Cook, stirring, for 1–2 minutes, or until fragrant. Add the corn, makrut leaves, stock and coconut milk, stir well and simmer for 1½ hours. Remove from the heat and cool. Remove the lemon grass and lime leaves and blend the mixture in batches in a food processor.

Push the mixture through a sieve. Repeat. Return to a saucepan, add the cream and warm gently.

Melt the butter in a frying pan over medium heat, add the remaining garlic, sambal oelek, remaining pepper and a pinch of salt and stir for 1 minute. Add the yabby meat, stir for 1 minute, then remove from the heat and stir in the coriander.

Using a sharp knife, carefully cut all the kernels from the corn cobs.

Rice soup with prawn and egg

preparation 15 minutes
cooking 15 minutes
serves 4

12 raw prawns (shrimp)
3 teaspoons dashi granules
60 ml (2 fl oz/¼ cup) Shoyu (Japanese soy sauce)
2 tablespoons sake
1 tablespoon mirin
750 g (1 lb 10 oz/4 cups) cold cooked Japanese short-grain rice, rinsed well
3 eggs, beaten
2 teaspoons ginger juice (see Notes)
2 spring onions (scallions), finely chopped
mitsuba or shiso, to garnish (see Notes)

Peel the prawns and gently pull out the dark vein from each prawn back, starting from the head end.

Dissolve the dashi granules in 1.5 litres (52 fl oz/6 cups) hot water, then combine with the Shoyu, sake, mirin and ½ teaspoon salt in a large saucepan and bring to the boil. Reduce the heat, then add the rice and simmer for 4 minutes, or until heated through. Add the prawns and cook for a further 3 minutes, or until the prawns are pink and starting to curl.

Remove the pan from the heat and drizzle the eggs over the top of the soup, cover and allow to sit for 1 minute. Stir the eggs through the soup along with the ginger juice and spring onion. Season to taste, garnish with mitsuba or shiso if desired, and serve immediately as the eggs should not be allowed to set completely.

Notes *Ginger juice is available in some health food stores.*

Mitsuba is a Japanese herb that resembles flat-leaf (Italian) parsley. Shiso (or perilla) is a member of the mint family.

Bottom: Rice soup with prawn and egg. Top: Corn and lemon grass soup with yabbies.

Ligurian fish stew

preparation 25 minutes
cooking 1 hour 10 minutes
serves 6

fish stock
250 g (9 oz) red snapper fillet, cut into chunks, bones reserved
250 g (9 oz) cod or turbot fillet, cut into chunks, bones reserved
250 g (9 oz) monkfish fillet, cut into chunks, bones reserved
6 large raw prawns (shrimp)
1 small onion, roughly chopped
1 carrot, roughly chopped
1 large handful flat-leaf (Italian) parsley, roughly chopped, stalks reserved

125 ml (4 fl oz/½ cup) olive oil
1 red onion, halved and thinly sliced
1 large fennel bulb, thinly sliced
3 garlic cloves, thinly sliced
800 g (1 lb 12 oz) tinned crushed tomatoes
310 ml (10¾ fl oz/1¼ cups) dry white vermouth or wine
large pinch of saffron threads
450 g (1 lb) waxy potatoes, quartered lengthways
450 g (1 lb) mussels

To make the fish stock, rinse the fish bones in cold water. Peel and devein the prawns and put the fish bones and prawn shells in a saucepan with water to cover. Bring to a simmer. Add the onion, carrot and the stalks from the parsley, then simmer for 20 minutes. Strain through a sieve and measure 1 litre (35 fl oz/4 cups) stock.

Heat the oil in a large saucepan and cook the onion and fennel for 5 minutes. Add the garlic and tomatoes. Bring to the boil, then reduce the heat and simmer until the tomatoes have reduced to a thick sauce. Season and add 200 ml (7 fl oz) of the vermouth, the saffron and the potatoes. Increase the heat and boil for about 5 minutes, then add the fish stock, reduce the heat and simmer for 10 minutes, or until the potatoes are cooked.

Scrub the mussels, pull off the beards and discard any that are broken or cracked. Bring the remaining vermouth to the boil in another saucepan and add the mussels. Cover and cook for about 1 minute, or until the shells just open. Remove the mussels from their shells and place in a bowl. Pour over the remaining cooking liquid, discarding any sediment left in the pan.

Add the prawns and fish to the soup. Stir briefly, season and simmer for 5 minutes, or until the fish is cooked. Add the mussels to reheat. Remove from the heat. Leave for 10 minutes before serving. Add the parsley and serve in bowls with bread.

Prawn, scallop and noodle soup

preparation 20 minutes
cooking 25 minutes
serves 4

4 dried shiitake mushrooms
100 g (3½ oz) dried soba (buckwheat) or somen noodles
10 g (¼ oz) sachet bonito-flavoured soup stock
80 g (2¾ oz) carrots, cut into thin batons
150 g (5½ oz) firm tofu, cut into cubes
16 raw prawns (shrimp), peeled and deveined, tails intact
8 scallops
2 spring onions (scallions), finely chopped
1 tablespoon mirin
shichimi togarashi (Japanese seven-spice seasoning mix), optional

Put the dried mushrooms in a bowl and cover with 300 ml (10½ fl oz) of boiling water. Place a saucer on top of the mushrooms to submerge them in the liquid, and leave to soak for 15 minutes.

Meanwhile, bring a saucepan of water to the boil for the noodles. Cook the noodles until just tender, then drain. Return the noodles to the pan and cover to keep warm.

In a saucepan, mix 1 litre (35 fl oz/4 cups) water with the stock. Drain the mushrooms and add the soaking liquid to the pan. Chop the mushroom caps, discarding the stalks.

Add the mushrooms and carrot to the pan and bring to the boil. Reduce the heat to a simmer and cook for 5 minutes. Add the tofu, prawns, scallops, spring onion and mirin to the pan. Cook at a gentle simmer for a further 3–4 minutes, until the prawns have turned pink and are cooked through and the scallops are firm and opaque.

Meanwhile, pour hot water over the noodles and swish the noodles around in the water to separate and warm them. Divide the noodles among four large bowls and pour the hot soup over them, dividing the seafood equally. Serve immediately, offering the shichimi togarashi to sprinkle over the top.

Notes *Although this recipe suggests soba or somen noodles you can use any type.*

If bonito stock sachets and shichimi togarashi are not available you could use a good-quality fish or chicken stock and omit the flavouring.

Trim the scallops, removing the hard white muscle and retaining the roe.

Drain the block of tofu, then carefully cut it into small cubes.

Fish ball and noodle soup

preparation 15 minutes
cooking 15 minutes
serves 4–6

500 g (1 lb 2 oz) skinless, boneless firm white fish fillets,
such as ling or perch
2 tablespoons rice flour
200 g (7 oz) dried somen noodles
2½ teaspoons dashi granules
2 tablespoons light soy sauce
1 tablespoon mirin
200 g (7 oz) Chinese cabbage (wong bok), shredded
2 spring onions (scallions), thinly sliced, to garnish
½ Lebanese (short) cucumber, peeled, seeded and cut into 5 cm (2 inch) strips

Put the fish in a food processor and process until smooth. Combine the rice flour and 80 ml (2½ fl oz/⅓ cup) water in a small bowl until smooth, then add to the fish and process for 5 seconds. Using 2 teaspoons of mixture at a time, shape into balls with wet hands.

Cook the noodles in a large saucepan of boiling water for 2 minutes, or until tender. Drain and set aside.

Pour 2 litres (70 fl oz/8 cups) water into a non-stick wok and bring to the boil. Reduce the heat to low, add the dashi granules and stir until dissolved. Increase the heat to high and bring to the boil, then add the soy sauce, mirin and salt to taste.

Add the fish balls, reduce the heat to medium and simmer for 3 minutes, or until they rise to the surface and are cooked through. Add the cabbage, increase the heat to high and return to the boil. Stir in the noodles and cook for 1 minute, or until warmed through.

To serve, divide the noodles and fish balls among serving bowls, then ladle the liquid over the top. Sprinkle with the spring onion and cucumber.

Shred the cabbage as finely as possible. This will ensure it wilts quickly in the broth.

Cut the spring onions into very thin slices to garnish the soup.

seafood soups

Eight treasure soup

preparation 15 minutes
cooking 1 hour
serves 4–6

12 small raw prawns (shrimp)
4 dried shiitake mushrooms
1 tablespoon vegetable oil
1 teaspoon sesame oil
2 teaspoons finely chopped fresh ginger
1 tablespoon finely chopped spring onion (scallion)
60 g (2¼ oz) Chinese bacon or ham, cut into thin strips (see Note)
1 litre (35 fl oz/4 cups) chicken stock
1 tablespoon soy sauce
1 tablespoon rice wine
250 g (9 oz) boneless, skinless chicken breast
1 carrot, cut into 1 cm (½ inch) slices
200 g (7 oz) firm tofu, cut into 2 cm (¾ inch) cubes
50 g (1¾ oz) sliced tinned bamboo shoots
100 g (3½ oz) baby English spinach, chopped
2 spring onions, thinly sliced, to serve

Peel the prawns and gently pull out the dark vein from each prawn back, starting from the head end.

Soak the mushrooms in 125 ml (4 fl oz/½ cup) boiling water for 20 minutes. Squeeze dry, reserving the soaking liquid. Discard the woody stalks and cut the caps into quarters.

Heat a wok over high heat. Add the oils and swirl to coat the base and side, then add the ginger, spring onion and bacon. Cook for 10 seconds, then add the stock, soy sauce, rice wine, mushroom liquid and ½ teaspoon salt. Bring to the boil and add the chicken. Reduce the heat to low, cover

with a lid and poach the chicken for 20 minutes. Remove the chicken with a slotted spoon and, when cool enough to handle, shred the meat.

Return the stock to the boil, add the carrot and cook for 5 minutes. Add the mushrooms, prawns, tofu, bamboo shoots, spinach and chicken and cook over low heat for a further 5 minutes. Serve with the extra spring onion.

Note *Chinese bacon has a dryish flesh with a strong flavour very much like prosciutto. You can substitute prosciutto.*

Dried shiitake mushrooms needed to be soaked in boiling water before use.

When the poached chicken is cool enough to handle, use your fingers to shred the meat.

Soupe de poisson (French seafood soup)

preparation 30 minutes
cooking 45 minutes
serves 6

1 large ripe tomato
1.5 kg (3 lb 5 oz) chopped fish bones from firm white fish
1 leek, white part only, chopped
1 carrot, chopped
1 celery stalk, chopped
1 garlic clove, chopped
1 bay leaf
3 flat-leaf (Italian) parsley stalks
6 black peppercorns
250 ml (9 fl oz/1 cup) dry white wine
1 tablespoon lemon juice
250 g (9 oz) skinless firm white fish fillets, such as snapper, perch, cod, cut into bite-sized pieces
ground white pepper, to taste
2 tablespoons chervil leaves
¼ lemon, cut into very fine slices

Score a cross in the base of the tomato. Put in a heatproof bowl and cover with boiling water. Leave for 30 seconds, then transfer to cold water and peel the skin away from the cross. Cut the tomato in half, scoop out the seeds and chop the flesh. Set aside.

Rinse the fish bones well in cold water and combine in a large saucepan with the leek, carrot, celery, garlic, bay leaf, parsley, peppercorns, wine, lemon juice and 2 litres (70 fl oz/8 cups) water. Slowly bring to the boil, skimming off any scum from the surface. Reduce the heat and simmer for 20 minutes.

Strain and discard the fish bones and vegetables. Strain the soup again, through a sieve lined with dampened muslin (cheesecloth), into a clean saucepan. Simmer, uncovered, for 10 minutes.

Add the fish pieces and simmer for 2 minutes, or until tender. Season with salt and ground white pepper.

Divide the chopped tomato and chervil among six warm bowls and ladle the hot soup over them. Float the lemon slices on top and serve immediately.

Note The straining muslin is dampened so it won't absorb too much of the cooking liquid.

New England clam chowder

preparation 35 minutes
cooking 45 minutes
serves 4

1.5 kg (3 lb 5 oz) clams (vongole) or pipis, in shell
2 teaspoons oil
3 bacon slices, chopped
1 onion, chopped
1 garlic clove, crushed
750 g (1 lb 10 oz) potatoes, diced
310 ml (10¾ fl oz/1¼ cups) fish stock
500 ml (17 fl oz/2 cups) milk
125 ml (4 fl oz/½ cup) cream
3 tablespoons chopped flat-leaf (Italian) parsley

Discard any clams that are broken, already open or do not close when tapped on the bench. If necessary, soak in cold water for 1–2 hours to remove any grit. Drain and put in a large heavy-based saucepan with 250 ml (9 fl oz/1 cup) water. Cover and simmer over low heat for 5 minutes, or until open. Discard any clams that do not open. Strain and reserve the liquid. Remove the clam meat from the shells.

Heat the oil in a clean saucepan. Add the bacon, onion and garlic and cook, stirring, over medium heat until the onion is soft and the bacon golden. Add the potato and stir well.

Measure the reserved clam liquid and add water to make 310 ml (10¾ fl oz/1¼ cups). Add to the pan with the stock and milk. Bring to the boil, then reduce the heat, cover and simmer for 20 minutes, or until the potato is tender. Uncover and simmer for 10 minutes, or until slightly thickened. Add the cream, clam meat and parsley and season to taste. Heat through gently before serving, but do not allow to boil or the liquid may curdle.

Simmer the clams until they open, then remove the meat from the shells.

Bottom: New England clam chowder. Top: Soupe de poisson.

Noodle soup with fish and prawn dumplings

preparation 20 minutes + chilling
cooking 15 minutes
serves 4

fish and prawn dumplings
200 g (7 oz) white fish fillets, skin and bones removed, chopped
100 g (3½ oz) peeled raw king prawns (shrimp), deveined and chopped
50 g (1¾ oz/½ cup) finely sliced sugar snap peas
1 tablespoon Chinese rice wine (optional)
1 egg white, lightly beaten
ground white pepper, to taste

100 g (3½ oz) dried vermicelli noodles
1.5 litres (52 fl oz/6 cups) chicken stock
2 tablespoons soy sauce
1 teaspoon fish sauce
1 tablespoon Chinese rice wine (optional)
2 cm (¾ inch) fresh ginger, peeled and bruised
1 bunch (500 g/1 lb 2 oz) baby bok choy (pak choy), chopped
2 long red chillies, finely sliced
2 spring onions (scallions), finely sliced
2 tablespoons soy sauce

To make the dumplings, put the fish and prawns in a food processor and blend to a coarse paste. Transfer to a large bowl and add the sugar snap peas, rice wine, if using, and egg white. Season with sea salt and ground white pepper and mix well. Take 1 heaped teaspoon of the mixture, roll it into a ball and place it on a baking tray lined with baking paper. Repeat with the remaining mixture and refrigerate for 15 minutes to firm slightly.

Meanwhile, put the vermicelli noodles in a heatproof bowl, pour boiling water over and leave to stand for 2 minutes, or until softened. Drain well and set aside.

Pour the stock, soy sauce, fish sauce and rice wine, if using, into a large saucepan. Add the ginger and bring to the boil over high heat, then reduce the heat to a simmer. Add the dumplings and simmer for 5–6 minutes, or until they are cooked through. Remove the ginger and stir in the noodles. Add the bok choy to the pan and cook for 2–3 minutes, or until softened.

Meanwhile, mix the chilli, spring onion and soy sauce together in a small bowl. Divide the soup, noodles and dumplings among four bowls and serve the soy sauce mixture on the side as a condiment.

vegetable soups

Italian bean soup

preparation 20 minutes
cooking 25 minutes
serves 4

2 x 400 g (14 oz) tins cannellini beans
1 tablespoon extra virgin olive oil
1 leek, white part only, finely chopped
2 garlic cloves, crushed
1 teaspoon thyme leaves
2 celery stalks, diced
1 carrot, diced
1 kg (2 lb 4 oz) silverbeet (Swiss chard), trimmed and
roughly chopped
1 ripe tomato, diced
1 litre (35 fl oz/4 cups) vegetable stock
2 small crusty rolls, each cut into 4 slices
2 teaspoons balsamic vinegar
shaved parmesan cheese, to serve

Put one tin of beans and liquid in a blender or small food processor and blend until smooth. Drain the other tin, reserving the beans and discarding the liquid.

Heat the oil in a large heavy-based saucepan, add the leek, garlic and thyme and cook for 2–3 minutes, until soft and aromatic. Add the celery, carrot, silverbeet and tomato. Cook for a further 2–3 minutes, until the silverbeet has wilted. Heat the stock in a separate saucepan.

Stir the puréed cannellini beans and stock into the vegetable mixture. Bring to the boil, then reduce the heat and simmer for 5–10 minutes, or until the vegetables are tender. Add the

drained beans and stir until heated through. Season to taste with salt and cracked black pepper.

Arrange two slices of bread in the base of each soup bowl. Stir the balsamic vinegar into the soup and ladle over the bread. Serve topped with shaved parmesan.

Note *This recipe is the authentic bean soup from Florence. If you like, spice it up by adding chopped chilli.*

Trim the silverbeet, removing the tough ends, then roughly chop the leaves.

Grate the parmesan cheese using the fine side of a grater.

Carrot and coriander soup

preparation 15 minutes
cooking 1 hour 10 minutes
serves 4

2 tablespoons olive oil
1 onion, sliced
800 g (1 lb 12 oz) carrots, roughly chopped
1 bay leaf
1 teaspoon ground cumin
1 teaspoon cayenne pepper
1 teaspoon ground coriander
2 teaspoons paprika
1.25 litres (44 fl oz/5 cups) chicken or vegetable stock
250 g (9 oz/1 cup) Greek-style yoghurt
2 tablespoons chopped coriander (cilantro) leaves
coriander (cilantro) leaves, extra, to garnish

Heat the oil in a saucepan, add the onion and carrot and cook over low heat for 30 minutes. Add the bay leaf, cumin, cayenne, ground coriander and paprika and cook for a further 2 minutes. Add the stock and bring to the boil, then reduce the heat. Simmer, uncovered, for 40 minutes, or until the carrot is tender.

Allow the soup to cool slightly before transferring to a food processor and blending, in batches, until smooth. Return to a clean saucepan and gently reheat. Season to taste.

Combine the yoghurt and coriander in a bowl. Pour the soup into bowls and serve with a dollop of the yoghurt mixture. Garnish with coriander.

Lentil and spinach soup

preparation 25 minutes
cooking 1 hour
serves 8

95 g (3¼ oz/½ cup) brown lentils
2 tablespoons oil
1 leek, white part only, chopped
1 onion, chopped
1 celery stalk, chopped
600 g (1 lb 5 oz) potatoes, chopped
1 litre (35 fl oz/4 cups) chicken stock
250 g (9 oz) English spinach

Put the lentils in a saucepan. Cover with water and bring to the boil, then reduce the heat and simmer for 20 minutes, or until tender; drain.

Heat the oil in a large saucepan. Cook the leek, onion and celery for 5 minutes, or until softened. Add the potato and cook, stirring frequently, for 10 minutes. Add the chicken stock and bring to the boil. Reduce the heat and simmer, covered, for 20 minutes, or until the potato is tender.

Remove the stalks from the spinach, wash the leaves well, add to the soup and cook for 1–2 minutes. Purée in a food processor, then return to the pan, add the lentils and stir until heated through.

Pour the stock into the carrot mixture and cook until the carrot is tender.

Purée the spinach mixture, then add the drained lentils and heat through.

Bottom: Lentil and spinach soup. Top: Carrot and coriander soup.

Cheese soup

preparation 20 minutes
cooking 15 minutes
serves 4–6

crusty bread rolls, to serve
75 g (2½ oz) butter
3 spring onions (scallions), finely chopped
60 g (2¼ oz/½ cup) plain (all-purpose) flour
875 ml (30 fl oz/3½ cups) chicken stock
250 ml (9 fl oz/1 cup) milk
100 g (3½ oz) pumpkin (winter squash), grated
150 g (5½ oz) grated cheddar cheese

Preheat the oven to 180°C (350°F/Gas 4). Cut the tops from the bread rolls and hollow out the centres. Set aside.

Melt the butter in a heavy-based saucepan and cook the spring onion for 3 minutes, or until soft. Add the flour and stir for 2 minutes, or until smooth. Gradually add the combined stock and milk, stirring until smooth.

Add the pumpkin and bring to the boil, then reduce the heat and simmer for 10 minutes.

Meanwhile, heat the bread rolls in the oven until warm.

Stir the cheese into the soup until melted and smooth. Spoon the soup into the warm bread rolls to serve.

Chilli, corn and red capsicum soup

preparation 20 minutes
cooking 45 minutes
serves 4

1 coriander (cilantro) sprig
4 corn cobs
30 g (1 oz) butter
2 red capsicums (peppers), seeded and diced
1 small onion, finely chopped
1 small red chilli, finely chopped
1 tablespoon plain (all-purpose) flour
500 ml (17 fl oz/2 cups) vegetable stock
125 ml (4 fl oz/½ cup) cream

Trim the leaves off the coriander and finely chop the root and stems. Cut the kernels off the corn cobs.

Heat the butter in a large saucepan over medium heat. Add the corn kernels, capsicum, onion and red chilli and stir to coat the vegetables in the butter. Cook, covered, over low heat, stirring occasionally, for 10 minutes, or until the vegetables are soft.

Increase the heat to medium and add the coriander root and stem. Cook, stirring, for 30 seconds, or until fragrant. Sprinkle with the flour and stir for 1 minute. Remove the pan from the heat and gradually stir in the vegetable stock. Add 500 ml (17 fl oz/2 cups) water and return to the heat. Bring to the boil, then reduce the heat to low and simmer, covered, for 30 minutes, or until the vegetables are tender. Cool slightly.

Ladle about 500 ml (17 fl oz/2 cups) of the soup into a blender and purée until smooth. Return the purée to the soup in the saucepan, pour in the cream and gently heat until warmed through. Season to taste with salt. Sprinkle with the coriander leaves to serve. Delicious with grilled (broiled) cheese on pitta bread.

Add the grated cheese to the simmering soup and stir until melted and smooth.

Trim the leaves off the coriander, and finely chop the root and stems.

Bottom: Chilli, corn and red capsicum soup. Top: Cheese soup.

Long and short noodle soup

preparation 30 minutes
cooking 10 minutes
serves 6

300 g (10½ oz) minced (ground) pork
4 spring onions (scallions), sliced
3 garlic cloves, roughly chopped
2 teaspoons grated fresh ginger
2 teaspoons cornflour (cornstarch)
125 ml (4 fl oz/½ cup) light soy sauce
60 ml (2 fl oz/¼ cup) Chinese rice wine
30 won ton wrappers
3 litres (104 fl oz/12 cups) ready-made Chinese chicken broth, or home-made
or ready-made chicken stock
200 g (7 oz) dried flat egg noodles
2 spring onions (scallions), extra, sliced on the diagonal
1 teaspoon sesame oil

Put the minced pork, spring onion, garlic, ginger, cornflour, 1½ tablespoons of the soy sauce and 1 tablespoon of the rice wine in a food processor. Process until well combined. Place 2 teaspoons of the mixture in the centre of a won ton wrapper and lightly brush the edges with water. Lift up the sides and tightly pinch around the filling to form a pouch. Repeat this process to make 30 won tons.

Place the chicken broth in a large saucepan and bring to a simmer over medium–high heat. Stir in the remaining soy sauce and rice wine.

Meanwhile, bring a large saucepan of water to the boil. Reduce the heat, add the won tons and simmer for 1 minute, or until they float to the surface and are cooked through, then remove with a slotted spoon. Return the water to the boil, add the egg noodles and cook for 3 minutes, or until tender. Drain and add to the chicken broth along with the cooked won tons. Simmer for 2 minutes, or until heated through.

Divide the broth, noodles and won tons among six serving bowls, sprinkle with the extra spring onion and drizzle each with a little sesame oil.

Place the filling in the centre of the wrapper, then pinch around the filling to form a pouch.

Simmer the won tons in boiling water until they float to the surface.

Split pea and vegetable soup

preparation 15 minutes
cooking 1 hour 20 minutes
serves 4

1 tablespoon peanut or vegetable oil
1 onion, chopped
2 garlic cloves, chopped
1½ teaspoons chopped fresh ginger
1½ tablespoons Madras curry paste
100 g (3½ oz) yellow split peas, rinsed and drained
1 large zucchini (courgette), peeled and chopped
1 large carrot, roughly chopped
170 g (6 oz) button mushrooms, roughly chopped
1 celery stalk, roughly chopped
1 litre (35 fl oz/4 cups) vegetable stock
125 ml (4 fl oz/½ cup) cream

Heat the oil in a saucepan, add the onion and cook over low heat for 5 minutes, or until soft. Add the garlic, ginger and curry paste and cook over medium heat for 2 minutes. Stir in the split peas until well coated with paste, then add the zucchini, carrot, mushroom and celery and cook for 2 minutes.

Add the stock, bring to the boil, then reduce the heat and simmer, partly covered, for 1 hour. Remove from the heat and allow to cool slightly.

Transfer the soup to a blender or food processor and process in batches until smooth. Return to the pan, stir in the cream and gently heat to warm through. Delicious served with naan bread.

Spicy parsnip soup

preparation 15 minutes
cooking 25 minutes
serves 6

1.25 litres (44 fl oz/5 cups) vegetable or chicken stock
30 g (1 oz) butter
1 white onion, cut into quarters and finely sliced
1 leek, white part only, finely sliced
500 g (1 lb 2 oz) parsnips, peeled and finely sliced
1 tablespoon Madras curry powder
1 teaspoon ground cumin
315 ml (10¾ fl oz/1¼ cups) cream
4 tablespoons coriander (cilantro) leaves

Pour the stock into a saucepan and bring to the boil. Reduce the heat and keep the stock at a low simmer.

Melt the butter in a large saucepan over medium heat. Cook the onion, leek and parsnip, covered, for 5 minutes. Add the curry powder and ground cumin and cook for 1 minute. Stir in the stock and cook, covered, over medium heat for about 10 minutes, or until tender.

Transfer the soup to a blender or food processor and blend in batches until smooth. Return to the pan. Stir in the cream and warm through over low heat. Season with sea salt and cracked black pepper and scatter with coriander leaves.

Note *This soup is also delicious without the cream.*

Sweet potato and chilli soup

preparation 10 minutes
cooking 25 minutes
serves 4

1 tablespoon oil
1 onion, chopped
2 garlic cloves, finely chopped
1–2 small red chillies, finely chopped
¼ teaspoon paprika
750 g (1 lb 10 oz) orange sweet potato, cut into small pieces
1 litre (35 fl oz/4 cups) vegetable or beef stock
chopped dried chilli, to garnish

Heat the oil in a large heavy-based saucepan, add the onion and cook for 1–2 minutes, until soft. Add the garlic, chilli and paprika and cook for 2 minutes, or until aromatic. Add the sweet potato to the pan and toss to coat with the spices.

Pour in the stock, bring to the boil, then reduce the heat and simmer for 15 minutes, or until the vegetables are tender. Cool slightly, then transfer to a blender or food processor and blend in batches until smooth, adding extra water if needed to reach the desired consistency. Do not overblend or the mixture may become gluey.

Season to taste with salt and black pepper. Ladle the soup into bowls, sprinkle with dried chilli and serve.

Top left: Split pea and vegetable soup. Top right: Spicy parsnip soup. Bottom left: Sweet potato and chilli soup.

Lentil and silverbeet soup

preparation 20 minutes
cooking 3 hours 30 minutes
serves 6

chicken stock
1 kg (2 lb 4 oz) chicken trimmings (necks, ribs, wings),
fat removed
1 small onion, roughly chopped
1 bay leaf
3–4 flat-leaf (Italian) parsley sprigs
1–2 oregano or thyme sprigs

280 g (10 oz/1½ cups) brown lentils, washed
850 g (1 lb 14 oz) silverbeet (Swiss chard)
60 ml (2 fl oz/¼ cup) olive oil
1 large onion, finely chopped
4 garlic cloves, crushed
2 large handfuls coriander (cilantro) leaves, finely chopped
80 ml (2½ fl oz/⅓ cup) lemon juice
lemon wedges, to serve

To make the stock, put the chicken trimmings, onion, bay
leaf and herbs in a large saucepan, add 3 litres (105 fl oz/
12 cups) water and bring to the boil. Skim off any scum
from the surface. Reduce the heat and simmer for 2 hours.
Strain the stock, discarding the chicken trimmings, onion
and herbs. You will need 1 litre (35 fl oz/4 cups) of stock for
the soup.

Skim any fat from the stock. Put the brown lentils in a large
saucepan, then add the stock and 1 litre (35 fl oz/4 cups)
water . Bring to the boil, then reduce the heat and simmer,
covered, for 1 hour.

Remove the stems from the silverbeet and shred the leaves.
Heat the oil in a saucepan over medium heat and cook the
onion for 2–3 minutes, until transparent. Add the crushed
garlic and cook for 1 minute. Add the silverbeet and toss for
2–3 minutes, until wilted. Stir the mixture into the lentils.
Add the coriander and lemon juice, season, and simmer,
covered, for 15–20 minutes. Serve with the lemon wedges.

Note *You can freeze any leftover stock for up to 3 months.*

Sweet potato and tofu laksa

preparation 30 minutes
cooking 25 minutes
serves 2

100 g (2½ oz/⅔ cup) chopped sweet potato
75 g (2½ oz/¾ cup) fresh thin rice noodles
3 teaspoons peanut oil
110 g (4 oz) laksa paste
500 ml (10 fl oz/2 cups) coconut milk
500 ml (10 fl oz/2 cups) chicken or vegetable stock or water
4 makrut (kaffir lime) leaves, shredded (optional)
½ lemon grass stem, white part only, trimmed and sliced in
half lengthways (optional)
10 cherry tomatoes, halved
150 g (5 oz) firm tofu, cut into 2 cm (¾ inch) cubes
3 teaspoons fish sauce
2 teaspoon sweet chilli sauce
2 teaspoon lime juice
100 g (2½ oz) trimmed snow peas (mangetout),
halved diagonally
2 small handfuls coriander (cilantro) leaves
1 red chilli, halved, seeded and thinly sliced (optional)

Cook the sweet potato in a steamer for 7–10 minutes, until
just tender.

Meanwhile, place the noodles in a heatproof bowl. Pour
over boiling water, cover and stand for 5–10 minutes, until
tender. Drain and divide among four deep serving bowls.

Heat the oil in a wok over high heat. Add the laksa paste
and cook, stirring, for 30 seconds, or until fragrant.

Pour in the coconut milk, stock or water and add the makrut
leaves and lemon grass, if using. Bring to the boil, reduce
the heat to medium and cook gently for 3 minutes. Add the
tomatoes and cook for 2–3 minutes, until just collapsing.
Stir in the tofu, fish sauce, sweet chilli sauce, lime juice and
snow peas. Cook for 1–2 minutes, until the tofu has warmed
through and the snow peas are tender. Remove the lime
leaves and lemon grass, if using.

Spoon the laksa over the noodles and top with the coriander
leaves and sliced chilli, if using. Serve immediately.

Bottom: Sweet potato and tofu laksa. Top: Lentil and silverbeet soup.

Roasted leek and celeriac soup

preparation 10 minutes
cooking 1 hour 10 minutes
serves 4

2 tablespoons olive oil
800 g (1 lb 12 oz/about 2 large) leeks, white part only,
cut into 5 cm (2 inch) lengths
1 garlic bulb, unpeeled, halved
800 g (1 lb 12 oz) celeriac, chopped
250 ml (9 fl oz/1 cup) milk
125 ml (4 fl oz/½ cup) thick (double/heavy) cream
2 tablespoons snipped chives
slices of toasted baguette, to serve

Preheat the oven to 200°C (400°F/Gas 6). Put the oil in a roasting tin and heat in the oven for 5 minutes.

Add the leek and garlic bulb halves and season with salt and freshly ground black pepper. Shake the roasting tin to coat the vegetables with the oil. Roast for 20–25 minutes, until the leek is tender. Remove the leek. Roast the garlic bulb for a further 10–15 minutes, or until tender when pierced with the tip of a knife.

Meanwhile, put the celeriac and 750 ml (26 fl oz/3 cups) water in a large saucepan. Cover and bring to the boil, then reduce the heat to medium–low and simmer for 20 minutes, or until tender. Add the roasted leek.

Squeeze or scoop the garlic into the saucepan. Season and mix well. Add the milk.

Remove the saucepan from the heat. Using an immersion blender fitted with the chopping blade, whizz for 45 seconds, or until puréed. Stir through the cream and gently reheat the soup. Add more milk if the soup is too thick. Sprinkle with the chives and serve topped with baguette slices.

Jerusalem artichoke soup

preparation 20 minutes
cooking 35 minutes
serves 4

50 g (1¾ oz) butter
1 onion, roughly chopped
1 leek, white part only, sliced
1 celery stalk, chopped
2 garlic cloves, chopped
800 g (1 lb 12 oz) Jerusalem artichokes,
cut into 5 cm (2 inch) pieces
2 potatoes, about 250 g (9 oz), cut into 5 cm (2 inch) pieces
1 teaspoon freshly grated nutmeg
500 ml (17 fl oz/2 cups) chicken or vegetable stock
500 ml (17 fl oz/2 cups) milk
2 tablespoons finely snipped chives

Melt the butter in a heavy-based saucepan over low heat and cook the onion, leek, celery and garlic for 2 minutes. Cover and simmer, stirring occasionally, for 5 minutes.

Add the Jerusalem artichokes, potato and nutmeg and stir to combine. Cook for 2 minutes, then add the stock and 250 ml (9 fl oz/1 cup) of the milk. Bring to the boil, cover and cook for another 20 minutes, or until the vegetables are tender.

Remove the saucepan from the heat. Using an immersion blender fitted with the chopping blade, whizz the soup for 10 seconds, or until roughly puréed. Season with salt and freshly ground black pepper. Stir in the rest of the milk and half the chives and gently reheat the soup.

Ladle the soup into four bowls and sprinkle with the rest of the chives and some freshly ground black pepper.

Potato, broccoli and coriander soup

preparation 15 minutes
cooking 35 minutes
serves 6

500 g (1 lb 2 oz) broccoli
cooking oil spray
2 onions, finely chopped
2 garlic cloves, finely chopped
2 teaspoons ground cumin
1 teaspoon ground coriander
750 g (1 lb 10 oz) potatoes, cubed
2 small chicken stock (bouillon) cubes
375 ml (13 fl oz/1½ cups) skim milk
3 tablespoons finely chopped coriander (cilantro) leaves

Cut the broccoli into small pieces. Lightly spray the base of a large saucepan with oil, then place over medium heat and add the onion and garlic. Add 1 tablespoon water to prevent sticking. Cover and cook, stirring occasionally, over low heat for 5 minutes, or until the onion has softened and is lightly golden. Add the cumin and coriander and cook for 2 minutes.

Add the potato and broccoli to the pan, stir well and add the stock cubes and 1 litre (35 fl oz/4 cups) water. Slowly bring to the boil, reduce the heat, cover and simmer over low heat for 20 minutes, or until the vegetables are tender. Allow to cool slightly.

Blend the soup in batches in a food processor or blender until smooth. Return to the pan and stir in the milk. Slowly reheat, without boiling. Stir the chopped coriander through and season well before serving.

Trim the leek, using only the white part, wash it well and cut it into slices.

Cut the broccoli into small pieces so that it will cook quickly and evenly.

Bottom: Potato, broccoli and coriander soup. Top: Jerusalem artichoke soup.

Spicy tomato and pea soup

preparation 15 minutes
cooking 20–25 minutes
serves 6

5 large very ripe tomatoes, chopped
2 tablespoons ghee or butter
1 large onion, thinly sliced
1 garlic clove, crushed
1 green chilli, seeded and sliced
2 teaspoons ground coriander
2 teaspoons ground cumin
½ teaspoon fennel seeds
2 bay leaves
375 ml (13 fl oz/1½ cups) coconut cream
235 g (8½ oz/1½ cups) frozen peas
1 tablespoon sugar
1 tablespoon chopped mint

Put the tomato and 500 ml (17 fl oz/2 cups) water in a saucepan and simmer until the tomato is very tender. Allow to cool slightly before transferring to a food processor and blending, in batches, until smooth.

Heat the ghee in a large saucepan, add the onion and garlic and cook over medium heat until very soft. Add the chilli, coriander, cumin, fennel seeds and bay leaves. Cook, stirring, for 1 minute. Add the coconut cream and puréed tomatoes, and bring to the boil. Reduce the heat, add the peas and cook until tender. Remove the bay leaves, stir in the sugar and chopped mint, and season with freshly ground black pepper to taste.

Using a small sharp knife, split the chilli in half and remove the seeds and membrane.

Spoon the coconut cream out of the tin and measure out the required quantity.

Cauliflower and almond soup
with hot cheese rolls

preparation 15 minutes
cooking 30 minutes
serves 4

75 g (2½ oz/½ cup) blanched almonds
1 tablespoon olive oil
1 large leek, white part only, chopped
2 garlic cloves, crushed
1 kg (2 lb 4 oz) cauliflower, cut into small florets
2 desiree potatoes (about 370 g/13 oz), cut into 1.5 cm (⅝ inch) pieces
1.75 litres (60 fl oz/7 cups) chicken stock

cheese rolls
4 round bread rolls
40 g (1½ oz) softened butter
125 g (4½ oz) cheddar cheese, grated
50 g (1¾ oz) parmesan cheese, finely grated

Preheat the oven to 180°C (350°F/Gas 4). Place the almonds on a baking tray and toast for 5 minutes, or until golden.

Heat the oil in a large saucepan and cook the leek over medium heat for 2–3 minutes, until softened. Add the garlic and cook for 30 seconds, then add the cauliflower florets, potato and chicken stock. Bring to the boil, then reduce the heat and simmer for 15 minutes, or until the vegetables are very tender. Cool for 5 minutes.

Meanwhile, to make the cheese rolls, split the rolls in half and butter both sides. Combine the grated cheeses and divide among the rolls. Sandwich together and wrap in foil. Bake for 15–20 minutes, or until the cheese has melted.

Blend the soup with the almonds in batches in a blender until smooth. Season to taste with salt and pepper. Return to the cleaned pan and stir over medium heat until heated through. Serve with the cheese rolls, if desired.

Cut the cauliflower into pieces, then into small florets that will cook quickly and evenly.

Grate the parmesan cheese using the fine side of a grater.

Risoni and mushroom broth

preparation 15 minutes
cooking 20–25 minutes
serves 4

90 g (3¼ oz) butter
2 garlic cloves, sliced
2 large onions, sliced
375 g (13 oz) mushrooms, thinly sliced
1.25 litres (44 fl oz/5 cups) chicken stock
125 g (4½ oz) risoni
310 ml (10¾ fl oz/1¼ cups) cream

Melt the butter in a large saucepan over low heat and cook the garlic and onion for 1 minute. Add the mushrooms and cook gently, without colouring, for 5 minutes. (Set aside a few mushroom slices to use as a garnish.) Add the chicken stock and cook for 10 minutes.

Allow the soup to cool slightly before transferring to a food processor and blending until smooth.

Meanwhile, add the risoni to a large saucepan of rapidly boiling salted water and cook until al dente, then drain and set aside.

Return the soup to a clean pan and stir in the risoni and cream. Heat through and season to taste. Garnish with the reserved mushrooms.

Carrot and orange soup

preparation 20 minutes
cooking 35 minutes
serves 4

500 g (1 lb 2 oz) carrots, peeled and sliced
30 g (1 oz) butter
125 ml (4 fl oz/½ cup) orange juice
1–1.25 litres (35–44 fl oz/4–5 cups) vegetable stock
1 small onion, roughly chopped
3–4 teaspoons chopped thyme
sour cream, to serve
freshly grated nutmeg, to serve

Put the sliced carrots and butter in a large heavy-based saucepan and cook over medium heat for 10 minutes, stirring occasionally. Add the orange juice, vegetable stock and onion. Bring to the boil, add the chopped thyme and season. Reduce the heat, cover and cook for 20 minutes, or until the carrots are tender. Allow to cool.

Process the mixture in a food processor or blender, in batches, until smooth. When ready to serve, return the mixture to the pan and reheat.

Spoon the soup into individual bowls. Top each with a dollop of sour cream and sprinkle with nutmeg. Garnish with a small sprig of thyme, if desired.

Spiced tomato soup

preparation 10 minutes
cooking 45 minutes
serves 2

2 tablespoons oil
1 onion, finely chopped
3 Indian bay leaves (cassia leaves)
5 cm (2 inch) piece of cinnamon stick
12 peppercorns
2 teaspoons ground cumin
2 teaspoons garam masala
2 x 400 g (14 oz) tins chopped tomatoes
1 teaspoon sugar
250 ml (9 fl oz/1 cup) chicken or vegetable stock
coriander leaves

Heat the oil over low heat in a heavy-based saucepan and fry the onion, bay leaves, cinnamon and peppercorns until the onion is soft. Add the cumin, garam masala and the tomatoes, mashing the tomatoes with a fork to break them up. Add the sugar and stock and slowly bring to the boil. Simmer over low heat for 30 minutes.

Strain the soup by pushing it through a sieve, using the back of a metal spoon to push against the solids and extract as much of the liquid as possible. Discard what's left in the sieve. Reheat, then season with salt, to taste, and garnish with the coriander leaves before serving.

Top left: Risoni and mushroom broth. Top right: Carrot and orange soup. Bottom left: Spiced tomato soup.

Lenten soup

preparation 15 minutes + soaking
cooking 1 hour 40 minutes
serves 4–6

250 g (9 oz) bacalao (salt cod)
250 g (9 oz) chickpeas
80 ml (2½ fl oz/⅓ cup) olive oil
1 red onion, roughly chopped
2 garlic cloves, chopped
1 leek, white part only, roughly chopped
2 carrots, roughly chopped
2 floury potatoes, roughly chopped
1 green capsicum (pepper), seeded and
roughly chopped
½ teaspoon sweet paprika (pimentón)

Put the bacalao in a large bowl and cover with cold water. Refrigerate for 20 hours, changing the water several times during the soaking process.

Put the chickpeas in a separate bowl, cover with cold water and soak overnight.

Heat the oil in a large, heavy-based saucepan over medium heat. Sauté the onion, garlic, leek and carrot for 5 minutes, or until softened.

Add the drained chickpeas and bacalao and cover with 1.5 litres (52 fl oz/6 cups) water . Bring to the boil, cover, reduce the heat to a simmer and cook for 30 minutes. Carefully remove the bacalao. When cool enough to handle, remove the skin and bones and return the flesh in large pieces back to the pan and continue simmering for a further 30 minutes.

Add the potato, capsicum and paprika to the pan. Cook for another 30 minutes, or until the potato is soft. Cool slightly, then blend in a food processor, in batches, until smooth. Season to taste, then gently reheat if necessary. Add more water if you prefer a thinner soup.

Cream of spinach soup

preparation 15 minutes
cooking 25 minutes
serves 4

3–4 bunches (about 750 g/1 lb 10 oz) English spinach, trimmed
1 tablespoon olive oil
1 onion, chopped
1 garlic clove, chopped
1 large (about 250 g/9 oz) potato, peeled and
cut into 1 cm (½ inch) dice
1.25 litres (44 fl oz/5 cups) salt-reduced chicken
or vegetable stock
750 ml (26 fl oz/3 cups) cream
90 g (3¼ oz/¾ cup) coarsely grated parmesan cheese

Pick the leaves from the spinach and wash thoroughly. (You will need about 400 g/14 oz leaves.) Roughly chop the leaves and set aside.

Put the oil, onion and garlic in a large saucepan over medium–low heat. Cook for 5 minutes, stirring occasionally, until soft.

Add the potato and stock, increase the heat to high and bring to the boil. Reduce the heat to low and simmer for 15 minutes, or until the potato is soft.

Increase the heat to medium, add half the cream and bring to a simmer. Stir through the chopped spinach and cook for 1 minute, or until just wilted. Stir through the rest of the cream and half the parmesan (this will cool the soup down slightly so you can blend it immediately).

Transfer the soup in batches to a food processor or blender and process until the spinach is finely chopped. Return the soup to the saucepan and reheat over medium heat. Season with salt. Serve sprinkled with the remaining parmesan.

Note To keep the spinach bright green, only cook it until it just wilts and then blend it as soon as possible.

Bottom: Cream of spinach soup. Top: Lenten soup.

Umbrian vegetable soup

preparation 20 minutes
cooking 1 hour 10 minutes
serves 6

60 ml (2 fl oz/¼ cup) olive oil
2 small onions, chopped
2 celery stalks, chopped
4 small carrots, chopped
2 large potatoes, diced
2 leeks, sliced
2 garlic cloves, crushed
100 g (3½ oz) runner beans
100 g (3½ oz) shelled green peas
1.75 litres (60 fl oz/7 cups) vegetable stock
150 g (5½ oz) cavolo nero or cabbage
12 asparagus spears
6 slices country-style bread, such as ciabatta,
crusts removed
1 garlic clove, cut in half
35 g (1¼ oz/⅓ cup) grated parmesan cheese
extra virgin olive oil, to drizzle

Heat the oil in a large saucepan and add the onion, celery, carrot, potato, leek and crushed garlic. Cook over low heat for 5–6 minutes, until the vegetables are softened but not browned. Season, add 375 ml (13 fl oz/1½ cups) water and bring to the boil. Reduce to low heat and simmer for 30 minutes.

Slice the beans diagonally and add to the pan. Add the peas and stock and simmer for a further 30 minutes. Finely shred the cabbage and slice the asparagus diagonally. Add both to the pan and simmer for a further 5 minutes.

Toast the bread and, while still hot, rub on both sides with the cut edge of the halved garlic clove.

Stir the parmesan into the soup and taste for seasoning. Place a slice of toast in the bottom of each serving bowl and ladle the soup over the top. Drizzle with olive oil and serve at once.

Curried sweet potato soup

preparation 20 minutes
cooking 40 minutes
serves 6

1 tablespoon oil
1 large onion, chopped
2 garlic cloves, crushed
3 teaspoons curry powder
1.25 kg (2 lb 12 oz) orange sweet potato,
peeled and cubed
1 litre (35 fl oz/4 cups) chicken stock
1 large apple, peeled, cored and grated
125 ml (4 fl oz/½ cup) light coconut milk

Heat the oil in a large saucepan over medium heat and cook the onion for 10 minutes, stirring occasionally, until very soft. Add the garlic and curry powder and cook for a further 1 minute.

Add the sweet potato, stock and apple. Bring to the boil, then reduce the heat and simmer, partially covered, for 30 minutes, or until very soft.

Cool the soup a little before processing in batches until smooth. Return to the pan, stir in the coconut milk and reheat gently without boiling. Serve the soup with warm pitta bread.

Note *Store this soup in the fridge for 1 day without the coconut milk – add this when you reheat it.*

Cabbage soup

preparation 15 minutes + overnight soaking
cooking 1 hour 30 minutes
serves 4

100 g (3½ oz) dried haricot beans
125 g (4½ oz) bacon, cubed
40 g (1½ oz) butter
1 carrot, sliced
1 onion, chopped
1 leek, white part only, roughly chopped
1 turnip, peeled and chopped
bouquet garni
1.25 litres (44 fl oz/5 cups) chicken stock
400 g (14 oz) white cabbage, finely shredded

Soak the beans overnight in cold water. Drain, then put in a saucepan and cover with cold water. Bring to the boil and simmer for 5 minutes, then drain.

Put the bacon in the same saucepan, cover with water and simmer for 5 minutes. Drain and pat dry with paper towel.

Melt the butter in a large heavy-based saucepan and cook the bacon for 5 minutes, without browning. Add the beans, carrot, onion, leek and turnip and cook for 5 minutes. Add the bouquet garni and chicken stock and bring to the boil. Cover and simmer for 30 minutes. Add the cabbage and simmer, uncovered, for 30 minutes, or until the beans are tender. Remove the bouquet garni. Season to taste.

Add the crushed garlic and curry powder to the softened onion.

Cook the bacon in the melted butter over low heat, without browning it.

Bottom: Cabbage soup. Top: Curried sweet potato soup.

Silverbeet and risoni soup with Gruyère croutons

preparation 20 minutes
cooking 20 minutes
serves 6

30 g (1 oz) butter
1 large onion, finely chopped
1 garlic clove, crushed
2 litres (70 fl oz/8 cups) vegetable or chicken stock
200 g (7 oz/1 cup) risoni
½ baguette, cut into 6 slices
15 g (½ oz) butter, extra, melted
1 teaspoon Dijon mustard
50 g (1¾ oz) Gruyère cheese, coarsely grated
500 g (1 lb 2 oz) silverbeet (Swiss chard), central stalk removed, shredded
1 large handful basil, torn

Heat the butter in a large heavy-based saucepan and cook the onion and garlic over medium heat for 2–3 minutes, or until the onion is softened. Meanwhile, place the stock in a separate pan and bring to the boil.

Add the stock to the onion mixture and bring to the boil. Stir in the risoni, reduce the heat and simmer for 8 minutes, stirring occasionally.

Meanwhile, place the baguette slices in a single layer on a baking tray and cook under a preheated grill (broiler) until golden brown on one side. Turn the slices over and brush with the combined melted butter and mustard. Top with the Gruyère and grill until the cheese has melted.

Add the shredded silverbeet and basil to the risoni mixture and simmer for 1 minute, or until the risoni is al dente and the silverbeet is cooked. Season with salt and freshly ground black pepper and serve with the Gruyère croutons.

Split pea and sweet potato soup

preparation 15 minutes
cooking 45 minutes
serves 4

80 ml (2½ fl oz/⅓ cup) olive oil
1 large onion, chopped
2 garlic cloves, finely chopped
2 teaspoons finely chopped fresh ginger
120 g (4¼ oz/½ cup) yellow split peas
1 red chilli, seeded and sliced
½ teaspoon sweet smoked paprika
1 litre (35 fl oz/4 cups) chicken stock
500 g (1 lb 2 oz) orange sweet potato, cubed
1 tablespoon finely chopped mint

Heat 1 tablespoon of oil in a large saucepan over medium heat. Fry the onion, garlic and ginger for about 5 minutes, or until soft and golden. Stir in the split peas, chilli and paprika, and cook for 1 minute. Add the stock and bring to the boil. Reduce the heat and simmer for 20 minutes.

Add the sweet potato, return to the boil, then reduce the heat and simmer for 15 minutes, or until the sweet potato is tender.

Meanwhile, heat the remaining oil in a small saucepan over low heat. Stir in the mint, then immediately remove the saucepan from the heat. Transfer the mint and oil to a small dish.

Remove the soup from the heat and cool slightly. Using an immersion blender fitted with the chopping blade, whizz for 30 seconds, or until puréed. Ladle the soup into four bowls and drizzle with a little of the minted oil.

Mushroom soup

preparation 10 minutes
cooking 30 minutes
serves 4

40 g (1½ oz) butter
1 onion, finely chopped
12 large (about 1.4 kg/3 lb 2 oz) field mushrooms, finely chopped
2 garlic cloves, crushed
2 tablespoons dry sherry
1 litre (35 fl oz/4 cups) chicken or vegetable stock
2 tablespoons flat-leaf (Italian) parsley, finely chopped
2 tablespoons cream

Melt the butter in a large saucepan and fry the onion until it is translucent but not browned.

Add the mushrooms and garlic and continue frying. Initially, the mushrooms may give off a lot of liquid, so keep frying until it is all absorbed back into the mixture. This will take 15–20 minutes.

Add the sherry to the pan, increase the heat and bring to the boil (this burns off the alcohol but retains the flavour). Cool slightly, then transfer to a blender and process until a smooth paste forms. Add the stock and parsley and blend until smooth.

Pour the soup into the saucepan and stir in the cream. Stir over low heat until heated through.

Bottom: Mushroom soup. Top: Split pea and sweet potato soup.

Watercress soup

preparation 15 minutes
cooking 15–20 minutes
serves 4–6

100 g (3½ oz) butter
1 onion, roughly chopped
4 spring onions (scallions), roughly chopped
450 g (1 lb) watercress, trimmed and roughly chopped
40 g (1½ oz/⅓ cup) plain (all-purpose) flour
750 ml (26 fl oz/3 cups) vegetable stock
sour cream or cream, to serve

Heat the butter in a large saucepan. Add the onion, spring onion and watercress. Stir over low heat for 3 minutes, or until the vegetables have softened. Stir in the flour.

Gradually add the stock and 310 ml (10¾ fl oz/1¼ cups) water. Stir until smooth and the mixture boils and thickens. Simmer, covered, over low heat for 10 minutes, or until the watercress is tender.

Allow to cool slightly, then transfer the mixture to a food processor and process, in batches, until smooth. Before serving, gently heat through and season to taste. Serve with a dollop of sour cream or cream.

Tofu miso soup

preparation 10 minutes
cooking 15 minutes
serves 4

80 g (2¾ oz/½ cup) dashi granules
100 g (3½ oz) miso paste
1 tablespoon mirin
250 g (9 oz) firm tofu, cubed
1 spring onion (scallion), sliced, to serve

Using a wooden spoon, combine 1 litre (35 fl oz/4 cups) water and the dashi granules in a small saucepan and bring to the boil.

Combine the miso paste and mirin in a small bowl, then add to the pan. Stir over medium heat, taking care not to let the mixture boil once the miso has dissolved, or it will lose its flavour.

Add the tofu cubes to the hot stock and heat, without boiling, over medium heat for 5 minutes. Serve in individual bowls, garnished with the spring onion.

Pick over the watercress stems, then trim and roughly chop them.

Drain the block of tofu, then carefully cut it into small cubes.

Bottom: Tofu miso soup. Top: Watercress soup.

Wild rice soup

preparation 15 minutes
cooking 1 hour
serves 6

95 g (3¼ oz/½ cup) wild rice
1 tablespoon oil
1 onion, finely chopped
2 celery stalks, finely chopped
1 green capsicum (pepper), seeded and
finely chopped
4 back bacon slices, finely chopped
4 open cap mushrooms, thinly sliced
1 litre (35 fl oz/4 cups) chicken stock
125 ml (4 fl oz/½ cup) cream
1 tablespoon finely chopped flat-leaf (Italian) parsley

Put the wild rice in a saucepan with 500 ml (17 fl oz/2 cups) water and bring to the boil. Cook for 40 minutes, or until the rice is tender. Drain and rinse well.

Heat the oil in a large saucepan and add the onion, celery, capsicum and bacon. Fry for 8 minutes, or until the onion has softened and the bacon has browned. Add the mushrooms and cook for 1–2 minutes. Pour in the chicken stock and bring to the boil, then add the wild rice, stir, and cook the mixture for 2 minutes. Remove from the heat.

Stir in the cream and parsley, then reheat until the soup is almost boiling. Serve in deep bowls.

Cook the wild rice in boiling water until tender, then drain and rinse well.

Remove the rind from the bacon slices and then finely chop it.

vegetable soups

Curried zucchini soup

preparation 20 minutes
cooking 20 minutes
serves 4

50 g (1¾ oz) butter
1 kg (2 lb 4 oz) zucchini (courgettes), chopped
1 onion, chopped
2 teaspoons mild curry powder
500 ml (17 fl oz/2 cups) chicken stock
plain yoghurt, to serve
naan bread, toasted, to serve

Melt the butter in a large saucepan over medium heat. Stir in the zucchini and onion and cook, covered, for 10 minutes, stirring occasionally, or until soft.

Stir in the curry powder. Add the stock and 500 ml (17 fl oz/ 2 cups) water. Bring to the boil over high heat, then reduce the heat and simmer, covered, for 5 minutes, or until the zucchini is almost tender.

Stand for 10 minutes to cool slightly and for the zucchini to finish cooking. Purée the soup in batches in a blender or food processor. Return to the saucepan and reheat over medium heat. Season to taste with salt and freshly ground black pepper. Serve with the yoghurt and naan bread.

Capsicum and tomato soup with couscous

preparation 10 minutes
cooking 20 minutes
serves 4

2 x 270 g (9½ oz) jars chargrilled red capsicums (peppers) in oil
1 tablespoon olive oil
1 red onion, chopped
2 garlic cloves, chopped
60 g (2¼ oz/¼ cup) tomato paste (concentrated purée)
2 x 400 g (14 oz) tins chopped tomatoes
1 litre (35 fl oz/4 cups) chicken stock
130 g (4½ oz/⅔ cup) couscous
plain yoghurt, to serve
chopped coriander (cilantro) leaves, to serve

Drain the oil from the capsicum (you will need about 400 g/ 14 oz capsicum). Put the capsicum in a food processor and pulse until almost smooth.

Put the oil and onion in a large saucepan over medium heat and cook, stirring occasionally, for 5 minutes, or until soft.

Add the garlic and cook for 1 minute, or until aromatic. Add the tomato paste and cook, stirring, for another 2 minutes.

Add the tomatoes, stock and puréed capsicum to the pan, increase the heat to high and bring to the boil. Reduce the heat and simmer for 5 minutes.

Stir through the couscous and simmer for 2 minutes. Turn off the heat and set aside for 3 minutes, or until the couscous is tender. Season with salt. Serve immediately, topped with the yoghurt and coriander.

Roasted tomato soup

preparation 20 minutes
cooking 1 hour 15 minutes
serves 4

1.5 kg (3 lb 5 oz) ripe tomatoes, cores removed, halved
2 onions, unpeeled, halved
1 whole garlic bulb
2 tablespoons olive oil
sea salt flakes, to sprinkle
1 litre (35 fl oz/4 cups) chicken stock
sugar, to taste
1 handful basil leaves, to serve
shaved parmesan cheese, to serve

Preheat the oven to 180°C (350°F/Gas 4). Put the tomato halves, onion halves and garlic in a roasting tin, drizzle with the oil and sprinkle with sea salt. Roast for 45–55 minutes, until soft. Set aside for 10 minutes, or until cool enough to handle.

Remove the outer skin from the onion halves, put in a food processor and pulse until roughly chopped. Transfer the onion to a large saucepan. Cut off the root end of the garlic and squeeze out the roasted pulp. Put the garlic in a food processor with half the roasted tomatoes and process until puréed. Add to the saucepan with the remaining roasted tomatoes and the stock.

Place the saucepan over high heat and bring to the boil. Reduce the heat to low and simmer for 15 minutes, or until the tomatoes partially break down.

Season with salt and a little sugar (the sugar is to round out the flavours – how much you need will depend upon the ripeness of the tomatoes). Serve immediately, topped with the basil and parmesan.

Top left: Curried zucchini soup. Top right: Capsicum and tomato soup with couscous. Bottom left: Roasted tomato soup.

Broad bean soup

preparation 10 minutes + soaking
cooking 1 hour 10 minutes
serves 6

350 g (12 oz/2 cups) dried, skinned and split broad (fava)
beans or whole dried broad (fava) beans
2 garlic cloves, peeled
1 teaspoon ground cumin, plus extra, to serve
1 teaspoon paprika, plus extra, to serve
extra virgin olive oil, to serve

Put the broad beans in a large bowl, cover with three times
their volume of cold water and leave to soak in a cool place
for 12 hours. Drain and rinse before cooking. (If you are
using whole beans, soak them for 48 hours in a cool place,
changing the water three or four times. Drain and remove
the skins.)

Place the beans in a large stockpot. Add 1.25 litres (44 fl oz/
5 cups) cold water, the garlic, cumin and paprika. Bring to
the boil, then reduce the heat and simmer, covered, over
low heat for 45–60 minutes, until the beans are mushy. Add
a little more water during cooking if the beans look dry. Do
not add salt or stir the beans during cooking.

Cool slightly and then purée the soup in batches in a food
processor or blender. Reheat the soup and season to taste.
Ladle into bowls and drizzle with a little olive oil. Finish with
a light dusting of paprika. Serve with extra olive oil on the
table, and cumin and paprika in little bowls, to be added if
desired. Serve with bread.

Spiced lentil soup

preparation 20 minutes + soaking
cooking 55 minutes
serves 4

1 eggplant (aubergine)
60 ml (2 fl oz/¼ cup) olive oil
1 onion, finely chopped
2 teaspoons brown mustard seeds
2 teaspoons ground cumin
1 teaspoon garam masala
¼ teaspoon cayenne pepper (optional)
2 large carrots, cut into cubes
1 celery stalk, diced
400 g (14 oz) tin chopped tomatoes
100 g (3½ oz/1 cup) puy or small blue-green lentils
1 litre (35 fl oz/4 cups) chicken stock
2 large handfuls coriander (cilantro) leaves, roughly chopped
125 g (4½ oz/½ cup) plain yoghurt

Cut the eggplant into cubes, place in a colander, sprinkle
with salt and leave for 20 minutes. Rinse well and pat the
eggplant dry with paper towel.

Heat the oil in a large saucepan over medium heat and
cook the onion for 5 minutes, or until softened. Add the
eggplant, stir to coat in oil and cook for 3 minutes, or
until softened.

Add the spices and the cayenne pepper (if using) and cook,
stirring, for 1 minute, or until fragrant and the mustard
seeds begin to pop. Add the carrot and celery and cook for
1 minute. Stir in the tomato, lentils and stock and bring to
the boil. Reduce the heat and simmer for 40 minutes, or
until the lentils are tender and the liquid is reduced to a
thick stew-like soup. Season to taste with salt and freshly
ground black pepper.

Stir the coriander into the soup just before serving. Ladle
the soup into four warmed bowls and serve with a dollop
of the yoghurt on top.

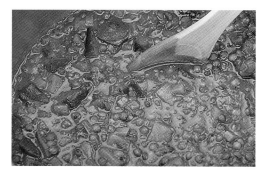

Add the tomato, lentils and stock to the soup and
simmer until the lentils are tender.

Bottom: Spiced lentil soup. Top: Broad bean soup.

Roast tomato, sweet potato and orange soup with basil oil

preparation 35 minutes
cooking 1 hour 15 minutes
serves 6

1.5 kg (3 lb 5 oz) sweet potato, peeled and cut into 3 cm (1¼ inch) chunks
2 tablespoons thyme leaves, plus extra, to garnish
100 ml (3½ fl oz) olive oil
4 vine-ripened tomatoes (about 550 g/1 lb 4 oz), chopped
3 garlic cloves, chopped
1 tablespoon chopped sage, plus extra sage leaves, to garnish
2 teaspoons balsamic vinegar
2 onions, thinly sliced
2 carrots, cut into 1 cm (½ inch) chunks
2 celery stalks, thinly sliced
2.5 litres (87 fl oz/10 cups) vegetable stock
60 ml (2 fl oz/¼ cup) freshly squeezed orange juice

basil oil
2 large handfuls basil leaves
125 ml (4 fl oz/½ cup) extra virgin olive oil

Preheat the oven to 180ºC (350ºF/Gas 4). Line two baking trays with baking paper.

Place the sweet potato on one baking tray. Sprinkle with half the thyme and drizzle with 2 tablespoons of the olive oil. Season to taste with sea salt and freshly ground black pepper and toss to coat.

Place the tomato, garlic and sage on the other baking tray. Drizzle with the vinegar and 1 tablespoon of the olive oil. Season to taste and toss to coat.

Roast the sweet potato and tomato, swapping the trays halfway through cooking, for 35 minutes, or until the sweet potato is tender and golden and the tomato is just collapsing. Remove from the oven and set aside.

Heat the remaining oil in a large saucepan over medium–low heat. Add the onion, carrot, celery and remaining thyme. Cook, stirring, for 10–15 minutes, until the vegetables start to soften. Pour in the vegetable stock and orange juice, then add the roasted sweet potato, tomato and cooking juices. Simmer for 25 minutes, or until the vegetables are tender. Remove from the heat and allow to cool slightly.

Meanwhile, to make the basil oil, place the basil and olive oil in a food processor and blend until combined.

Transfer the soup in batches to a food processor and process until smooth. Return the soup to the saucepan and bring to a simmer. Season to taste. Ladle the soup into serving bowls and drizzle with the basil oil. Garnish with extra thyme and sage, and serve.

Sweet potato and pear soup

preparation 10 minutes
cooking 30 minutes
serves 4

25 g (1 oz) butter
1 small white onion, finely chopped
750 g (1 lb 10 oz) orange sweet potato, peeled
and cut into 2 cm (¾ inch) dice
2 firm pears (500 g/1 lb 2 oz), peeled, cored and cut into
2 cm (¾ inch) dice
750 ml (26 fl oz/3 cups) vegetable or chicken stock
250 ml (9 fl oz/1 cup) cream
mint leaves, to garnish

Melt the butter in a saucepan over medium heat, add the onion and cook for 2–3 minutes, or until softened but not brown. Add the sweet potato and pear, and cook, stirring, for 1–2 minutes. Add the stock to the pan, bring to the boil and cook for 20 minutes, or until the sweet potato and pear are soft.

Cool slightly, then place the mixture in a blender or food processor and blend in batches until smooth. Return to the pan, stir in the cream and gently reheat without boiling. Season with salt and freshly ground black pepper. Garnish with the mint leaves.

Green soup with pistou

preparation 25 minutes
cooking 20 minutes
serves 4

60 ml (2 fl oz/¼ cup) olive oil
1 onion, finely chopped
2 garlic cloves, crushed
1 celery stalk, chopped
1 zucchini (courgette), cut into 1 cm (½ inch) rounds
1 head broccoli, cut into 1 cm (½ inch) pieces
1.5 litres (52 fl oz/6 cups) vegetable or chicken stock
150 g (5½ oz) green beans, trimmed and
cut into 1 cm (½ inch) pieces
155 g (5½ oz/1 cup) green peas
155 g (5½ oz/1 bunch) asparagus, ends trimmed and
cut into 1 cm (½ inch) pieces
80 g (2¾ oz/2 cups) shredded silverbeet (Swiss chard) leaves

pistou
3 garlic cloves, peeled
1 large handful basil
80 ml (2½ fl oz/⅓ cup) olive oil
50 g (1¾ oz/½ cup) grated parmesan cheese

Heat the oil in a large saucepan and cook the onion, garlic and celery until golden. Add the zucchini and broccoli, and cook for 5 minutes.

Add the stock and bring to the boil. Simmer for 5 minutes, then add the green beans, peas, asparagus and silverbeet. Simmer for 5 minutes, or until the vegetables are tender. Season well with salt and pepper.

To make the pistou, place the garlic and basil in a mortar and pestle or small food processor and crush together. Slowly add the oil, and blend until a smooth paste. Stir in the parmesan, and season well with salt and pepper.

Ladle the soup into bowls and serve topped with a dollop of pistou.

Peel the sweet potato, then cut it into small, evenly sized cubes.

Cut the broccoli off the stalk, then cut it into small pieces that will cook quickly.

vegetable soups

Bottom: Green soup with pistou. Top: Sweet potato and pear soup.

Carrot soup with spices

preparation 15 minutes
cooking 40 minutes
serves 4

500 g (1 lb 2 oz) carrots
1 onion, grated
30 g (1 oz) butter
2 garlic cloves, crushed
½ teaspoon ground turmeric
½ teaspoon ground ginger
½ teaspoon ground cinnamon
½ teaspoon paprika
½ teaspoon ground cumin
pinch of cayenne pepper
1.25 litres (44 fl oz/5 cups) chicken stock
50 g (1¾ oz/¼ cup) couscous
2 teaspoons lemon juice
chopped flat-leaf (Italian) parsley, to garnish

Using the shredding side of a grater, grate the carrots. Put the onion in a saucepan with the butter and cook over medium heat for 3 minutes.

Add the garlic, turmeric, ginger, cinnamon, paprika, cumin, cayenne pepper and grated carrot. Cook for a few seconds, then add the chicken stock.

Bring to the boil, then cover and reduce to a simmer for 15 minutes. Add the couscous, stir until boiling, then cover and simmer gently for a further 20 minutes. Add the lemon juice and serve hot, topped with a little parsley.

Caramelised onion and parsnip soup

preparation 10 minutes
cooking 40 minutes
serves 4

30 g (1 oz) butter
3 large onions, halved and thinly sliced
2 tablespoons soft brown sugar
250 ml (9 fl oz/1 cup) dry white wine
3 large parsnips, peeled and chopped
1.25 litres (44 fl oz/5 cups) vegetable stock
60 ml (2 fl oz/¼ cup) cream
thyme leaves, to garnish

Melt the butter in a large saucepan over low heat. Add the onion and sugar and cook for 10 minutes. Add the wine and parsnip, and simmer, covered, for 20 minutes, or until the onion and parsnip are golden and tender.

Pour in the stock, bring to the boil, then reduce the heat and simmer, covered, for 10 minutes. Cool slightly, then place in a blender or food processor and blend in batches until smooth. Season and drizzle with a little cream. Sprinkle the thyme leaves over the top.

Mixed vegetable soup

preparation 20 minutes
cooking 10 minutes
serves 4

500 g (1 lb 2 oz) mixed vegetables, such as carrots, baby corn, bamboo shoots, Chinese (shiitake) or button mushrooms, asparagus, English spinach leaves, lettuce, cucumber, Chinese cabbage (wong bok) or tomato
120 g (4¼ oz) soft tofu, drained
750 ml (26 fl oz/3 cups) vegetable or chicken stock
1 tablespoon light soy sauce
½ teaspoon roasted sesame oil
chopped spring onion (scallion) or snipped chives, to serve

Cut your selection of vegetables and the tofu into a roughly uniform shape and size. You can cut into shreds, cubes or slices, but make the pieces small enough for a spoonful of soup to include several at once to give a balance of flavours.

Bring the stock to a rolling boil in a large saucepan or clay pot. Add your selection of the carrots, corn, bamboo shoots and mushrooms first and cook for 2–3 minutes, then add the tofu and any other vegetables and cook for 1 minute. Do not overcook the vegetables or they will become soggy and lose their crispness and delicate flavour.

Season with salt and white pepper. Add the soy sauce, drizzle with the sesame oil and sprinkle with the spring onion or chives.

Top left: Carrot soup with spices. Top right: Caramelised onion and parsnip soup. Bottom left: Mixed vegetable soup.

Stilton and apple soup

preparation 20 minutes
cooking 30 minutes
serves 8

40 g (1½ oz) butter
2 tablespoons plain (all-purpose) flour
750 ml (26 fl oz/3 cups) chicken stock
4 red apples, peeled, cored and sliced
500 ml (17 fl oz/2 cups) milk
250 g (9 oz) Stilton cheese
2 tablespoons snipped chives

Melt the butter in a large heavy-based saucepan. Sprinkle with the flour and stir over low heat for 2 minutes, or until lightly golden. Gradually add the stock, stirring until smooth.

Add the apples to the pan. Cook, covered, over medium heat for 20 minutes, or until tender. Cool, then purée in a food processor in batches until smooth.

Return the soup to the pan, add the milk and gently reheat, stirring. Simmer gently and add the crumbled Stilton and chives. Stir until the soup is smooth and serve immediately.

Test to see if the apple is cooked by piercing it with the tip of a small sharp knife.

Roasted red capsicum soup

preparation 50 minutes
cooking 1 hour
serves 6

4 large red capsicums (peppers)
4 ripe tomatoes
2 tablespoons oil
1 red onion, chopped
1 garlic clove, crushed
1 litre (35 fl oz/4 cups) vegetable stock
1 teaspoon sweet chilli sauce
pesto, to serve
shaved parmesan cheese, to garnish

Cut the capsicums into large flat pieces, removing the seeds and membrane. Place skin-side-up under a hot grill (broiler) until blackened. Leave covered with a tea towel until cool. Peel off the skin and chop the flesh.

Cut a small cross in the base of each tomato, place in a large heatproof bowl and cover with boiling water. Leave for 1 minute, then plunge into cold water and peel the skin from the cross. Cut the tomatoes in half, scoop out the seeds and roughly chop the flesh.

Heat the oil in a large heavy-based saucepan and add the onion. Cook over medium heat for 10 minutes, stirring frequently, until very soft. Add the garlic and cook for a further minute. Add the capsicum, tomato and stock. Bring to the boil, then reduce the heat and simmer for about 20 minutes.

Allow the soup to cool slightly before processing in batches until smooth. Return to the pan to reheat gently and stir in the sweet chilli sauce (vary the amount according to your taste). This soup is delicious topped with a spoonful of pesto and shavings of parmesan.

Score a cross in the base of the tomatoes, soak in boiling water for 1 minute, then drain and peel.

Bottom: Roasted red capsicum soup. Top: Stilton and apple soup.

Spicy corn and coconut soup

preparation 15 minutes
cooking 30 minutes
serves 4

1 tablespoon oil
1 large onion, chopped
1 celery stalk, chopped
2 garlic cloves, chopped
1 teaspoon ground coriander
1½ teaspoons ground cumin
1–2 teaspoons sambal oelek (see Note)
500 g (1 lb 2 oz) potatoes, chopped
750 ml (26 fl oz/3 cups) chicken or vegetable stock
420 g (14¾ oz) tin corn kernels, drained
270 ml (9½ fl oz) light coconut milk
1 handful coriander (cilantro) leaves
310 g (11 oz) tin creamed corn
extra coriander (cilantro) leaves, to serve

Heat the oil in a large heavy-based saucepan over medium–low heat. Add the onion, celery and garlic. Stir for 2 minutes to coat the vegetables in the oil. Reduce the heat, cover and simmer, stirring occasionally, for 5 minutes. Do not allow the vegetables to brown. Add the ground coriander, cumin and 1 teaspoon of the sambal oelek and stir for 1 minute.

Add the potato and stock. Bring slowly to the boil, then reduce the heat and simmer, covered, for 15 minutes, or until the potato is cooked. Stir in the corn kernels, coconut milk and coriander leaves. Set aside to cool slightly.

Using a stick blender fitted with the chopping blade, whizz the soup for 20–30 seconds, or until smooth. Stir in the creamed corn and gently reheat the soup. Add a little hot water if you prefer a thinner consistency. Season well with salt and freshly ground black pepper. Ladle into four warm bowls and add the remaining sambal oelek, to taste. Serve sprinkled with the extra coriander leaves.

Note Sambal oelek is a condiment made from red chillies, vinegar and sugar. It is used in Singaporean, Indonesian and Malaysian cuisines and is available from Asian supermarkets.

Potato and cheese soup

preparation 20 minutes
cooking 40 minutes
serves 4–6

30 g (1 oz) butter
4 rashers bacon, cut into strips
1 onion, finely chopped
½ teaspoon sweet paprika
1 kg (2 lb 4 oz) potatoes, chopped
750 ml (26 fl oz/3 cups) chicken stock
125 g (4½ oz/1 cup) grated cheddar
snipped chives, to serve

Melt the butter in a large saucepan, add the bacon and cook until crisp. Remove the bacon from the pan with a slotted spoon, leaving as much fat as possible. Add the onion to the same pan and cook for 5 minutes, or until very soft and golden. Add the paprika and cook for a further 30 seconds.

Return the bacon to the pan and add the potato and chicken stock. Bring to the boil, then reduce the heat and simmer for 30 minutes, or until the potato is very soft. Stir or mash lightly to break up the potato. Add the cheddar and stir well, until it is melted through. Season with salt and pepper and serve topped with a sprinkling of chopped chives.

Roasted apple and pumpkin soup

preparation 20 minutes
cooking 1 hour 30 minutes
serves 4

2 red apples
60 ml (2 fl oz/¼ cup) olive oil
1 onion, finely chopped
2 teaspoons ground cumin
¼ teaspoon chilli powder
1 kg (2 lb 4 oz) butternut pumpkin (squash), peeled and chopped
2 potatoes, chopped
2 teaspoons plain (all-purpose) flour
1 litre (35 fl oz/4 cups) vegetable stock
315 ml (10¾ fl oz/1¼ cups) cream

Preheat the oven to 200°C (400°F/Gas 6). Cut the unpeeled apples into thick wedges and cut away the core. Lay in a baking dish and pour over 1 tablespoon of the oil. Roast for 25–30 minutes, turning occasionally, until golden brown. Set aside.

Heat the remaining oil in a large saucepan, add the onion, cumin and chilli and cook for 10 minutes over low heat, or until the onion is very soft and golden. Add the pumpkin and potato and cook for 15 minutes, over medium–high heat, tossing regularly, or until slightly brown. Add the flour and cook, stirring, for 1 minute.

Remove from the heat and gradually pour in the vegetable stock, stirring. Return to the heat and bring to the boil, then reduce the heat and simmer, covered, for 30 minutes. Drain, reserving the vegetables and stock.

Set aside eight pieces of the roasted apple. Put the rest in a food processor, with half the vegetables and 250 ml (9 fl oz/ 1 cup) of the reserved stock. Purée until smooth and return to the pan. Repeat with the remaining vegetables and the same amount of stock, then add to the pan with the cream and any remaining stock. Reheat and season well. Serve the remaining roasted apple as a garnish.

Creamy beetroot soup

preparation 15 minutes
cooking 50 minutes
serves 6

1 tablespoon oil
1 small onion, chopped
1.5 kg (3 lb 5 oz) beetroot, peeled and chopped
1.25 litres (44 fl oz/5 cups) vegetable stock
2 teaspoons caraway seeds
2 tablespoons horseradish cream
250 g (9 oz) sour cream

Heat the oil in a heavy-based saucepan. Cook the onion over medium heat for 5 minutes, or until soft.

Add the beetroot, stock and caraway seeds and bring to the boil. Simmer, partially covered, for 40 minutes.

Cool slightly, then process in batches until smooth. Reheat gently and stir in the horseradish and sour cream to serve.

Stir the horseradish cream and sour cream into the puréed soup.

Top left: Potato and cheese soup. Top right: Roasted apple and pumpkin soup. Bottom left: Creamy beetroot soup.

Capsicum, spinach and chickpea soup

preparation 15 minutes
cooking 25 minutes
serves 4

1 tablespoon olive oil
8 spring onions (scallions), finely sliced
1 red capsicum (pepper)
1 garlic clove, crushed
1 teaspoon cumin seeds
375 ml (13 fl oz/1½ cups) tomato passata (puréed tomatoes)
750 ml (26 fl oz/3 cups) vegetable or beef stock
300 g (10½ oz) tin chickpeas,
rinsed and drained
2 teaspoons red wine vinegar
1–2 teaspoons sugar
100 g (3½ oz) baby English spinach leaves

Heat the oil in a large heavy-based saucepan and stir in the spring onion. Reduce the heat and cook, covered, for 2–3 minutes, or until softened. Meanwhile, remove the seeds and membrane from the capsicum and finely dice. Add the capsicum, garlic and cumin seeds to the pan and cook for 1 minute.

Add the tomato passata and stock and bring the mixture to the boil. Reduce the heat and simmer for 10 minutes. Add the chickpeas, red wine vinegar and sugar to the soup and simmer for a further 5 minutes.

Stir in the baby spinach and season to taste with salt and ground black pepper. Cook until the spinach begins to wilt, then serve immediately.

The chickpeas need to be rinsed well and drained before adding to the soup.

Saffron and Jerusalem artichoke soup

preparation 20 minutes
cooking 30 minutes
serves 4

pinch of saffron threads
250 g (9 oz) Jerusalem artichokes
2 tablespoons lemon juice
1 tablespoon olive oil
1 large onion, finely chopped
1 litre (35 fl oz/4 cups) vegetable or chicken stock
3 teaspoons ground cumin
500 g (1 lb 2 oz) desiree potatoes, grated
2 teaspoons lemon juice, extra

Place the saffron threads in a bowl with 2 tablespoons boiling water and leave until needed. Peel and thinly slice the artichokes, dropping the slices into a bowl of water mixed with lemon juice to prevent discolouration.

Heat the oil in a large heavy-based saucepan, add the onion and cook over medium heat for 2–3 minutes, or until the onion is softened.

Bring the stock to the boil in a separate saucepan.

Add the cumin to the onion mixture and cook for a further 30 seconds, or until fragrant. Add the drained artichokes, grated potato, saffron mixture, stock and extra lemon juice. Bring to the boil, then reduce the heat and simmer for 15–18 minutes, or until the artichokes are very soft.

Transfer to a blender and process in batches until smooth. Return the soup to the pan and season to taste with salt and cracked pepper. Reheat over medium heat and serve.

Soak the saffron threads in 2 tablespoons boiling water while you prepare the other ingredients.

Bottom: Saffron and Jerusalem artichoke soup. Top: Capsicum, spinach and chickpea soup.

Zucchini and basil soup

preparation 20 minutes
cooking 20 minutes
serves 4

1 large onion, finely chopped
3 garlic cloves, very finely chopped
½ teaspoon coriander seeds
2 celery stalks, finely diced
6 zucchini (courgettes), roughly diced
3 large waxy potatoes, diced
1.25 litres (44 fl oz/5 cups) chicken stock
125 g (4½ oz/½ cup) crème fraîche or sour cream
1 large handful basil, torn
2 tablespoons finely chopped flat-leaf (Italian) parsley
sea salt, to serve

Place the onion, garlic, coriander seeds, celery, zucchini, potato and stock in a large heavy-based saucepan. Bring to the boil over medium heat. Partially cover the pan and gently simmer for 12–15 minutes, or until the vegetables are cooked through.

Meanwhile, put the crème fraîche or sour cream in a small bowl with half the basil and the parsley. Combine, using a fork, then set aside.

Remove the saucepan from the heat. Using an immersion blender fitted with the chopping blade, whizz the soup for 20 seconds, or until semi-smooth. Stir in the remaining basil. Season with salt and freshly ground black pepper, to taste.

Divide the crème fraîche mixture among four bowls and ladle in the soup. Sprinkle with sea salt and freshly ground black pepper and serve.

Creamy brussels sprout and leek soup

preparation 15 minutes
cooking 30 minutes
serves 4

1 tablespoon olive oil
2 rindless bacon slices, chopped
2 garlic cloves, chopped
3 leeks, white part only, sliced
300 g (10½ oz) brussels sprouts, roughly chopped
750 ml (26 fl oz/3 cups) chicken or vegetable stock
185 ml (6 fl oz/¾ cup) cream or milk
slices of toasted crusty bread, to serve

Heat the oil in a large saucepan over medium heat. Add chopped bacon and fry for 3 minutes. Add the garlic and leek, cover and fry, stirring often, for a further 5 minutes. Add brussels sprouts, stir to combine, cover and cook, stirring often, for 5 minutes.

Add the stock and season with salt and freshly ground black pepper. Bring to the boil, then reduce the heat, cover the pan and simmer for 10 minutes, or until the vegetables are very tender. Set aside to cool for 10 minutes.

Using an immersion blender fitted with a chopping blade, whizz the soup for 25–30 seconds, until puréed. Stir in the cream or milk and gently reheat the soup. Serve with slices of toasted crusty bread.

Tip *For a vegetarian version of this soup, simply omit the bacon and use vegetable stock rather than chicken stock.*

Remove the stems from the parsley, then finely chop the leaves.

Fry the chopped bacon in a large saucepan over medium heat.

Bottom: Creamy brussels sprout and leek soup. Top: Zucchini and basil soup.

Carrot and ginger soup

preparation 10 minutes
cooking 25 minutes
serves 4

750 ml (26 fl oz/3 cups) vegetable stock
1 tablespoon oil
1 onion, chopped
1 tablespoon grated fresh ginger
1 kg (2 lb 4 oz) carrots, chopped
2 tablespoons chopped coriander (cilantro) leaves

Place the stock in a saucepan and bring to the boil. Heat the oil in a large heavy-based pan, add the onion and ginger and cook for 2 minutes, or until the onion has softened.

Add the stock and carrots. Bring to the boil, then reduce the heat and simmer for 10–15 minutes, or until the carrot is cooked and tender.

Place in a blender or food processor and process in batches until smooth. Return to the pan and add a little more stock or water to thin the soup to your preferred consistency.

Stir in the chopped coriander and season to taste. Heat gently before serving.

Mushroom and tortellini soup

preparation 15 minutes
cooking 20 minutes
serves 4

1 tablespoon olive oil
175 g (6 oz) small flat mushrooms, sliced
6 spring onions (scallions), sliced
1 small garlic clove, crushed
1.25 litres (44 fl oz/5 cups) vegetable or chicken stock
1 tablespoon port
2 teaspoons Worcestershire sauce
200 g (7 oz) fresh large ricotta tortellini
shaved parmesan cheese, to garnish

Heat the oil in a large heavy-based saucepan. Add the mushrooms and cook over high heat for 2 minutes, browning the mushrooms before turning. Add the spring onion and garlic and cook for a further 1 minute.

Meanwhile, bring the stock to the boil in a separate saucepan. Add the stock, port and Worcestershire sauce to the mushroom mixture and bring to the boil. Add the tortellini and simmer for 8 minutes, or until the tortellini is al dente.

Season the soup with salt and cracked black pepper to taste and serve topped with shaved parmesan.

Potato and sweet corn chowder

preparation 15 minutes
cooking 40 minutes
serves 6

6 cobs sweet corn
2 tablespoons oil
1 onion, finely diced
3 garlic cloves, crushed
1 celery stalk, diced
1 carrot, peeled and diced
2 large potatoes, peeled and diced
1 litre (35 fl oz/4 cups) vegetable or chicken stock
2 tablespoons finely chopped flat-leaf (Italian) parsley

Bring a large pot of salted water to the boil, and cook the sweet corn for 5 minutes. Reserve 250 ml (9 fl oz/1 cup) of the cooking water. Cut the corn kernels from the cob, place half in a blender with the reserved cooking water, and blend until smooth.

Heat the oil in a large saucepan and cook the onion, garlic, celery and a large pinch of salt for 5 minutes. Add the carrot and potatoes and cook for a further 5 minutes, then add the stock, corn kernels and blended corn. Reduce the heat and simmer for 20 minutes, or until the vegetables are tender. Season well, and stir in the chopped parsley before serving.

Top left: Carrot and ginger soup. Top right: Mushroom and tortellini soup. Bottom left: Potato and sweet corn chowder.

Cream of fennel and leek soup

preparation 20 minutes
cooking 30 minutes
serves 6

30 g (1 oz) butter
2 large fennel bulbs, thinly sliced
2 leeks, white part only, thinly sliced
1 litre (35 fl oz/4 cups) hot vegetable or chicken stock
2 rosemary sprigs
1/8 teaspoon ground nutmeg
80 g (2¾ oz/1/3 cup) sour cream
25 g (1 oz/¼ cup) finely grated parmesan cheese
1 tablespoon oil
1 leek, extra, cut in half lengthways, and cut into 4 cm (1½ inch) lengths
grated parmesan cheese, extra, to garnish
sour cream, extra, to garnish

Heat the butter in a large heavy-based saucepan, add the fennel and leek, and cook, covered, over medium heat for 2–3 minutes, stirring occasionally.

Put the hot stock, rosemary and nutmeg in a saucepan and bring to the boil. Simmer over low heat for 15 minutes, then remove the rosemary sprigs and add the fennel and leek mixture to the pan.

Transfer the soup to a blender or food processor and blend in batches until smooth. Return to the pan, and stir in the sour cream and parmesan. Reheat over medium heat until hot. Season to taste with salt and freshly ground black pepper and keep warm.

Heat the oil in a frying pan and cook the extra leek for about 2–3 minutes, or until soft but not browned.

Spoon the soup into six warm soup bowls and top with the fried leek. Garnish with the extra parmesan and sour cream and serve immediately.

White bean and rocket soup with basil pesto

preparation 20 minutes
cooking 8 hours 20 minutes
serves 4–6

1 large onion, chopped
2 garlic cloves, crushed
2 x 400 g (14 oz) tins cannellini beans, drained and rinsed
300 g (10½ oz/2 bunches) rocket (arugula), trimmed and chopped
2 litres (70 fl oz/8 cups) chicken stock
125 ml (4 fl oz/½ cup) cream
crusty bread, to serve

basil pesto
2 tablespoons pine nuts, toasted
1 garlic clove, crushed
125 g (4½ oz/1 bunch) basil, leaves picked
35 g (1¼ oz/⅓ cup) grated parmesan cheese
60 ml (2 fl oz/¼ cup) olive oil

Place the onion, garlic, beans, rocket and stock in a slow cooker. Gently mix until well combined. Cover and cook on low for 8 hours. Using a stick blender, process the soup until smooth, then stir the cream through. Cover and cook for a further 20 minutes, or until warmed through.

Meanwhile, to make the basil pesto, place the pine nuts, garlic and basil in a food processor and blend until smooth and combined. Add the parmesan and process for 1 minute. With the motor running, add the oil in a slow steady stream until the pesto is smooth. Season to taste with sea salt and freshly ground black pepper.

Ladle the soup into large serving bowls and sprinkle with freshly ground black pepper. Add a generous dollop of the basil pesto and serve with crusty bread.

Tunisian chickpea and silverbeet soup

preparation 20 minutes
cooking 3 hours 40 minutes
serves 4

1 tablespoon olive oil
1 onion, finely sliced
1 teaspoon ground white pepper
1 teaspoon freshly grated nutmeg
½ teaspoon ground cumin
¼ teaspoon ground cloves
¼ teaspoon ground cinnamon
2 x 400 g (14 oz) tins chickpeas, drained and rinsed
1 bunch silverbeet (Swiss chard), about 900 g (2 lb)
625 ml (21½ fl oz/2½ cups) chicken or vegetable stock
Greek-style yoghurt, to serve
crusty bread, to serve
lemon wedges, to serve

Heat the oil in a frying pan over medium–high heat. Add the onion and cook for 3 minutes, or until it starts to brown, stirring occasionally. Reduce the heat to low and cook for another 5 minutes, or until the onion is soft.

Add the white pepper, nutmeg, cumin, cloves and cinnamon and continue to cook, stirring, for another 30 seconds. Add the chickpeas and stir until they are coated in the spiced onion. Transfer the mixture to a slow cooker.

Wash the silverbeet leaves well and shake dry. Discard the stem below the leaf. Slice across the leaves and stems, cutting the silverbeet into 2 cm (¾ inch) ribbons. Add the silverbeet to the slow cooker and pour in the stock. Gently mix together.

Cover and cook on low for 2½–3½ hours, until the silverbeet is just tender. Using a stick blender, process the soup in a few short bursts, just to blend a portion of the soup, but not to make it smooth — most of the chickpeas should still be whole. Season to taste with sea salt and freshly ground black pepper.

Ladle the soup into bowls and top with a small dollop of yoghurt. Serve with crusty bread and lemon wedges.

Bottom: Tunisian chickpea and silverbeet soup. Top: White bean and rocket soup with basil pesto.

Curried cauliflower and red lentil soup

preparation 15 minutes
cooking 3 hours
serves 4

1 kg (2 lb 4 oz) cauliflower
1 large onion
2 celery stalks
100 g (3½ oz/½ cup) red lentils
1½ tablespoons mild curry paste
400 ml (14 fl oz) tin coconut milk
1 litre (35 fl oz/4 cups) vegetable stock
2 tablespoons finely shredded mint
lime wedges, to serve

Cut the cauliflower, onion and celery into 2 cm (¾ inch) chunks. Place in a slow cooker with the lentils. In a small bowl, mix the curry paste and coconut milk until smooth. Pour into the slow cooker, then pour in the stock.

Cover and cook on high for 3 hours, or until the vegetables are tender.

Remove and reserve a large ladleful of the cauliflower. Blend the remaining soup in a blender or food processor in several batches until smooth. Season to taste with sea salt and freshly ground black pepper.

Ladle the soup into serving bowls. Top with the reserved cauliflower florets and the shredded mint and serve with lime wedges.

Fresh mushroom, shallot and sour cream soup

preparation 15 minutes
cooking 20 minutes
serves 4

2 tablespoons butter
100 g (3½ oz/about 4) French shallots, roughly chopped
3 garlic cloves, crushed
2 large handfuls flat-leaf (Italian) parsley
315 ml (10¾ fl oz/1¼ cups) vegetable or chicken stock
315 ml (10¾ fl oz/1¼ cups) milk
600 g (1 lb 5 oz) button mushrooms
¼ teaspoon ground nutmeg
¼ teaspoon cayenne pepper
150 g (5½ oz) light sour cream
cayenne pepper, to garnish

Melt the butter in a large heavy-based saucepan and add the shallots, garlic and parsley. Cook over medium heat for 2–3 minutes. Put the stock and milk in a separate saucepan and bring to the boil.

Gently wipe the mushrooms clean, then chop and add to the shallot mixture. Season with salt and pepper, then stir in the nutmeg and cayenne pepper. Cook, stirring, for 1 minute. Add the stock and milk and bring to the boil, then reduce the heat and simmer for 5 minutes.

Transfer the soup to a blender or food processor and blend until smooth. Return to the pan.

Stir in the sour cream, adjust the seasoning and reheat gently. Serve sprinkled with cayenne pepper.

Note *For an ideal garnish, fry diced button mushrooms in a little butter until golden. This can be prepared during the soup's final simmering.*

Gently wipe the mushrooms with a damp cloth to remove any dirt.

Bottom: Fresh mushroom, shallot and sour cream soup. Top: Curried cauliflower and red lentil soup.

Zucchini corn chowder

preparation 15 minutes
cooking 25 minutes
serves 4

500 g (1 lb 2 oz) desiree potatoes, diced
1 onion, chopped
2 celery stalks, finely chopped
1 litre (35 fl oz/4 cups) chicken stock
200 g (6½ oz/1 cup) fresh or frozen corn kernels
4 zucchini (courgettes), chopped
125 g (4 oz/1 cup) grated cheddar cheese
70 g (2¼ oz/1½ cups) roughly chopped rocket
(arugula) leaves
250 ml (9 fl oz/1 cup) milk
4 slices prosciutto, chopped, to serve

Place the potato, onion, celery and stock in a large saucepan and bring to the boil. Simmer, covered, for 20 minutes, or until the vegetables are tender. Leave to cool slightly.

Process the vegetables in a food processor until smooth. Return to a clean pan and then bring gently to the boil.

Reduce the heat, add the corn and zucchini and cook until the zucchini is tender but still firm. Stir in the cheddar, rocket leaves and milk. Reheat gently, while stirring, but do not allow the soup to boil.

Adjust the consistency of the soup with a little extra stock if necessary. Season to taste with salt and freshly ground black pepper and serve topped with the chopped prosciutto.

Stir the cheddar, rocket and milk into the zucchini and corn mixture and reheat gently, without boiling.

Tortellini vegetable soup with pistou

preparation 30 minutes
cooking 55 minutes
serves 6–8

1 tablespoon olive oil
1 leek, finely chopped
1 onion, finely chopped
2 carrots, finely chopped
2 potatoes, finely chopped
2 zucchini (courgettes), finely chopped
1 celery stalk, finely chopped
2 tomatoes, chopped
2.5 litres (87 fl oz/10 cups) vegetable stock
375 g (13 oz) tortellini pasta
3 large handfuls basil leaves
3 garlic cloves, chopped
100 g (3½ oz/1 cup) finely grated parmesan cheese
100 ml (3½ fl oz) olive oil, extra

Heat the oil in a very large saucepan, add the leek and onion and cook over low heat for 5 minutes, or until just soft. Add the carrot, potato, zucchini and celery and cook over medium heat for 5 minutes, stirring continuously. Add the tomato and stock and bring to the boil. Simmer, covered, over low heat for 20–30 minutes, or until the vegetables are tender.

Bring a large saucepan of salted water to the boil and cook the pasta for 6–8 minutes, until al dente. Drain, add to the soup and season well.

To make the pistou, place the basil in a food processor with the garlic and parmesan and process until chopped. Add the extra oil with the motor running.

Ladle the soup into bowls and add a spoonful of the pistou to each.

Add the drained tortellini to the simmering soup and season well.

Bottom: Tortellini vegetable soup with pistou. Top: Zucchini corn chowder.

Rich red onion soup

preparation 20 minutes
cooking 50 minutes
serves 6

1 tablespoon oil
20 g (¾ oz) butter
1 kg (2 lb 4 oz) red onions, thinly sliced
1 tablespoon plain (all-purpose) flour
1 litre (35 fl oz/4 cups) vegetable stock
250 ml (9 fl oz/1 cup) red wine
250 ml (9 fl oz/1 cup) tomato paste (concentrated puréed)
French bread, cut diagonally into 12 slices,
2 cm (¾ inch) thick
60 g (2¼ oz/½ cup) finely grated cheddar cheese

Heat the oil and butter in a large heavy-based saucepan. Add the sliced red onion and stir-fry over high heat for 3 minutes, or until soft and starting to become golden. Reduce the heat to medium–low and cook the onion for 25 minutes, stirring occasionally, or until very soft and golden.

Sprinkle the flour over the onion and stir well with a wooden spoon. Cook for 2 minutes, stirring constantly. Add the stock, red wine and puréed tomato and stir until the mixture boils and thickens slightly. Season. Reduce the heat and simmer, uncovered, for 20 minutes.

Toast the bread on both sides under a grill (broiler). Top with grated cheese, return to the grill and cook until melted and golden. To serve, ladle the soup into deep bowls and float-bread slices on the top.

Provencal vegetable soup with pesto

preparation 25–30 minutes
cooking 35–40 minutes
serves 8

3 stalks parsley
1 large sprig rosemary
1 large sprig thyme
1 large sprig marjoram
60 ml (2 fl oz/¼ cup) olive oil
2 onions, thinly sliced
1 leek, white part only, thinly sliced
1 bay leaf
375 g (13 oz) pumpkin (winter squash),
cut into small pieces
250 g (9 oz) potato, cut into small pieces
1 carrot, cut in half lengthways and thinly sliced
2 small zucchini (courgettes), finely chopped
2 litres (70 fl oz/8 cups) water or vegetable stock
1 teaspoon salt
95 g (3¼ oz/½ cup) fresh or frozen broad (fava) beans
80 g (2¾ oz/½ cup) fresh or frozen peas
2 tomatoes, peeled and roughly chopped
80 g (2¾ oz/½ cup) short macaroni or shell pasta

pesto
1 handful basil leaves
2 large garlic cloves, crushed
½ teaspoon black pepper
35 g (1¼ oz/⅓ cup) grated parmesan cheese
80 ml (2½ fl oz/⅓ cup) olive oil

Tie the parsley, rosemary, thyme and marjoram with string. Heat the oil in a heavy-based saucepan; add the onion and leek. Cook over low heat for 10 minutes, or until soft. Add the herbs, bay leaf, pumpkin, potato, carrot, zucchini, and water or stock; add the salt. Cover and simmer for 10 minutes, or until the vegetables are almost tender.

Add the beans, peas, tomato and pasta. Cover and cook for another 15 minutes, or until the vegetables are very tender (add more water if necessary). Remove the herbs.

To make the pesto, process the basil, garlic, pepper and parmesan in a food processor for 20 seconds, or until finely chopped. Gradually add the oil and process until smooth.

Ladle the soup into bowls. Serve the pesto separately for diners to help themselves.

Bottom: Provencal vegetable soup with pesto. Top: Rich red onion soup.

Lemon grass, corn and coconut soup

preparation 25 minutes
cooking 1 hour
serves 4

1½ tablespoons coarsely chopped fresh ginger
2 garlic cloves, chopped
2 lemon grass stems, white part only, thinly sliced
½ teaspoon ground turmeric
½ teaspoon chilli flakes, or to taste
60 ml (2 fl oz/¼ cup) peanut oil
1 large onion, finely chopped
4 corn cobs, kernels removed
2 desiree or other all-purpose potatoes (about 325 g/11½ oz),
peeled and cut into 5 mm (¼ inch) cubes
1.25 litres (44 fl oz/5 cups) vegetable stock
2½ tablespoons soy sauce
400 ml (14 fl oz) tin coconut cream
2 spring onions (scallions), thinly sliced
ground white pepper, to taste
1 small handful chopped coriander (cilantro) leaves
2 makrut (kaffir lime) leaves, very thinly sliced
1 small red chilli, or to taste, thinly sliced
80 g (2¾ oz/½ cup) roasted peanuts, coarsely chopped

In a small food processor, combine the ginger, garlic, lemon grass, turmeric and chilli flakes and 1 tablespoon of the oil. Blend until a coarse paste forms.

Heat the remaining oil in a large saucepan over medium–low heat. Add the onion and corn and cook, stirring often, for 10 minutes, or until the corn is starting to soften.

Add the ginger mixture and potato cubes, and stir until well combined. Cook over low heat for 2 minutes, or until the mixture is aromatic.

Stir in the stock, soy sauce and coconut cream and slowly bring to a simmer. Simmer gently for 35–40 minutes, until the corn and potato are very tender.

Transfer 750 ml (26 fl oz/3 cups) of the soup to a food processor and blend to a smooth purée. Return the puréed soup to the pan and reheat gently. Stir in the spring onion and season to taste with sea salt and ground white pepper.

Ladle the soup into serving bowls. Serve garnished with the coriander, lime leaves, chilli and peanuts.

Slice the kernels off the corn cobs with a large sharp knife.

Return the puréed soup to the saucepan and reheat over low heat.

breads *and* accompaniments

Sourdough rye bread

preparation 2 hours
cooking 40 minutes
makes 2 loaves

sourdough starter
2 teaspoons dried yeast
1 teaspoon caster (superfine) sugar
200 g (7 oz/2 cups) rye flour

bread dough
100 g (3½ oz/1 cup) rye flour
550 g (1 lb 4 oz/4½ cups) unbleached plain (all-purpose) flour
45 g (1¾ oz/¼ cup) soft brown sugar
3 teaspoons caraway seeds
2 teaspoons dried yeast, extra
60 ml (2 fl oz/¼ cup) oil
rye flour, extra, to sprinkle

To make the sourdough starter, combine the yeast, sugar, rye flour and 435 ml (15¼ fl oz/1¾ cups) warm water in a bowl. Cover with plastic wrap and set aside overnight at room temperature to sour. For a stronger flavour, leave for up to 3 days.

To make the bread dough, brush a large baking tray with oil or melted butter. In a large bowl, combine the rye flour, 440 g (15½ oz/3½ cups) of the plain flour, sugar, caraway seeds and 2 teaspoons salt. Dissolve the yeast in 250 ml (9 fl oz/1 cup) warm water. Make a well in the centre of the dry ingredients and add the sourdough starter, dissolved yeast and oil. Mix, using a wooden spoon then your hands, until the dough forms a rough, slightly sticky ball, which leaves the side of the bowl. Add some of the remaining flour, if necessary — you may not need to use it all.

Turn onto a lightly floured surface. Knead for 10 minutes, or until smooth and elastic. Incorporate the remaining flour, if needed. Place the dough in a large, lightly oiled bowl. Leave, covered with plastic wrap, in a warm place for 45 minutes, or until well risen. Punch down and knead for 1 minute. Divide into two even-sized portions. Shape into round or oblong loaves and place on the baking tray. Sprinkle with rye flour and use the end of a wooden spoon handle to press holes 2 cm (¾ inch) deep in the top, or make three slashes. Leave, covered with plastic wrap, in a warm place for 45 minutes, or until the dough is well risen.

Preheat the oven to 180°C (350°F/Gas 4). Sprinkle the loaves with flour. Bake for 40 minutes, or until a skewer inserted in the centre comes out clean. Cool on a wire rack.

Layered cob

preparation 45 minutes
cooking 10 minutes
serves 6–8

2 red capsicums (peppers), seeded and cut into large pieces
500 g (1 lb 2 oz) eggplant (aubergine)
400 g (14 oz) baby English spinach, trimmed
22 cm (8½ inch) cob (round) loaf
2 tablespoons oil
2 garlic cloves, crushed
500 g (1 lb 2 oz/2 cups) ricotta cheese
2 tablespoons chopped flat-leaf (Italian) parsley
25 g (1 oz/¼ cup) freshly grated parmesan cheese
150 g (5½ oz) sliced ham

Cook the capsicum, skin side up, under a hot grill (broiler) until the skins blacken and blister. Cool in a plastic bag, then peel and slice the flesh. Cut the eggplant into 1 cm (½ inch) slices and grill until golden on both sides. Steam the spinach briefly until wilted, then cool and squeeze out any excess liquid.

Cut a large round from the top of the cob loaf and reserve. Scoop out the white bread, leaving a 1 cm (½ inch) border. Combine the oil and garlic and brush the insides of the loaf and lid.

Combine the ricotta, parsley and parmesan in a bowl. Place half the eggplant slices in the loaf, layer the capsicum on top, then the ham. Top with the ricotta mixture and season. Spread the spinach leaves over the top, then add the remaining eggplant. Put the 'lid' on and wrap tightly with plastic wrap. Place a plate on top, weigh down with tins and chill overnight. Serve hot or cold in wedges. To heat, wrap in foil and bake in a 200°C (400°F/Gas 6) oven for 15–20 minutes.

Soy and linseed loaf

preparation 30 minutes
cooking 50 minutes
makes 1 loaf

110 g (3¾ oz/½ cup) pearl barley
2 teaspoons dried yeast
1 teaspoon caster (superfine) sugar
1 tablespoon linseeds (flax seeds)
2 tablespoons soy flour
2 tablespoons gluten flour
150 g (5½ oz/1 cup) wholemeal (whole-wheat)
strong flour
310 g (11 oz/2½ cups) white strong flour
2 tablespoons olive oil

Brush a 10 x 26 cm (4 x 10½ inch) bread tin with oil. Put the barley in a saucepan with 500 ml (17 fl oz/2 cups) water, bring to the boil and boil for 20 minutes, or until softened. Drain.

Put the yeast, sugar and 150 ml (5 fl oz) warm water in a small bowl and mix well. Leave in a warm, draught-free place for 10 minutes, or until bubbles appear on the surface. The mixture should be frothy and slightly increased in volume. If your yeast doesn't foam, it is dead, so you will have to discard it and start again.

Put the barley, linseeds, soy and gluten flours, wholemeal flour, 250 g (9 oz/2 cups) of the white flour and 1 teaspoon salt in a large bowl. Make a well in the centre and add the yeast mixture, oil and 150 ml (5 fl oz) warm water. Mix with a wooden spoon to a soft dough. Turn out onto a floured surface and knead for 10 minutes, or until smooth and elastic. Incorporate enough of the remaining flour until the dough is no longer sticky.

Place in an oiled bowl and brush the dough with oil. Cover with plastic wrap or a damp tea towel (dish towel) and leave in a warm, draught-free place for 45 minutes, or until doubled in size. Punch down and knead for 2–3 minutes.

Pat the dough into a 20 x 24 cm (8 x 9½ inch) rectangle. Roll up firmly from the long side and place, seam side down, in the bread tin. Cover with plastic wrap or a damp tea towel and set aside in a warm, draught-free place for 1 hour, or until risen to the top of the tin. Preheat the oven to 200°C (400°F/Gas 6).

Brush the dough with water and make two slits on top. Bake for 30 minutes, or until golden. Remove from the tin and cool on a wire rack.

Cheats' sourdough

preparation 30 minutes (+ 12 hours standing and 2 hours 45–50 minutes proving)
cooking 35 minutes
makes 35 cm (14 inch) loaf

starter
150 g (5½ oz/1 cup) plain (all-purpose) flour
50 g (1¾ oz/⅓ cup) plain (all-purpose) wholemeal (whole-wheat) flour
2 g (¹⁄₁₂ oz/½ teaspoon) dried yeast
1 teaspoon caster (superfine) sugar
250 ml (9 fl oz/1 cup) lukewarm water

185 g (6½ oz/1¼ cups) plain (all-purpose) flour, plus extra, to dust
70 g (2½ oz/½ cup) plain (all-purpose) wholemeal (whole-wheat) flour
2 g (¹⁄₁₂ oz/½ teaspoon) dried yeast
1½ teaspoons salt
80 ml (2½ fl oz/⅓ cup) lukewarm water

For the starter, put all the ingredients in the bowl of a stand mixer and use the paddle attachment to mix at low speed for 2–3 minutes or until smooth. (Alternatively, if mixing by hand, put all the ingredients except the water in a bowl and mix well. Add the water in a steady stream while stirring constantly, then continue to stir vigorously for 3–4 minutes or until very smooth.) Cover the bowl with plastic wrap and set aside at room temperature for 12 hours. The mixture will be foamy.

Add the flours, yeast, salt and lukewarm water to the starter and use the paddle attachment to mix on low speed until a coarse dough forms. Switch to the dough hook attachment and knead the dough for 5 minutes or until smooth and slightly sticky. If the dough is too dry, add a little water and if it is too wet, add a little extra flour. (If mixing by hand, add all the ingredients to the starter and use a wooden spoon to mix until a coarse dough forms. Turn the dough out onto a lightly floured work surface and knead until a smooth, soft, slightly sticky dough forms.)

Shape the dough into a ball and place in a lightly oiled large bowl, turning to coat in the oil. Cover the bowl with plastic wrap and set aside at room temperature for 1 hour or until doubled in size. Knock back the dough with just one punch to expel the air, then cover the bowl with plastic wrap and set aside at room temperature for another hour or until doubled in size.

Knock back the dough. Turn out onto a lightly floured work surface and pat into a square, about 30 cm (12 inches). Roll it up, like a Swiss roll (jelly roll), then gently work with your hands to form a torpedo-like shape, about 35 cm (14 inches) long. Place on a baking tray lined with non-stick baking paper, cover with a tea towel (dish towel) and set aside at room temperature for 45–50 minutes or until nearly doubled in size.

Meanwhile, preheat the oven to 240°C (475°F/Gas 8) or the maximum temperature. Use a razor blade or sharp knife to make 3–4 diagonal slashes in the surface of the loaf and dust with flour. Bake for 10 minutes, then reduce the temperature to 180°C (350°F/Gas 4) and bake for a further 25 minutes or until the loaf sounds hollow when tapped on the base. Transfer to a wire rack to cool.

Ciabatta

preparation 30 minutes
cooking 30 minutes
makes 1 loaf

2 teaspoons dried yeast
1 teaspoon sugar
375 g (13 oz/3 cups) white strong flour
50 ml (1¾ fl oz) olive oil
extra flour, to sprinkle

Put the yeast, sugar and 80 ml (2½ oz/⅓ cup) warm water in a small bowl and stir well. Leave in a warm, draught-free place for 10 minutes, or until bubbles appear on the surface. The mixture should be frothy and slightly increased in volume.

Put 250 g (9 oz/2 cups) of the flour in a large bowl with 2 teaspoons salt and make a well in the centre. Add the yeast mixture, oil and 230 ml (7¾ fl oz) water to the bowl and stir to combine. Use a cupped hand to knead the wet dough, lifting and stirring for 5 minutes. The dough will be quite wet at this stage. Shape the dough into a ball and put in a clean bowl. Cover with plastic wrap or a damp tea towel (dish towel) and leave in a warm place for 4 hours, or until doubled in size.

Stir in the remaining flour, using a cupped hand, and mix until the flour has been incorporated. Scrape down the side of the bowl. Cover with plastic wrap or a clean tea towel and leave in a warm place for 1–1¼ hours.

Liberally sprinkle a large baking tray with flour. Do not punch down the dough but carefully tip it out onto the tray. Use floured hands to spread the dough into an oval about 12 x 30 cm (4½ x 12 inches). Use heavily floured hands to spread evenly and tuck under the dough edges to plump up the dough. Sprinkle liberally with flour. Cover with plastic wrap and leave for 30 minutes.

Preheat the oven to 210°C (415°F/Gas 6–7). Place a heatproof container of ice on the base of the oven. Bake the ciabatta for 30 minutes, or until puffed and golden. Remove the melted ice after about 20 minutes. The loaf is cooked when it sounds hollow when tapped.

Fougasse

preparation 30 minutes
cooking 35 minutes
makes 4 small loaves

2 teaspoons dried yeast
1 teaspoon sugar
500 g (1 lb 2 oz/4 cups) white strong flour
60 ml (2 fl oz/¼ cup) olive oil
185 g (6½ oz/1 cup) black pitted olives, chopped (optional)
1 handful chopped mixed herbs, such as parsley, oregano and basil (optional)

Put the yeast, sugar and 125 ml (4 fl oz/½ cup) warm water in a small bowl and stir until dissolved. Leave in a warm, draught-free place for 10 minutes, or until bubbles appear on the surface. The mixture should be frothy and slightly increased in volume.

Sift the flour and 2 teaspoons salt into a bowl and make a well in the centre. Add the yeast mixture, olive oil and 185 ml (6 fl oz/¾ cup) warm water. Mix to a soft dough and gather into a ball with floured hands.

Turn out onto a floured surface and knead for 10 minutes, or until smooth. Place the dough in a large, lightly oiled bowl, cover loosely with plastic wrap or a damp tea towel (dish towel) and leave in a warm place for 1 hour, or until doubled in size.

Punch down the dough and add the olives and herbs, if desired. Knead for 1 minute. Divide the mixture into four equal portions. Press each portion into a large, oval shape about 1 cm (½ inch) thick and make several cuts on either side of each. Lay the dough on large, floured baking trays, cover with plastic wrap and leave to rise for 20 minutes.

Preheat the oven to 210°C (415°F/Gas 6–7). Bake the fougasse for 35 minutes, or until crisp. To make the crust crispy, spray the inside of the oven with water after 15 minutes cooking.

Note *Although fougasse is traditionally made as a plain bread, these days bakeries often incorporate ingredients such as fresh herbs, olives, chopped ham and anchovies into the dough.*

Bottom: Fougasse. Top: Ciabatta

Basic white bread

preparation 35 minutes + 2 hours 15 minutes proving
cooking 40 minutes
makes 2 loaves

310 ml (10¾ fl oz/1¼ cups) lukewarm water
Large pinch of caster (superfine) sugar
9 g (¼ oz/2½ teaspoons) dried yeast
60 g (2¼ oz) butter, melted
250 ml (9 fl oz/1 cup) milk, warmed
900 g (2 lb/6 cups) plain (all-purpose) flour
2 teaspoons salt

Combine 125 ml (4 fl oz/½ cup) of the water and the sugar in a large bowl. Sprinkle over the yeast and set aside for 5–6 minutes or until foamy.

Add the butter, milk, remaining water, half the flour and the salt and use a wooden spoon to mix well. Add the remaining flour, 150 g (5½ oz/1 cup) at a time, stirring until a coarse dough forms. Turn the dough out onto a lightly floured work surface and knead for 8–10 minutes or until it feels smooth, elastic and fairly soft, adding a little extra flour if it is too sticky.

Put the dough in a lightly oiled, large bowl, turning to coat in the oil. Cover the bowl with plastic wrap and set aside in a warm, draught-free place for 1½ hours or until the dough has doubled in size.

Preheat the oven to 200°C (400°F/Gas 6). Lightly grease two 8 x 17.5 cm (3¼ x 6¾ inch) loaf (bar) tins.

Knock back the dough with just one punch to expel the air. Turn out onto a lightly floured work surface and use a large sharp knife to cut in half. Working with one portion at a time, use your hands to pat the dough out into a rough rectangle, about 1.5 cm (⅝ inch) thick. Roll each rectangle up, like a Swiss roll (jelly roll), and place in the greased tins, seam side down, pushing them in to fit. Cover with a damp tea towel (dish towel) and set aside in a warm, draught-free place for 45 minutes or until the dough has risen just above the edge of each tin.

Use a sharp serrated knife or razor blade to make 3–4 diagonal slashes in the top of each loaf, taking care not to deflate the dough. Bake for 10 minutes, then reduce the heat to 180°C (350°F/Gas 4) and bake for 30 minutes more or until the loaves are deep golden and sound hollow when tapped on the base. Turn out onto a wire rack to cool.

Potato bread

preparation 45 minutes
cooking 35 minutes
makes 1 loaf

2 teaspoons dried yeast
500 g (1 lb 2 oz/4 cups) unbleached plain (all-purpose) flour
2 tablespoons full-cream milk powder
235 g (8½ oz/1 cup) warm cooked mashed potato
25 g (1 oz) snipped chives
1 egg white, to glaze
2 teaspoons cold water
sunflower seeds and pepitas (pumpkin seeds), to sprinkle

Lightly grease a 25 cm (10 inch) round cake tin and line the base with baking paper. Put the yeast and 60 ml (2 fl oz/¼ cup) warm water in a small bowl and stir well. Leave in a warm, draught-free place for 10 minutes, or until bubbles appear on the surface. The mixture should be frothy and slightly increased in volume.

Sift 440 g (15½ oz/3½ cups) of the flour, the milk powder and 1 teaspoon salt into a large bowl. Using a fork, mix the potato and chives through the dry ingredients. Add the yeast mixture and 250 ml (9 fl oz/1 cup) warm water and mix until combined. Add enough of the remaining flour to make a soft dough.

Turn the dough onto a lightly floured surface. Knead for 10 minutes, or until the dough is smooth and elastic. Place in an oiled bowl, then brush the surface with oil. Cover with plastic wrap and leave in a warm place for 1 hour, or until well risen.

Punch down the dough, then knead for 1 minute. Divide into 12 equal pieces and form each piece into a smooth ball. Place evenly spaced balls in a daisy pattern in the tin, piling two balls in the centre. Cover with plastic wrap and leave to rise for 45 minutes, or until the dough has risen to the top of the tin. Preheat the oven to 210°C (415°F/Gas 6–7).

Brush the top with the combined egg white and water and sprinkle the sunflower seeds and pepitas over the top. Bake for 15 minutes. Reduce the oven to 180°C (350°F/Gas 4) and bake for another 20 minutes, or until a skewer inserted into the centre of the loaf comes out clean.

Leave for 10 minutes, then turn out onto a wire rack.

Note *Depending on the moisture content of the potato, extra flour may have to be added to make a soft, slightly sticky dough. The bread will keep for 3 days in an airtight container.*

Potoato bread

Rye bread

preparation 30 minutes
(+ 2 hours standing and 1 hour 45–50 minutes proving)
cooking 45 minutes
makes 1 loaf

starter
110 g (3¾ oz/¾ cup) plain (all-purpose) wholemeal
(whole-wheat) flour
30 g (1 oz/¼ cup) rye flour
2 g (¹⁄₁₂ oz/½ teaspoon) dried yeast
¾ teaspoon caster (superfine) sugar
250 ml (9 fl oz/1 cup) lukewarm water

205 g (7¼ oz/1²⁄₃ cups) rye flour
150 g (5½ oz/1 cup) plain (all-purpose) wholemeal (whole-
wheat) flour
2 g (¹⁄₁₂ oz/½ teaspoon) dried yeast
2 teaspoons salt
1½ teaspoons molasses
140 ml (4½ fl oz) lukewarm water

For the starter, put all ingredients in the bowl of a stand mixer and use the paddle attachment to mix at low speed for 2–3 minutes or until smooth. (Alternatively, if mixing by hand, put all ingredients except the water in a bowl and mix well. Add water in a steady stream while stirring constantly, then continue to stir vigorously for 3–4 minutes or until very smooth.) Cover bowl with plastic wrap and set aside at room temperature for 12 hours. The mixture will be foamy.

Add flours, yeast, salt, molasses and lukewarm water to the starter and use the paddle attachment to mix on low speed until a coarse dough forms. Switch to the dough hook attachment and knead for 5 minutes or until smooth, but slightly sticky. If dough is too dry, add water and if it is too wet, add extra flour. (Alternatively, if mixing by hand, add all ingredients to the starter and use a wooden spoon to mix until a coarse dough forms. Turn dough out onto a lightly floured work surface and knead until a smooth, soft, slightly sticky dough forms.) Shape dough into a ball and place in a lightly oiled large bowl, turning to coat in the oil. Cover bowl with plastic wrap and set aside at room temperature for 1 hour or until dough has doubled in size.

Knock back dough with just one punch to expel the air, then turn out onto a clean work surface. Shape dough (it will be slightly sticky) into a 15 cm (6 inch) long log and place in a greased 9 x 15 cm (3½ x 6 inch) loaf (bar) tin. Cover with a tea towel (dish towel) and set aside at room temperature for 45–50 minutes or until nearly doubled in size.

Preheat the oven to 200°C (400°F/Gas 6). Bake the bread for 45 minutes or until the loaf sounds hollow when tapped on the base. Cool for 5 minutes in the tin, then transfer to a wire rack to cool to room temperature.

Pumpkin bread

preparation 35 minutes
cooking 50 minutes
makes 1 round loaf

300 g (10½ oz) pumpkin (winter squash), chopped
7 g (¼ oz) sachet dried yeast
1 teaspoon salt
560 g (1 lb 2 oz/4½ cups) white bread flour
1 egg, beaten
pumpkin seeds (pepitas), to decorate

Boil the pumpkin for 10 minutes, or until tender. Drain thoroughly, then mash.

Grease a 20 cm (8 inch) cake tin and line the base with baking paper.

Place the yeast and 60 ml (2 fl oz/¼ cup) warm water in a small bowl and stir well. Leave in a warm, draught-free place for 10 minutes. The mixture should be frothy. If your yeast doesn't foam it is dead, so you will have to discard it and start again.

Sift the salt and 500 g (1 lb 2 oz/4 cups) of the flour into a large bowl. Add the pumpkin, yeast mixture and 60 ml (2 fl oz/¼ cup) warm water. Mix until combined.

Turn onto a floured surface. Knead for 10 minutes, or until the dough is smooth and elastic. Incorporate enough of the remaining flour to form a smooth dough. Place the dough in a lightly oiled bowl and brush the dough with oil. Cover with plastic wrap and leave in a warm place for 1 hour, or until well risen.

Punch down the dough, knead for 1 minute, then pull away a golf ball-sized piece of dough. Shape the remaining dough into a smooth ball and place in the tin. Roll the smaller ball into a rope 35 cm (14 in) long. Tie into a loose knot and place across the top of the dough, then seal with water to hold in place. Cover with plastic wrap and leave in a warm place for 1 hour, or until risen to the top of the tin.

Preheat the oven to hot 210°C (415°F/Gas 6–7). Beat 2 teaspoons water into the egg and brush over the dough.

Four-seed bread

preparation 40 minutes (+ 1–1½ hours proving)
cooking 25 minutes
makes 1 loaf

500 g (1 lb 2 oz/3⅓ cups) plain (all-purpose) wholemeal
(whole-wheat) flour
1½ teaspoons salt
350 ml (12 fl oz) lukewarm water
7 g (⅛ oz/2 teaspoons) dried yeast
1 tablespoon honey
1 tablespoon olive oil
1½ tablespoons poppy seeds
1½ tablespoons linseeds (flax seeds)
2 tablespoons sunflower seeds
40 g (1½ oz/¼ cup) sesame seeds

Sift the flour and salt into a large bowl. Place 50 ml
(1½ fl oz) of the lukewarm water in a small bowl, add
the yeast and stir to dissolve. Set aside for 5–6 minutes or
until foamy.

Add the yeast mixture to the flour with the honey, oil and
remaining lukewarm water and use a wooden spoon to mix
until a rough dough forms. Turn out onto a lightly floured
work surface and knead for 5 minutes or until smooth
and elastic.

Return the dough to the bowl, add the seeds and knead
until incorporated. Turn out onto a lightly floured work
surface and knead for 3 minutes to distribute the seeds.

Shape the dough into a ball and place in a lightly oiled
large bowl, turning to coat in the oil. Cover the bowl with
plastic wrap and set aside in a warm, draught-free place
for 30–45 minutes or until the dough has doubled in size.

Knock back the dough with just one punch to expel the air,
then turn out onto a clean work surface. Shape into a round,
about 20 cm (8 inches) in diameter and place on a greased
baking tray. Cover with a damp tea towel (dish towel) and
set aside in a warm, draught-free place for 30–45 minutes or
until the dough has nearly doubled in size.

Meanwhile, preheat the oven to 220°C (425°F/Gas 7).
Bake the bread for 10 minutes, then turn to ensure even
cooking and bake for a further 12–15 minutes or until it
sounds hollow when tapped on the base. Cool on the
tray for 5 minutes, then transfer to a wire rack to cool to
room temperature.

Four-seed bread

Pumpernickel

preparation 1 hour
cooking 50 minutes
makes 2 loaves

1 tablespoon dried yeast
1 teaspoon caster (superfine) sugar
90 g (3¼ oz/¼ cup) molasses
60 ml (2 fl oz/¼ cup) cider vinegar
90 g (3¼ oz) butter
30 g (1 oz) dark chocolate, chopped
1 tablespoon instant coffee powder
560 g (1 lb 4 oz/4½ cups) unbleached plain (all-purpose) flour
300 g (10½ oz/3 cups) rye flour
75 g (2¾ oz/1 cup) bran
1 tablespoon caraway seeds
2 teaspoons fennel seeds
1 egg white
caraway seeds, extra, to sprinkle

Grease a 20 cm (8 inch) round cake tin and a 12 x 28 cm (4½ x 11¼ inch) loaf (bar) or bread tin, or use any baking tin that has a 1.75 litre capacity. Line the base of each tin with baking paper. Put 125 ml (4 fl oz/½ cup) warm water, the yeast and sugar in a small bowl and stir well. Leave in a warm, draught-free place for 10 minutes, or until bubbles appear on the surface. The mixture should be frothy and slightly increased in volume.

Put the molasses, vinegar, butter, chocolate, coffee powder and 500 ml (17 fl oz/2 cups) cold water into a saucepan and stir over low heat until the butter and chocolate have melted and the mixture is just warmed.

Put the rye flour, bran, caraway and fennel seeds, 440 g (15½ oz/3½ cups) of the plain flour and 1 teaspoon salt in a large bowl. Make a well in the centre and add the yeast and chocolate mixtures. Using a wooden spoon, and then your hands, combine the dough until it leaves the side of the bowl and forms a firm, sticky ball.

Turn out onto a heavily floured surface and knead for 10 minutes. Incorporate enough of the remaining plain flour to make a dense but smooth and elastic dough. Divide in half and place in separate lightly oiled bowls. Brush the surface of the dough with melted butter or oil. Cover with plastic wrap or a damp tea towel (dish towel) and leave in a warm, draught-free place for 1¼ hours, or until well risen. Punch down the dough and knead each portion for 1 minute. Shape each portion to fit a tin and place one in each tin. Cover with lightly oiled plastic wrap or a damp tea towel and leave in a warm place for 1 hour, or until well risen.

Preheat the oven to 180°C (350°F/Gas 4). Glaze the dough with combined egg white and 1 tablespoon water and sprinkle with caraway seeds. Bake for 50 minutes, or until well browned. During the last 15 minutes, cover with foil to prevent excess browning. Leave in the tins for 15 minutes before turning out onto a wire rack to cool.

Note *Pumpernickel is a dense rye bread that originated in Germany.*

Feta and olive pull-apart

preparation 50 minutes (+ 2½ hours proving)
cooking 50 minutes
makes 22.5 cm (8¾ inch) loaf

½ quantity basic white bread dough (see page 352)
80 g (2¾ oz/½ cup) pitted kalamata olives, coarsely chopped
150 g (5½ oz) feta cheese, crumbled
2½ tablespoons oregano leaves, coarsely chopped
1½ tablespoons olive oil

Follow the basic white bread recipe to the end of paragraph 3. Knock back the dough with just one punch to expel the air and turn out onto a lightly floured work surface. Use a rolling pin to roll out the dough into a rectangle about 26 x 40 cm (10½ x 16 inches). With a long side facing you, scatter the olives, feta and oregano lengthways over half the dough, leaving a 1 cm (½ inch) border around the edges. Drizzle the oil over the filling. Grease a 8 x 22.5 cm (3¼ x 8¾ inch) loaf (bar) tin with olive oil.

Fold the dough over to enclose the filling and use your fingertips to press the edges of the dough all the way around to seal. Use a large sharp knife to cut the dough widthways into 10 even slices. Working with one piece of dough at a time, roll up lengthways and place, cut side down, in the tin pushing in the ends to fit and taking care not to drop too much filling. Continue packing in the pieces of dough so they fit snugly in the tin, scattering with any dropped pieces of filling as you go.

Use your hands to press down on the surface of the dough to make it even, then cover with a tea towel (dish towel). Set aside in a warm, draught-free place for 1 hour or until the dough has risen to the top of the tin. Preheat the oven to 180°C (350°F/Gas 4).

Bake for 50 minutes or until the loaf is deep golden all over and the base sounds hollow when tapped. Cool in the tin for 5 minutes, then transfer to a wire rack.

Variation Pesto, tomato and parmesan pull-apart: *Omit the olives, feta and oregano. Spread 60 g (2¼ oz/¼ cup) pesto lengthways over half of the rolled dough, leaving a 1 cm (½ inch) border around the edges. Scatter 80 g (2¾ oz/¾ cup) finely grated parmesan cheese and 110 g (3¾ oz/½ cup) chopped semi-dried tomatoes over the pesto, then proceed as for the main recipe.*

Focaccia

preparation 50 minutes
cooking 25 minutes
makes 1 loaf

2 teaspoons dried yeast
1 teaspoon caster (superfine) sugar
2 tablespoons olive oil
405 g (14¼ oz/3¼ cups) white strong flour
1 tablespoon full-cream milk powder

topping
1 tablespoon olive oil
1–2 garlic cloves, crushed
black olives
rosemary sprigs or leaves
1 teaspoon dried oregano
1–2 teaspoons coarse sea salt

Lightly grease a 18 x 28 cm (7 x 11¼ inch) baking tin. Put the yeast, sugar and 250 ml (9 fl oz/1 cup) warm water in a small bowl and stir well. Leave in a warm, draught-free place for 10 minutes, or until bubbles appear on the surface. The mixture should be frothy and slightly increased in volume. If your yeast doesn't foam, it is dead, so you will have to discard it and start again. Add the oil.

Sift 375 g (13 oz/3 cups) of the flour, the milk powder and ½ teaspoon salt into a large bowl. Make a well in the centre and add the yeast mixture. Beat with a wooden spoon until the mixture is well combined. Add enough of the remaining flour to form a soft dough, and then turn onto a lightly floured surface.

Knead for 10 minutes, or until the dough is smooth and elastic. Place dough in a large, lightly oiled bowl. Brush the surface of dough with oil. Cover with plastic wrap or a damp tea towel (dish towel) and leave in a warm place for 1 hour, or until well risen. Punch down the dough and knead for 1 minute. Roll into a rectangle, 18 x 28 cm (7 x 11¼ inches) and place in the prepared tin. Cover with plastic wrap and then leave to rise in a warm place for 20 minutes. Using the handle of a wooden spoon, form indents 1 cm (½ inch) deep all over the dough at regular intervals. Cover with plastic wrap and set aside for 30 minutes, or until dough is well risen. Preheat the oven to 180°C (350°F/Gas 4).

To make the topping, brush the combined olive oil and garlic over the surface of the dough. Top with olives and rosemary sprigs, then sprinkle with the oregano and salt.

Bake for 20–25 minutes, or until golden and crisp. Cut into large squares and serve warm.

Note *Focaccia is best eaten on the day of baking. It can be reheated if necessary.*

Olive bread

preparation 30 minutes
cooking 35 minutes
makes 1 loaf

375 g (13 oz/3 cups) plain (all-purpose) flour
2 teaspoons dry yeast
2 teaspoons sugar
2 tablespoons olive oil
110 g (3¾ oz/⅔ cup) pitted and halved Kalamata olives
2 teaspoons plain (all-purpose) flour, extra, to coat
1 small oregano sprig, leaves removed
and torn into small pieces (optional)
olive oil, to glaze

Put one-third of the flour in a large bowl and stir in 1 teaspoon salt. Put yeast, sugar and 250 ml (9 fl oz/1 cup) warm water in a small bowl and stir well. Leave in a warm, draught-free place for 10 minutes, or until bubbles appear on the surface. The mixture should be frothy and slightly increased in volume. If your yeast doesn't foam, it is dead, so you will have to discard it and start again.

Add yeast mixture to flour mixture and stir to make a thin, lumpy paste. Cover with a tea towel (dish towel) and set aside in a warm, draught-free place for 45 minutes, or until doubled in size. Stir in remaining flour and the oil and 125 ml (4 fl oz/½ cup) warm water. Mix with a wooden spoon until a rough dough forms. Transfer to a lightly floured work surface and knead for 10–12 minutes, incorporating as little extra flour as possible to keep dough soft and moist, but not sticky. Form into a ball. Oil a clean large bowl and roll dough around in it to lightly coat in the oil. Cut a cross on top, cover bowl with a tea towel and set aside in a warm place for 1 hour, or until doubled in size.

Lightly grease a baking tray and dust with flour. Punch down the dough on a lightly floured surface. Roll out to 1 x 25 x 30 cm (½ x 10 x 12 inch). Squeeze any excess liquid from the olives and toss to coat in extra flour. Scatter over dough and top with oregano. Roll up tightly lengthways, pressing firmly to expel any air pockets as you roll. Press ends together to form an oval loaf 25 cm (10 inches) long. Transfer to the prepared tray, join side down. Make three shallow diagonal slashes across the top. Slide the tray into a large plastic bag and leave in a warm place for 45 minutes, or until doubled in bulk.

Preheat the oven to 220°C (425°F/Gas 7). Brush the top of the loaf with olive oil and bake for 30 minutes. Reduce the heat to 180°C (350°F/Gas 4) and bake for another 5 minutes. Cool on a wire rack. Serve warm or cold.

Olive bread

Damper

preparation 20 minutes
cooking 25 minutes
makes 1 damper

375 g (13 oz/3 cups) self-raising flour
90 g (3¼ oz) butter, melted
125 ml (4 fl oz/½ cup) milk
milk, extra, to glaze
flour, extra, to dust

Preheat the oven to 210°C (415°F/Gas 6–7). Grease a baking tray. Sift the flour and 1–2 teaspoons salt into a bowl and make a well in the centre. Combine the butter, milk and 125 ml (4 fl oz/½ cup) water and pour into the well. Stir with a knife until just combined. Turn the dough onto a lightly floured surface and knead for 20 seconds, or until smooth. Place the dough on the baking tray and press out to a 20 cm (8 inch) circle.

Using a sharp pointed knife, score the dough into eight sections about 1 cm (½ inch) deep. Brush with milk, then dust with flour. Bake for 10 minutes. Reduce the oven to 180°C (350°F/Gas 4) and bake the damper for another 15 minutes, or until the damper is golden and sounds hollow when the surface is tapped. Serve with butter.

Note Damper is the Australian version of soda bread. It is traditionally served warm with slatherings of golden syrup. If you prefer, you can make four rounds instead of one large damper and slightly reduce the cooking time. Cut two slashes in the form of a cross on the top.

Cottage loaf

preparation 30 minutes
cooking 40 minutes
makes 1 large loaf

2 teaspoons dried yeast
1 tablespoon soft brown sugar
250 g (9 oz/2 cups) white strong flour
300 g (10½ oz/2 cups) wholemeal (whole-wheat) strong flour
1 tablespoon vegetable oil

Put the yeast, 1 teaspoon of the sugar and 125 ml (4 fl oz/½ cup) warm water in a small bowl and mix well. Leave in a warm, draught-free place for 10 minutes, or until bubbles appear on the surface. The mixture should be frothy and slightly increased in volume.

Put the flours and 1 teaspoon salt in a large bowl. Make a well in the centre and add the yeast mixture, oil, the remaining sugar and 250 ml (9 fl oz/1 cup) warm water.

Mix with a wooden spoon then turn out onto a lightly floured surface. Knead for 10 minutes, or until smooth and elastic. Incorporate a little extra flour into the dough as you knead, to stop the dough from sticking.

Place the dough in an oiled bowl and lightly brush oil over the dough. Cover with plastic wrap or a damp tea towel (dish towel) and leave in a warm place for 45 minutes, or until doubled in size.

Punch down the dough then turn out onto a lightly floured surface and knead the dough for 3–4 minutes. Pull away one-third of the dough and knead both portions into a smooth ball. Place the large ball on a large floured baking tray and brush the top with water. Sit the smaller ball on top and, using two fingers, press down into the centre of the dough to join the two balls together. Cover with plastic wrap or a damp tea towel (dish towel) and set aside in a warm place for 40 minutes, or until well risen.

Preheat oven to 190°C (375°F/Gas 5). Sift some white flour over top of the loaf and bake for 40 minutes, or until golden brown and cooked. Leave on the tray for 2–3 minutes to cool slightly, then turn out onto a wire rack to cool.

Irish soda bread

preparation 15 minutes
cooking 45–50 minutes
makes 1 loaf

200 g (7 oz/1⅓ cups) plain (all-purpose) flour
200 g (7 oz/1⅓ cups) plain (all-purpose) wholemeal (whole-wheat) flour
1 teaspoon baking powder
1 teaspoon bicarbonate of soda (baking soda)
2 teaspoons salt
60 g (2¼ oz) chilled unsalted butter, chopped
300 ml (10½ fl oz) buttermilk

Preheat the oven to 180°C (350°F/Gas 4). Grease and flour a baking tray.

Sift the flours, baking powder, bicarbonate of soda and salt into a large bowl, returning the husks from the wholemeal flour to the bowl. Use your fingertips to rub in the butter until the mixture resembles coarse breadcrumbs. Add the buttermilk and mix with a flat-bladed knife, using a cutting action, until a dough forms.

Turn the dough out onto a floured surface and knead briefly until smooth. Shape the dough into a ball about 18 cm (7 inches) in diameter and place on the prepared tray. Use a large sharp knife to cut a deep cross into the surface.

Bake for 45–50 minutes or until the loaf is golden and sounds hollow when tapped on the base. Transfer to a wire rack to cool.

Bottom: Cottage loaf. Top: Damper.

Greek lemon, dill and feta bread

preparation 30 minutes
cooking 30 minutes
makes 2 loaves

375 g (13 oz/3 cups) white strong flour
125 g (4½ oz/1 cup) semolina
1 tablespoon (12 g) instant dried yeast
1 teaspoon caster (superfine) sugar
2 tablespoons olive oil
60 g (2¼ oz/1 bunch) dill, finely chopped
grated zest of 1 lemon
200 g (7 oz/1⅓ cups) coarsely crumbled feta cheese,
well drained

Combine the flour, semolina, yeast, sugar and
1½ teaspoons salt in the bowl of an electric mixer with a
dough hook attachment and make a well in the centre.
Pour 250 ml (9 fl oz/1 cup) warm water and the oil into
the well. With the mixer set to the lowest speed, mix for
3 minutes, or until a dough forms. Increase the speed
to medium, add the dill and lemon zest and knead for
another 8 minutes, or until the dough is smooth and elastic.
Add the feta and knead for 2 minutes, or until the feta is
incorporated into the dough.

Alternatively, mix the dough by hand using a wooden
spoon, then turn out onto a floured work surface, sprinkle
over the dill and lemon zest and knead for 8 minutes or
until the dill and zest are incorporated and the dough
is smooth and elastic. Pat the dough into a rectangle
approximately 20 x 10 cm (8 x 4 inch) and sprinkle over
the feta. Fold the dough over several times, then knead for
2 minutes, or until the feta is incorporated.

Grease a large bowl with oil, then transfer the dough to
the bowl, turning the dough to coat in the oil. Cover with
plastic wrap and leave to rise in a draught-free place for
1½–2 hours, or until the dough has doubled in size.

Knock back the dough by punching it, then turn out onto
a floured work surface. Divide the dough in half and form
each into a loaf shape and place, seam side down, into two
greased 20 x 10 cm (8 x 4 inch) loaf tins. Cover with a damp
cloth and leave for 30 minutes, or until doubled in size.

Meanwhile, preheat the oven to 200°C (400°F/Gas 6). Bake
the bread for 10 minutes, then reduce the oven to 180°C
(350°F/Gas 4) and bake for a further 20 minutes, or until
golden and hollow sounding when tapped on the base.
Transfer to a wire rack to cool.

Chunky croutons

preparation 5 minutes
cooking 10 minutes
makes 2 cups

½ loaf (about 350 g/12 oz) rustic bread
(sourdough or ciabatta)
125 ml (4 fl oz/½ cup) olive oil
30 g (1 oz) butter, chopped
4 garlic cloves, lightly bruised

Remove the crust from the bread and tear the bread into
rough 2–3 cm (¾–1¼ inch) pieces. (You will need about 4
cups loosely packed.)

Heat the oil, butter and garlic in a large frying pan over
medium–low heat. (It should just be gently bubbling not
sizzling.) Add the croutons and use tongs to turn to coat in
the oil. Cook for 8–10 minutes, turning occasionally, until
light golden and crisp. Remove with tongs and drain on
paper towel. Serve warm or at room temperature.

Herb bread

preparation 10 minutes
cooking 20 minutes
serves 4

125 g (4 oz) butter, softened
30 g (1 oz) chopped mixed herbs
1 garlic clove, finely chopped (optional)
1 baguette

Preheat the oven to 180°C (350°F/Gas 4).

Combine the butter, mixed herbs and garlic, if using. Slice
the baguette, diagonally, almost all the way through, and
spread each piece with the herb butter. Reshape into a loaf,
wrap in foil and bake for 20 minutes, or until the loaf is
crisp and hot.

Garlic bread

preparation 10 minutes
cooking 10 minutes
serves 4

4 small long rolls
100 g (3½ oz) butter, just softened
1 garlic clove, finely chopped
1 tablespoon finely chopped flat-leaf (Italian) parsley
3 teaspoons finely snipped chives
sea salt flakes

Preheat oven to 200°C (400°F/Gas 6). Make three diagonal cuts through the top of each roll but don't go all the way through. Combine the butter, garlic, herbs and a pinch of sea salt. Spread onto both sides of the cut bread.

Wrap each roll individually in foil, place on a baking tray and bake for 10 minutes or until crisp on the outside and the butter has melted. Serve immediately as whole rolls or broken into individual slices.

Variation Replace the garlic and herbs with 3 teaspoons finely chopped sun-dried tomatoes (not in oil) and 50 g (1¾ oz/⅓ cup) finely grated parmesan cheese.

Onion and buttermilk bread

preparation 15 minutes
cooking 30 minutes
makes 4 small loaves

375 g (13 oz/3 cups) self-raising flour
35 g (1¼ oz) dried French onion soup
2 tablespoons snipped chives
435 ml (15¼ fl oz/1¾ cups) buttermilk, plus a little extra

Preheat the oven to 180°C (350°F/Gas 4).

Sift the flour into a large bowl and stir in the dried soup and chives. Mix in the buttermilk with a flat-bladed knife, using a cutting action, until the mixture forms a soft dough. Add extra buttermilk if the mixture is too dry.

Turn the dough out onto a lightly floured surface and quickly knead into a smooth ball. Cut into four even-sized pieces and shape each into a ball. Place on a floured baking tray, allowing room for each to rise. Sift extra flour over the top and make a slash with a sharp knife across the top of each loaf. Bake the loaves for 25–30 minutes, or until cooked and golden.

Lemon pepper bread

preparation 20 minutes
cooking 25 minutes
makes 2 loaves

250 g (9 oz/2 cups) self-raising flour
2 teaspoons lemon pepper, or 1 teaspoon grated lemon zest
and 2 teaspoons black pepper
50 g (1¾ oz) butter, chopped
1 tablespoon snipped chives
90 g (3¼ oz/¾ cup) grated cheddar cheese
2 teaspoons white vinegar
185 ml (6 fl oz/¾ cup) milk

Preheat the oven to 210°C (415°F/Gas 6–7). Brush two baking trays with melted butter or oil. Sift the flour and 1 teaspoon salt into a large bowl and add the lemon pepper, or lemon zest and pepper. Using your fingertips, rub in the butter until the mixture resembles coarse breadcrumbs. Stir in the chives and cheese.

In a separate bowl, stir the vinegar into the milk (it should look slightly curdled). Add to the flour mixture and mix to a soft dough, adding more milk if the dough is too stiff.

Turn the dough out onto a lightly floured surface and knead until smooth. Divide the dough into two portions. Place on the prepared trays and press each portion out into a circle approximately 2.5 cm (1 inch) thick. Score each with a knife into eight wedges, cutting lightly into the top of the bread. Dust lightly with flour. Bake for 20–25 minutes, or until the bread is a deep golden colour and sounds hollow when tapped on the base. Serve warm with butter.

Skillet bread

preparation 20 minutes
cooking 30 minutes
serves 8

190 g (6¾ oz/1 cup) polenta
150 g (5½ oz/1 cup) self-raising flour
2 teaspoons sea salt
2 eggs, lightly whisked
375 ml (13 fl oz/1½ cups) buttermilk
100 g (3½ oz) butter, softened

Preheat the oven to 200°C (400°F/Gas 6). Place a 6 cm (2½ inch) deep, 26 cm (10½ inch) (top diameter) and 20 cm (8 inch) (base diameter) frying pan with a heatproof handle in the oven.

Meanwhile, combine the polenta, sifted flour and salt in a large bowl. Make a well in the centre. Slowly pour in the combined egg and buttermilk while mixing with a fork to gradually incorporate the dry ingredients, mixing until smooth. Take care not to overmix the batter, it doesn't matter if there are a few lumps.

Remove the hot pan from the oven. Add the butter and swirl it around to coat the base and side of the pan. Pour the excess butter into the batter and stir to combine. Pour the batter into the pan and bake for 30 minutes or until golden and a skewer inserted into the centre comes out clean. Turn out onto a wire rack. Serve warm.

Walnut and cheddar soda bread

preparation 30 minutes
cooking 40 minutes
makes 1 loaf

250 g (9 oz/2 cups) plain (all-purpose) flour
225 g (8 oz/1½ cups) wholemeal (whole-wheat) flour
1 tablespoon baking powder
1 teaspoon bicarbonate of soda (baking soda)
1 tablespoon soft brown sugar
60 g (2¼ oz/½ cup) walnut pieces, chopped
175 g (6 oz/1½ cups) grated mature cheddar cheese
40 g (1½ oz) butter, melted and cooled
2 eggs, lightly beaten
250 ml (9 fl oz/1 cup) buttermilk

Preheat the oven to 180°C (350°F/Gas 4). Line a baking tray with baking paper.

Sift the flours, baking powder and bicarbonate of soda into a large bowl (tip any husks from the wholemeal flour left in the sieve back into the mixture). Stir in the sugar, walnuts and cheese. Make a well in the centre. Combine the butter, eggs and buttermilk in a bowl and pour into the well. Stir with a wooden spoon until a soft dough forms, then turn out onto a lightly floured work surface. Using lightly floured hands, knead briefly just until smooth, then shape the dough into a 20 cm (8 inch) round. Transfer to a baking tray.

Using a sharp, lightly floured knife, cut a 1 cm (½ inch) deep cross into the top of the loaf. Bake for 30–40 minutes, or until golden.

Bottom: Skillet bread. Top: Lemon pepper bread.

Ham, cheese and onion quickbread

preparation 25 minutes
cooking 1 hour 5 minutes
makes 1 loaf

1 tablespoon oil
3 onions, thinly sliced into rings
2 teaspoons soft brown sugar
200 g (7 oz) sliced ham, finely chopped
375 g (13 oz/3 cups) self-raising flour
100 g (3½ oz) chilled butter
90 g (3¼ oz/¾ cup) grated cheddar cheese
125 ml (4 fl oz/½ cup) milk

Heat half of the oil in a large, heavy-based frying pan. Add the onion and cook over medium heat for 10 minutes, stirring occasionally. Add the sugar and continue to cook for 10–15 minutes, or until the onion is golden brown. Set aside to cool.

Heat the remaining oil in a small frying pan, add the ham and cook over moderately high heat until golden brown. Drain on crumpled paper towel and add to the onion. Allow to cool slightly.

Preheat the oven to 210°C (415°F/Gas 6–7). Lightly grease a baking tray. Sift the flour into a large bowl and rub in the butter with your fingertips until the mixture resembles fine breadcrumbs.

Add three-quarters of the onion mixture and 60 g (2¼ oz/ ½ cup) of the cheddar to the flour and mix well. Make a well in the centre and add the milk and about 125 ml (4 fl oz/½ cup) water (add enough water to bring the dough together). Mix with a flat-bladed knife, using a cutting action, until the mixture forms a soft dough. Gently gather together into a ball.

Lay the dough on the tray and press out to form a 22 cm (8½ inch) circle. Using a sharp knife, mark the dough into quarters, cutting two-thirds of the way through. Sprinkle with the rest of the onion mixture and the remaining cheddar. Bake for 15 minutes, then reduce the oven to 180°C (350°F/Gas 4). Cover the top loosely with foil if it starts getting too brown. Bake for another 20 minutes, or until the base sounds hollow when tapped.

Malt bread

preparation 45 minutes
cooking 40 minutes
makes 1 loaf

2 teaspoons dried yeast
1 teaspoon sugar
300 g (10½ oz/2 cups) plain (all-purpose) wholemeal (whole-wheat) flour
125 g (4½ oz/1 cup) plain (all-purpose) flour
2 teaspoons ground cinnamon
60 g (2¼ oz/½ cup) raisins
30 g (1 oz) butter, melted
1 tablespoon treacle
1 tablespoon liquid malt extract
1 tablespoon hot milk
½ teaspoon liquid malt extract, extra

Brush a 7 x 14 x 21 cm (2¾ x 5½ x 8¼ inch) loaf (bar) tin with oil and line the base with baking paper. Combine 250 ml (9 fl oz/1 cup) lukewarm water, the yeast and sugar in a small bowl. Cover with plastic wrap and set aside in a warm place for 10 minutes, or until bubbles appear on the surface. The mixture should be frothy and slightly increased in volume.

Sift the flours and cinnamon into a large bowl, then add the raisins and stir. Make a well in the centre. Add the melted butter, treacle, 1 tablespoon of malt extract and the yeast mixture. Mix to a soft dough using a flat-bladed knife. Turn onto a lightly floured surface and knead for 10 minutes, or until smooth. Shape the dough into a ball and place in a lightly oiled bowl. Set aside, covered with plastic wrap, in a warm place for 1 hour, or until well risen. Punch down the dough, then knead until smooth.

Roll into a 20 cm (8 inch) square and then roll up. Place the dough in the tin, with the seam underneath, and set aside, covered with plastic wrap, in a warm place for 40 minutes, or until well risen.

Preheat the oven to 180°C (350°F/Gas 4). Brush the dough with the combined milk and extra malt. Bake for 40 minutes or until a skewer inserted into the centre of the bread comes out clean. Set aside for 3 minutes in the tin before transferring to a wire rack to cool.

Cheese and herb pull-apart

preparation 30 minutes
cooking 30 minutes
makes 1 loaf

2 teaspoons dried yeast
1 teaspoon sugar
500 g (1 lb 2 oz/4 cups) plain (all-purpose) flour
2 tablespoons chopped flat-leaf (Italian) parsley
2 tablespoons snipped chives
1 tablespoon chopped thyme
60 g (2¼ oz) cheddar cheese, grated
milk, to glaze

Put the yeast, sugar and 125 ml (4 fl oz/½ cup) warm water in a small bowl and stir well. Leave in a warm place for 10 minutes, or until bubbles appear on the surface. The mixture should be frothy and slightly increased in volume.

Sift the flour and 1½ teaspoons salt in a large bowl. Make a well in the centre and add the yeast mixture and 250 ml

(9 fl oz/1 cup) warm water. Mix to a soft dough. Turn onto a lightly floured surface and knead for 10 minutes, or until smooth. Place the dough in an oiled bowl, cover with plastic wrap or a damp tea towel (dish towel) and leave for 1 hour, or until doubled in size.

Punch down the dough and knead for 1 minute. Divide the dough in half and shape each half into 10 flat discs, 6 cm (2½ inches) in diameter. Mix the herbs with the cheddar and put 2 teaspoons of the mixture on one of the discs. Press another disc on top, then repeat with the remaining discs and herb mixture.

Grease a 6 x 10.5 x 21 cm (2½ x 4¼ x 8¼ inches) loaf (bar) tin. Stand the filled discs upright in the prepared tin, squashing them together. Cover the tin with plastic wrap or a damp tea towel (dish towel) and leave in a warm place for 30 minutes, or until the dough is well risen.

Preheat the oven to 210°C (415°F/Gas 6–7). Lightly brush the loaf with a little milk and bake for 30 minutes, or until the bread is brown and crusty and sounds hollow when tapped on the base.

Wheatless loaf

preparation 40 minutes
cooking 35 minutes
makes 1 loaf

canola oil, for greasing
2 x 7g sachets dried yeast (4 teaspoons)
1 tablespoon sugar
625 ml (2½ cups) warm water
525 g (3½ cups) soy-free, gluten-free plain (all-purpose) flour
2 teaspoons ground sea salt
80 ml (⅓ cup) canola oil
2 tablespoons roasted buckwheat, optional
2 tablespoons canola oil, extra, to glaze

Preheat the oven to 220°C (425°F/Gas 7). Lightly grease a 14 x 20 cm (5½ x 8 inches) loaf (bar) tin.

Combine the yeast, sugar and warm water in a bowl, then stir to dissolve the yeast. Stand the bowl in a warm place for about 10 minutes, or until the mixture is frothy.

Sift the flour into a large bowl and add the salt. Make a well in the centre and add the yeast mixture and oil. Beat well with a wooden spoon.

Pour into the prepared tin and sprinkle with buckwheat, if using. Cover loosely and place in a warm place for about 20 minutes, or until the mixture comes to the top of the tin.

Bake for 20 minutes, then reduce heat to 200°C (400°F/Gas 6) and bake for a further 30–35 minutes, or until cooked. Brush with extra oil during cooking at least twice to help promote browning.

Hints *Bread is best eaten on the day of baking; alternatively, you can slice it and then freeze until required. For a high fibre loaf, add 45 g (½ cup) rice bran with the dry ingredients.*

Walnut bread

preparation 45 minutes
cooking 50 minutes
makes 1 loaf

2½ teaspoons dried yeast
90 g (3¼ oz/¼ cup) liquid malt
2 tablespoons olive oil
300 g (10½ oz/3 cups) walnut halves, lightly toasted (see Note)
540 g (1 lb 3 oz/4⅓ cups) white strong flour
1 egg, lightly beaten

Grease a baking tray. Put the yeast, liquid malt and 330 ml (11¼ fl oz/1⅓ cups) warm water in a small bowl and stir well. Leave in a warm, draught-free place for 10 minutes, or until bubbles appear on the surface. The mixture should be frothy and slightly increased in volume. Stir in the oil.

Process 200 g (7 oz/2 cups) of the walnuts in a food processor until they resemble coarse meal. Combine 500 g (1 lb 2 oz/4 cups) of the flour with 1½ teaspoons salt in a large bowl and stir in the walnut meal. Make a well and add the yeast mixture. Mix with a large metal spoon until just combined. Turn out onto a lightly floured surface and knead for 10 minutes, or until smooth, incorporating enough of the remaining flour to keep the dough from sticking — it should be soft and moist, but it won't become very springy. Shape the dough into a ball. Place in a lightly oiled bowl, cover with plastic wrap or a damp tea towel (dish towel) and leave in a warm place for up to 1½ hours, or until doubled in size.

Punch down the dough and turn out onto a lightly floured surface with very little kneading, shape the dough into a flattened 20 x 25 cm (8 x 10 inch) rectangle. Spread with the remaining walnuts and roll up firmly from the short end. Place the loaf on the baking tray, cover with plastic wrap or a damp tea towel (dish towel) and leave to rise for 1 hour, or until doubled in size.

Preheat oven to 190°C (375°F /Gas 5). Glaze the loaf with the egg and bake for 45–50 minutes, or until golden and hollow sounding when tapped. Transfer to a wire rack to cool.

Note *Use good-quality pale and plump walnuts as cheaper varieties can be bitter.*

Walnut bread

Traditional corn bread

preparation 15 minutes
cooking 25 minutes
makes 1 loaf

150 g (5½ oz/1 cup) polenta
2 tablespoons caster (superfine) sugar
125 g (4½ oz/1 cup) plain (all-purpose) flour
2 teaspoons baking powder
½ teaspoon bicarbonate of soda (baking soda)
1 egg, lightly beaten
250 ml (9 fl oz/1 cup) buttermilk
60 g (2¼ oz) butter, melted

Preheat the oven to 210°C (415°F/Gas 6–7). Brush a 20 cm (8 inch) square cake tin with oil or melted butter and line the base with baking paper.

Put the polenta and sugar in a large bowl. Add the sifted flour, baking powder, bicarbonate of soda and ½ teaspoon salt and mix thoroughly.

In a separate bowl, combine the beaten egg, buttermilk and melted butter. Stir the mixture quickly into the dry ingredients. Stir only until the ingredients are moistened. Pour the mixture into the prepared tin and smooth the surface. Bake for 20–25 minutes, or until a skewer inserted in the centre of the bread comes out clean.

Place on a wire rack and leave to cool for 10 minutes before turning out. Cut into squares and serve warm.

Beer bread rolls

preparation 15 minutes
cooking 20 minutes
makes 4

405 g (14¼ oz/3¼ cups) plain (all-purpose) flour
3 teaspoons baking powder
1 tablespoon sugar
50 g (1¾ oz) butter, chopped
375 ml (13 fl oz/1½ cups) beer

Process the flour, baking powder, sugar, butter and 1 teaspoon salt in a food processor until crumbly. Add the beer and process in bursts to form a soft dough.

Preheat the oven to 210°C (415°F/Gas 6–7). Turn the dough out onto a well-floured surface and knead until smooth, adding extra flour if needed. Divide the dough into four

balls, place on greased oven trays and flatten slightly. Brush with a little water and slash the tops with a knife. Bake for 10 minutes. Reduce the oven to 180°C (350°F/Gas 4) and bake for about 10 minutes, or until cooked. Cool on a wire rack. Serve with butter.

Scottish baps

preparation 40 minutes
cooking 30 minutes
makes 12 baps

2 teaspoons dried yeast
1 teaspoon caster (superfine) sugar
440 g (15½ oz/3½ cups) white strong flour
250 ml (9 fl oz/1 cup) lukewarm milk
50 g (1¾ oz) butter, melted
1 tablespoon plain (all-purpose) flour

Lightly dust two baking trays with flour. Put the yeast, sugar and 2 tablespoons of the white strong flour in a small bowl. Gradually add the milk, blending until smooth and dissolved. Leave in a warm, draught-free place for 10 minutes, or until bubbles appear on the surface. The mixture should be frothy and slightly increased in volume.

Sift the remaining flour and 1½ teaspoons salt into a large bowl. Make a well in the centre and add the yeast mixture and butter. Using a flat-bladed knife, mix to form a soft dough. Turn the dough onto a lightly floured surface and knead for 3 minutes, or until smooth. Shape into a ball and place in a large oiled bowl. Cover with plastic wrap or a damp tea towel (dish towel) and leave in a warm place for 1 hour, or until well risen.

Preheat the oven to 210°C (415°F/Gas 6–7). Punch down the dough with your fist. Knead the dough again for 2 minutes, or until smooth. Divide into 12 pieces. Knead one portion at a time on a lightly floured surface for 1 minute, roll into a ball and shape into a flat oval. Repeat with the remaining dough.

Place the baps on the trays and dust with the plain flour. Cover with plastic wrap and leave in a warm place for 15 minutes, or until well risen. Make an indent in the centre of each bap with your finger. Bake for 30 minutes until browned and cooked through. Serve warm.

Top left: Traditional corn bread. Top right: Beer bread rolls. Bottom left: Scottish baps.

Bagels

preparation 1 hour (+ overnight chilling and 1½–2 hours proving)
cooking 35 minutes
makes 10

5 g (⅛ oz/1½ teaspoons) dried yeast
750 g (1 lb 10 oz/5 cups) plain (all-purpose) flour
1½ tablespoons vegetable oil
90 g (3¼ oz/¼ cup) malt extract
2 teaspoons salt
1 tablespoon bicarbonate of soda (baking soda)
1 egg, whisked with 1 tablespoon water
Poppy and sesame seeds, to sprinkle

Put the yeast, 250 ml (9 fl oz/1 cup) room-temperature water and 375 g (13 oz/2½ cups) of the flour in a bowl and use a fork to stir until a coarse dough forms. Turn the dough out onto a very lightly floured work surface and knead for 4–5 minutes, until a smooth dough forms. Place the dough in a lightly floured bowl, turning to coat in the flour. Cover the bowl with plastic wrap and refrigerate overnight.

Use a large sharp knife to cut the dough into 7 or 8 pieces and place in the bowl of a stand mixer. Add 250 ml (9 fl oz/1 cup) warm water, oil, malt extract, salt and 335 g (11¾ oz/2¼ cups) of the remaining flour. Use the dough hook attachment to knead on low speed for 10–15 minutes or until the dough is smooth and very elastic and comes away from the side of the bowl. The dough should be a little soft.

Cover the bowl with plastic wrap and set aside at room temperature for 1½–2 hours or until the dough has doubled in size.

Knock back the dough with just one punch to expel the air, then turn out onto a lightly floured work surface and divide into 10 equal portions. Preheat the oven to 180°C (350°F/Gas 4). Lightly grease 2 baking trays with oil.

Place 8–10 cm (3¼–4 inches) water in a large, deep frying pan or shallow saucepan and bring to the boil. Add the bicarbonate of soda. Meanwhile, working with one portion of dough at a time, shape it into a ball on a lightly floured surface. Push your finger through the middle of the ball to form a hole, then pick it up and work it in your hands to enlarge the hole and form a ring around it, about 10–12 cm (4–4½ inches) in diameter.

Cook the bagels, in batches, in the boiling water for 2 minutes, then turn and boil for a further 90 seconds. Turn again, then use a slotted spoon to remove from the water and drain well. Transfer to the greased trays. Brush the bagels with the egg wash, then sprinkle with the poppy or sesame seeds. Bake for 20 minutes, swapping the trays halfway through cooking, or until golden and cooked through. Transfer to a wire rack to cool.

Crumpets

preparation 25 minutes (+ 1 hour proving)
cooking 44–56 minutes
makes about 12

250 ml (9 fl oz/1 cup) warm milk
2½ teaspoons caster (superfine) sugar
375 ml (13 fl oz/1½ cups) lukewarm water
10 g (¼ oz/3 teaspoons) dried yeast
450 g (1 lb/3 cups) plain (all-purpose) flour
1 teaspoon salt
½ teaspoon bicarbonate of soda (baking soda)
20 g (¾ oz) butter
Butter and berry jam, to serve

Combine the warm milk, sugar and 250 ml (9 fl oz/1 cup) of the lukewarm water in a large bowl or the bowl of a stand mixer. Sprinkle over the yeast, then set aside for 7–8 minutes or until foamy.

Add the flour and salt and use a wooden spoon or the stand mixer's paddle attachment to beat for 3–4 minutes or until smooth and elastic. Cover the bowl with plastic wrap and set aside in a warm, draught-free place for 1 hour or until the mixture is well risen and bubbly.

Stir the bicarbonate of soda into the remaining lukewarm water, then stir the mixture into the batter. Cover and set aside for 10 minutes.

Preheat the oven to 120°C (235°F/Gas ½). Heat the butter in a large non-stick frying pan over low heat and place 3–4 greased 10 cm (4 inch) egg rings in the pan (this will depend on the size of your pan). Spoon about 80 ml (2½ fl oz/⅓ cup) crumpet batter into each ring. Cook the crumpets for 8–10 minutes or until they have risen, the bases are deep golden and the tops are dry to touch, with a few small holes.

Remove the rings, turn the crumpets and cook for a further 3–4 minutes or until the tops are light golden. Transfer to a plate, cover loosely with foil and keep warm in the preheated oven while cooking the remaining crumpets. Wash, dry and grease the rings before cooking each batch. Serve the crumpets warm, with butter and jam, if desired.

Mini wholemeal loaves

preparation 40 minutes
cooking 45 minutes
makes 4 small loaves

2 teaspoons dried yeast
1 tablespoon caster (superfine) sugar
125 ml (4 fl oz/½ cup) warm milk
600 g (1 lb 5 oz/4 cups) wholemeal (whole-wheat) strong flour
60 ml (2 fl oz/¼ cup) oil
1 egg, lightly beaten

Grease four 13 x 6½ x 5 cm (5 x 2¾ x 2 inch) baking tins. Put the yeast, sugar and milk in a small bowl and mix well. Leave in a warm, draught-free place for 10 minutes, or until bubbles appear on the surface. The mixture should be frothy and slightly increased in volume.

Put the flour and 1 teaspoon salt in a large bowl, make a well in the centre and add the yeast mixture, oil and 250 ml (9 fl oz/1 cup) warm water. Mix to a soft dough and gather into a ball. Turn out onto a floured surface and knead for 10 minutes. Add a little extra flour if the dough is too sticky.

Place the dough in a large oiled bowl, cover loosely with plastic wrap or a damp tea towel (dish towel) and leave in a warm place for 1 hour, or until well risen. Punch down the dough, turn out onto a floured surface and knead for 1 minute, or until smooth. Divide into four portions, knead into shape and put in the tins. Cover loosely with plastic wrap or a damp tea towel and leave in a warm place for 45 minutes, or until risen.

Preheat the oven to 210°C (415°F/Gas 6–7). Brush the loaf tops with the beaten egg. Bake for 10 minutes, then reduce the oven temperature to 180°C (350°F/Gas 4) and bake for a further 30–35 minutes, or until the base sounds hollow when tapped. Cover with foil if the tops become too brown.

Semit

preparation 45 minutes
cooking 15 minutes
makes 20

2 teaspoons dried yeast
1 teaspoon sugar
375 g (13 oz/3 cups) plain (all-purpose) flour
125 ml (4 fl oz/½ cup) milk
125 g (4½ oz/1 cup) plain (all-purpose) flour, extra
1 egg, lightly beaten
80 g (2¾ oz/½ cup) sesame seeds

Place the yeast, sugar and 60 ml (2 fl oz/¼ cup) warm water in a small bowl and stir until dissolved. Leave in a warm, draught-free place for 10 minutes, or until bubbles appear on the surface. The mixture should be frothy and slightly increased in volume. If your yeast doesn't foam, it is dead, so you will have to discard it and start again.

Sift the flour into a bowl and season well with 1 teaspoon salt. Heat the milk and 125 ml (4 fl oz/½ cup) water together until tepid. Make a well in the flour and pour in the liquid and the yeast mixture. Mix with a wooden spoon, adding the extra flour, a little at a time (you may not need all of it), until a soft dough forms. Turn onto a lightly floured board and knead for 10 minutes, or until smooth and elastic. Place in an oiled bowl, cover and leave in a warm, draught-free place for 15 minutes, or until doubled in size.

Turn the dough onto a floured board and knock down. Break off pieces the size of an egg and roll each into a rope 1 cm (½ inch) thick and 20 cm (8 inches) long. Form the rope into a ring. Moisten the edges to seal. Continue until you have used all the dough.

Preheat the oven to 200°C (400°F/Gas 6). Place an ovenproof dish filled with hot water on the bottom of the oven to create steam while cooking the rings.

Grease two baking trays and dust with flour. Place the rings on the trays. Brush the surface with the beaten egg and sprinkle with the sesame seeds. Cover the rings with a damp tea towel (dish towel) and leave to rise in a warm place for 30 minutes. Bake the rings for 15 minutes, or until cooked and golden. While still hot, brush the rings with hot water to help create crisp crusts while they are cooling.

Rosettas

preparation 40 minutes
cooking 25 minutes
makes 10

7 g (¼ oz) dried yeast
1 teaspoon sugar
560 g (1 lb 4 oz/4½ cups) unbleached plain
(all-purpose) flour, sifted
50 g (1¾ oz) butter, softened
60 ml (2 fl oz/¼ cup) olive oil
55 g (2 oz/¼ cup) caster (superfine) sugar
milk, to glaze
plain (all-purpose) flour, extra, to dust

Grease two baking trays. Put the yeast, sugar and 125 ml (4 fl oz/½ cup) warm water in a bowl and stir well. Leave in a warm, draught-free place for 10 minutes, or until bubbles appear on the surface. The mixture should be frothy and increased in volume. If your yeast doesn't foam it is dead, so you will have to discard it.

Set aside 30 g (1 oz/¼ cup) of the flour and put the rest in a bowl with 1 teaspoon salt. Make a well in the centre. Add the yeast mixture, butter, oil, sugar and 315 ml (10¾ fl oz/1¼ cups) warm water. Stir with a wooden spoon until the dough leaves the side of the bowl and forms a rough, sticky ball. Turn out onto a floured surface. Knead for 10 minutes, or until the dough is smooth and elastic. Add enough of the reserved flour, if necessary, to make a smooth dough. Put in a lightly oiled bowl and brush the surface with melted butter or oil. Cover with plastic wrap and leave in a warm place for 1 hour, or until well risen.

Punch down the dough, then knead for 1 minute. Divide into ten portions and shape each into a smooth ball. Place balls 5 cm (2 inch) apart on trays. Using a 3 cm (1¼ inch) round cutter, press a 1 cm (½ inch) deep indent into the centre of each ball. With a sharp knife, score five evenly spaced, 1 cm (½ inch) deep cuts down side of each roll. Cover with plastic wrap and leave in a warm place for 1 hour.

Preheat the oven to 180°C (350°F/Gas 4). Brush the rolls with milk and sift a fine layer of the extra flour over them. Bake for 25 minutes, or until golden. Rotate the trays in the oven if one tray is browning faster than the other. Cool on a wire rack.

Mini baguettes

preparation 25 minutes
cooking 30 minutes
makes 3 loaves

2 teaspoons dried yeast
1 teaspoon sugar
90 g (3¼ oz/¾ cup) plain (all-purpose) flour
375 g (13 oz/3 cups) white strong flour
2 tablespoons polenta, to sprinkle

Put the yeast, sugar and 310 ml (10¾ fl oz/1¼ cups) warm water in a small bowl and mix well. Leave in a warm, draught-free place for 10 minutes, or until bubbles appear on the surface. The mixture should be frothy and slightly increased in volume.

Mix together the flours and ½ teaspoon salt and transfer half the dry ingredients to a large bowl. Make a well in the centre and add the yeast mixture. Using a large metal spoon fold the flour into the yeast mixture. This should form a soft dough. Cover the bowl with a damp tea towel (dish towel) or plastic wrap and set aside for 30–35 minutes, or until frothy and risen by about one third of its original size.

Mix in the remaining dry ingredients and add up to 60 ml (2 fl oz/¼ cup) warm water, enough to form a soft, but slightly sticky dough. Knead the dough on a lightly floured surface for about 10 minutes, or until smooth and elastic. If the dough sticks to the work surface while kneading, flour the surface sparingly, but try to avoid adding too much flour. Shape the dough into a ball and place in a large lightly greased bowl. Cover with a damp tea towel or plastic wrap and leave in a warm place for about 1 hour, until the dough has doubled in size.

Lightly grease two large baking trays and sprinkle with polenta. Punch down the dough and knead for 2–3 minutes. Divide the dough into three portions and press or roll each into a rectangle about 20 x 40 cm (8 x 16 inches). Roll each up firmly into a long sausage shape and place, seam side down, well spaced on the prepared trays. Cover loosely with a damp tea towel or plastic wrap and set aside in a warm place for 40 minutes, or until doubled in size.

Preheat the oven to 220°C (425°F/Gas 7). Lightly brush the loaves with water and make diagonal slashes across the top at 6 cm (2½ inch) intervals. Place the trays in the oven and spray the oven with water.

Bake the bread for 20 minutes, spraying inside the oven with water twice during this time. Lower the temperature to 180°C (350°F/Gas 4) and bake for another 5–10 minutes, or until the crust is golden and firm and the base sounds hollow when tapped underneath. Cool on a wire rack. Baguettes are best eaten within a few hours of baking.

Mini baguettes

Potato and olive scones

preparation 25 minutes
cooking 15 minutes
makes 15

250 g (9 oz) potatoes, chopped
125 ml (4 fl oz/½ cup) milk
250 g (9 oz/2 cups) self-raising flour
30 g (1 oz) butter, chopped
3 tablespoons black olives, pitted and chopped
3–4 teaspoons chopped rosemary
milk, extra, to glaze

Preheat the oven to 210°C (415°F/Gas 6–7). Brush a baking tray with melted butter or oil. Boil or microwave potatoes until tender. Mash the potatoes with the milk and season with freshly ground black pepper.

Sift the flour into a large bowl. Rub in the butter, using your fingertips. Add the olives and rosemary and stir until just combined. Make a well in the centre and add the mashed potato and almost all of 125 ml (4 fl oz/½ cup) water. Mix with a flat-bladed knife, using a cutting action, until the mixture forms a soft dough. Add more water if the dough is too dry.

Knead the dough briefly on a lightly floured surface until smooth. Press out to a thickness of 2 cm (¾ inch). Using a floured 5 cm (2 inch) plain round cutter, cut 15 rounds from the dough and place them on the prepared tray. Brush the tops with the extra milk and cook for about 10–15 minutes until the scones are golden brown.

Zucchini and carrot muffins

preparation 20 minutes
cooking 20 minutes
makes 12

2 zucchini (courgettes)
2 carrots
250 g (9 oz/2 cups) self-raising flour
1 teaspoon ground cinnamon
½ teaspoon freshly grated nutmeg
60 g (2¼ oz/½ cup) chopped pecans
2 eggs
250 ml (9 fl oz/1 cup) milk
90 g (3¼ oz) butter, melted

Preheat the oven to 210°C (415°F/Gas 6–7). Brush a 12-hole muffin tin with melted butter or oil. Grate the zucchinis and carrots. Sift the flour, cinnamon, nutmeg and a pinch of salt into a large bowl. Add carrot, zucchini and chopped pecans. Stir thoroughly until all the ingredients are well combined.

Combine the eggs, milk and melted butter in a separate bowl and whisk well until combined.

Make a well in the centre of the flour mixture and add the egg mixture all at once. Mix quickly with a fork or rubber spatula until all the ingredients are just moistened. (Do not over-mix — the batter should be quite lumpy.)

Spoon the batter evenly into the prepared tin. Bake for 15–20 minutes, or until golden. Loosen the muffins with a flat-bladed knife or spatula and leave in the tin for 2 minutes, before turning out onto a wire rack to cool.

Cheese and chive scones

preparation 20 minutes
cooking 12 minutes
makes 9

250 g (9 oz/2 cups) self-raising flour
30 g (1 oz) butter, chopped
60 g (2¼ oz/½ cup) grated cheddar cheese
3 tablespoons shredded parmesan cheese
2 tablespoons snipped chives
125 ml (4 fl oz/½ cup) milk
3 tablespoons grated cheddar cheese, extra

Preheat the oven to 210°C (415°F/Gas 6–7). Brush a baking tray with melted butter or oil. Sift the flour and a pinch of salt into a bowl. Rub in the butter using your fingertips. Stir in the cheeses and the chives. Make a well in the centre, add the milk and almost all of 125 ml (4 fl oz/½ cup) water. Mix lightly with a flat-bladed knife to form a soft dough, adding more water if the dough is too dry.

Knead the dough briefly on a lightly floured surface until smooth. Press out the dough to 2 cm (¾ inch) thick. Using a floured 5 cm (2 inch) plain round cutter, cut nine rounds from the dough. Place the rounds on the prepared tray and sprinkle with extra cheese. Bake for 12 minutes, or until the cheese is golden.

Top left: Potato and olive scones. Top right: Zucchini and carrot muffins. Bottom left: Cheese and chive scones.

Cheesy herb rolls

preparation 10 minutes
cooking 15 minutes
serves 4

125 g (4½ oz) butter, softened
1 tablespoon chopped basil
1 tablespoon chopped flat-leaf (Italian) parsley
1 tablespoon snipped chives
30 g (1 oz/1¼ cups) grated cheddar cheese
4 crusty rosetta rolls

Preheat the oven to 160°C (315°F/Gas 2–3). Combine the butter with the herbs and cheese and season. Cut the rolls into thin slices, but don't cut all the way through. Spread each side of each slice with the flavoured butter. Bake for 15 minutes, or until the rolls are crisp and golden.

Potato rolls

preparation 1 hour 45 minutes
cooking 30 minutes
makes 18–20 rolls

canola oil, to grease
400 g (14 oz) white-skinned potatoes,
peeled and roughly chopped
1 x 7 g sachet (2 teaspoons) dry yeast
55 g (¼ cup) sugar
60 ml (¼ cup) canola oil
ground sea salt
300–375 g (2–2½ cups) potato flour
2 eggs, or equivalent
egg replacer

Preheat the oven to 190°C (375°F/Gas 5). Lightly oil two baking trays.

Boil or steam the potatoes for 15 minutes, or until tender. Drain well, and mash until smooth. You will need 230 g (8⅛ oz/1 cup) warm mashed potato for this recipe.

In a large bowl, combine 250 ml (1 cup) warm water, yeast and half the sugar. Allow to stand for 10 minutes, or until frothy.

Add the oil, mashed potatoes and salt to the yeast mixture. Stir in 150 g (5½ oz/1 cup) of the potato flour and the remaining sugar. Beat for 1 minute with a wooden spoon. Stand in a warm place until the mixture forms a sponge. It will rise and look foamy.

Add the rest of the flour to make a firm dough. Stand in a warm place until doubled in bulk.

Turn the dough out onto a board dusted with potato flour. Using a little extra potato flour, shape the dough into rolls. Place on the prepared baking trays. Cover with plastic wrap. Stand in a warm place and let rise for 10 minutes. Brush with egg and then bake for 12 minutes.

Capsicum and corn muffins

preparation 15 minutes
cooking 20 minutes
makes 12

125 g (4½ oz/1 cup) plain (all-purpose) flour
1 tablespoon baking powder
150 g (5½ oz/1 cup) fine polenta
1 tablespoon caster (superfine) sugar
1 egg
170 ml (5½ fl oz/⅔ cup) milk
¼ teaspoon Tabasco sauce (optional)
60 ml (2 fl oz/¼ cup) oil
½ red capsicum (pepper), seeded and finely chopped
440 g (15½ oz) tinned corn kernels, drained
3 tablespoons finely chopped flat-leaf
(Italian) parsley

Preheat the oven to 210°C (415°F/Gas 6–7). Brush a 12-hole muffin tin with oil or melted butter. Sift the flour, baking powder and ¼ teaspoon salt into a large bowl. Add the polenta and sugar. Stir thoroughly until all the ingredients are well mixed. Make a well in the centre.

Combine the egg, milk, Tabasco and oil in a separate bowl. Add the egg mixture, capsicum, corn and parsley all at once to the dry ingredients. Stir quickly with a wooden spoon or rubber spatula until all the ingredients are just moistened. (Do not over-mix — the batter should be quite lumpy.)

Spoon the mixture into the tin. Bake for 20 minutes, or until golden. Loosen with a knife but leave in the tin for 2 minutes. Cool on a wire rack.

Capsicum and corn muffins

Popovers

preparation 5 minutes
cooking 35 minutes
makes 12

250 g (9 oz/2 cups) plain (all-purpose) flour
4 eggs, lightly beaten
125 ml (4 oz/½ cup) pouring (whipping) cream
250 ml (9 oz/1 cup) milk
45 g (¾ oz) butter, melted

Preheat the oven to 200°C (400°F/Gas 6). Put the flour in a food processor. With the machine running, add the eggs, cream, milk and butter and process until smooth. Pour into a jug.

Butter a 12-hole 125 ml (4 fl oz/½ cup) muffin tin and divide the mixture evenly among the holes. Place in the oven and bake for 35 minutes, or until the popovers are golden and puffy.

Clover leaf rolls

preparation 40 minutes
cooking 20 minutes
makes 16–24 rolls

2 teaspoons dried yeast
1 teaspoon caster (superfine) sugar
500 g (1 lb 2 oz) white strong flour
2 tablespoons dried whole milk powder
1 tablespoon caster (superfine) sugar, extra
60 ml (2 fl oz/¼ cup) vegetable oil

Put the yeast, sugar and 125 ml (4 fl oz/½ cup) warm water in a small bowl and stir well to combine. Leave in a warm, draught-free place for 10 minutes, or until bubbles appear on the surface. The mixture should be frothy and slightly increased in volume.

Sift the flour, milk powder, extra sugar and 1 teaspoon salt into a large bowl. Make a well in the centre, add the yeast mixture, vegetable oil and 250 ml (9 fl oz/1 cup) warm water. Mix to a soft dough using a large metal spoon. The moisture content of flour can vary greatly between brands and even between batches so add extra water or flour, 1 tablespoon at a time, if the dough is too dry or too sticky. Do not add too much flour because the dough will absorb more flour during kneading.

Divide the dough into 16–24 even pieces. Divide each piece into three even-sized balls. Place the trio of balls from each piece close together on lightly oiled baking trays and 5 cm (2 inches) apart. Cover with plastic wrap and leave in a warm place for 20 minutes, or until well risen. Preheat the oven to 180°C (350°F/Gas 4). Brush the rolls with a glaze or topping. Bake for 15–20 minutes, or until risen and golden.

Mini onion and parmesan scones

preparation 25 minutes
cooking 12 minutes
makes 24

30 g (1 oz) butter
1 small onion, finely chopped
250 g (9 oz/2 cups) self-raising flour, sifted
50 g (1¾ oz/½ cup) finely grated fresh parmesan cheese
125 ml (4 oz/½ cup) milk
cayenne pepper, to sprinkle

Preheat the oven to 210°C (415°F/Gas 6–7). Brush a baking tray with a little melted butter or oil.

Melt the butter in a small frying pan, add the onion and cook, over low heat, for 2–3 minutes or until soft. Cool slightly.

Combine the sifted flour, parmesan and a pinch salt in a bowl. Make a well in the centre and add the onion. Combine the milk with 125 ml (4 oz/½ cup) water and add almost all to the bowl. Mix lightly, with a flat-bladed knife, using a cutting action, until the mixture forms a soft dough. Add more liquid if the dough is too dry. Knead dough briefly on a lightly floured surface until smooth and press out to 2 cm (¾ inch) thick. Cut the dough into 24 rounds with a 3 cm (1¼ inch) plain round cutter. Place the rounds on the prepared tray and sprinkle each lightly with cayenne pepper. Cook for 10–12 minutes until golden brown.

Note Handle scone dough with a light touch. Cut the liquid in with a knife and then take care not to over-knead or you'll have tough scones.

Mini onion and parmesan scones

Yorkshire puddings

preparation 10 minutes
cooking 20 minutes
makes 12

60 ml (2 fl oz/¼ cup) olive oil
250 ml (9 fl oz/1 cup) milk
2 eggs, lightly whisked
150 g (5½ oz/1 cup) plain (all-purpose) flour
1 teaspoon sea salt

Preheat the oven to 200°C (400°F/Gas 6). Divide the oil among twelve 80 ml (2½ fl oz/⅓ cup) muffin tin holes. Place the tin in the oven and heat for 10 minutes.

Meanwhile, use a whisk to combine the milk, egg, flour and salt in a jug. Working quickly, remove muffin tin from the oven and pour the batter evenly among the holes. Bake for 20 minutes or until golden and puffed. Serve immediately.

Variation Herbed Yorkshire puddings: *Add 2½ tablespoons chopped chives or parsley, or 2¼ teaspoons thyme leaves, when whisking the batter to combine.*

Grissini

preparation 40 minutes + 1 hour 30 minutes proving
cooking 35 minutes
makes about 26

large pinch of caster (superfine) sugar
150 ml (5 fl oz) lukewarm water
5 g (⅛ oz/1½ teaspoons) dried yeast
1 tablespoon extra virgin olive oil
225 g (8 oz/1½ cups) plain (all-purpose) flour
1 teaspoon salt

Combine the sugar and lukewarm water in a large bowl, sprinkle over the yeast and set aside for 5–6 minutes or until foamy. Stir in the olive oil. Add the flour and salt and use a wooden spoon to stir until a coarse dough forms.

Turn out onto a lightly floured work surface and knead for 5–6 minutes or until smooth and elastic. Place in an oiled bowl, turning to coat in the oil. Cover the bowl with plastic wrap and set aside in a warm, draught-free place for 1½ hours or until doubled in size.

Preheat the oven to 180°C (350°F/Gas 4). Lightly grease 2 baking trays with oil. Knock back the dough with just one punch to expel the air. Turn out onto a lightly floured work surface and use a rolling pin to roll out to a rough

rectangle, about 22 x 34 cm (8½ x 13½ inches) (pic 1). Turn the dough so a long edge is facing you, then use a large, sharp knife to cut it widthways into 26 strips.

Use your hands to roll each strip into a thin log, about 26 cm (10½ inches) long. Some will be longer than others. Place on the greased trays and bake for 35 minutes or until golden and crisp. Transfer to wire racks to cool.

Pretzels

preparation 50 minutes
cooking 15 minutes
makes 12

1 teaspoon dried yeast
¼ teaspoon sugar
150 ml (5 fl oz) warm milk
185 g (6½ oz/1½ cups) white strong flour
30 g (1 oz) butter, melted
1 egg yolk, lightly beaten
coarse sea salt, to sprinkle

Put the yeast, sugar and warm milk in a small bowl and stir well. Leave in a warm, draught-free place for 10 minutes, or until bubbles appear on the surface. The mixture should be frothy and slightly increased in volume.

Put the flour and ¼ teaspoon salt in a large bowl and make a well in the centre. Add the yeast mixture and butter and mix to a rough dough with a wooden spoon. Turn out onto a floured surface and knead for 10 minutes until smooth and elastic.

Place into an oiled bowl, oil the surface of the dough, cover with plastic wrap or a clean tea towel (dish towel) and set aside in a warm place for 1 hour until doubled in size.

Preheat oven to 190°C (375°F/Gas 5). Line a large baking tray with baking paper. Punch down the dough and knead again for 2–3 minutes. Divide into 12 pieces. Cover the dough while working with each piece. Roll each piece into a long rope 40 cm (16 inch) long. Circle and knot into a pretzel shape. Place well spaced on the tray. Cover with a tea towel. Leave to rise in a warm, draught-free place for 20–30 minutes.

Lightly brush pretzels with the beaten egg yolk and sprinkle with sea salt. Place the pretzels in the oven and spray them twice with water before baking for 12–15 minutes, or until crisp and golden brown. Transfer to a wire rack to cool.

Top left: Yorkshire puddings. Top right: Grissini. Bottom left: Pretzels

Gozleme

preparation 40 minutes (+ 30 minutes proving)
cooking 16–24 minutes
makes 4

1 teaspoon caster (superfine) sugar
125 ml (4 fl oz/½ cup) lukewarm water
9 g (¼ oz/2½ teaspoons) dried yeast
450 g (1 lb/3 cups) plain (all-purpose) flour
½ teaspoon salt
160 ml (5¼ fl oz/⅔ cup) lukewarm milk
1 tablespoon olive oil
1 large onion, thinly sliced
2 garlic cloves, crushed
1 teaspoon paprika
¼ teaspoon cayenne pepper
100 g (3½ oz) baby spinach leaves, coarsely chopped
2 tablespoons finely chopped mint
100 g (3½ oz) firm, fresh ricotta cheese
200 g (7 oz) crumbled feta cheese
lemon wedges, to serve

Combine the sugar and lukewarm water in a small bowl. Sprinkle over the yeast, then set aside for 7–8 minutes or until foamy. Sift the flour and salt into a large bowl. Make a well in the centre, then add the yeast mixture and lukewarm milk. Use a flat-bladed knife in a cutting action to gradually mix together until a coarse dough forms. Turn out onto a lightly floured work surface and knead until smooth and elastic. Place in a lightly oiled bowl, turning to coat in the oil. Cover the bowl with plastic wrap and set aside in a warm, draught-free place for 30 minutes.

Meanwhile, heat the oil in a large frying pan over medium–high heat. Add the onion and cook, stirring, for 5 minutes. Add the garlic, paprika and cayenne pepper and cook for 1 minute or until aromatic. Add the spinach and cook, stirring occasionally, for 2 minutes or until just wilted. Transfer to a bowl, add the mint and stir to combine. Cool to room temperature.

Combine the ricotta and feta in a separate bowl. Divide dough into 4 equal portions. Working with one portion at a time, use a rolling pin to roll out on a lightly floured work surface into a 20 x 35 cm (8 x 14 inch) rectangle, about 3 mm (⅛ inch) thick. Place one-quarter of the spinach mixture over half of the rectangle, leaving a 1 cm (½ inch) border. Top with one-quarter of cheese mixture. Fold dough over to enclose the filling, then press the edges together to seal.

Preheat a large non-stick frying pan or barbecue plate over medium heat. Lightly brush the pan or plate with a little oil. Cook the gozleme, one at a time, for 2–3 minutes each side or until cooked through. Transfer to a serving plate, cut into quarters and serve immediately with lemon wedges.

Savoury flat bread

preparation 20 minutes
cooking 40 minutes
makes 6–8 rounds

canola oil, to grease
70 g (2½ oz/½ cup) brown rice flour
50 g (1¾ oz/½ cup) arrowroot
¾ teaspoon bicarbonate of soda (baking soda)
1½ teaspoons cream of tartar
90 g (3¾ oz/ 1cup) rice bran
250 ml (9 fl oz/1 cup) chicken stock or water
60 ml (2 fl oz/¼ cup) canola oil
canola oil, extra, for
greasing and glazing
1 tablespoon ground sea salt
1 tablespoon poppy seeds

Preheat the oven to 190°C (375°F/Gas 5). Grease two baking trays well.

Sift the flour, arrowroot, bicarbonate of soda and cream of tartar into a large bowl. Add the rice bran. Make a well in the centre, then add the combined stock and oil. Beat until smooth with a wooden spoon. Spoon heaped tablespoons of the dough onto the prepared trays.

Bake for 20 minutes. Remove from the oven, brush with oil and sprinkle with salt and poppy seeds. Return to the oven and bake for a further 15–20 minutes.

Moroccan flatbread

preparation 1 hour
cooking 12 minutes
makes 16

375 g (13 oz/2½ cups) wholemeal (whole-wheat) flour
1 teaspoon caster (superfine) sugar
2 teaspoons dried yeast
½ teaspoon sweet paprika
50 g (1¾ oz/⅓ cup) cornmeal
1 tablespoon oil
1 egg, lightly beaten
2 tablespoons sesame seeds

Preheat the oven to 180°C (350°F/Gas 4). Lightly grease a baking tray. Put 75 g (2¾ oz/½ cup) of the flour, the sugar, yeast, 1 teaspoon salt and 310 ml (10¾ fl oz/1¼ cups) lukewarm water in a bowl and stir until dissolved. Cover and leave in a warm, draught-free place for 10 minutes, or until bubbles appear on the surface. The mixture should be frothy and slightly increased in volume.

Sift the paprika, cornmeal and remaining flour into a bowl. Add the oil then stir in the yeast mixture. Mix to a firm dough and knead until smooth. Cover and leave in a warm, draught-free place for 20 minutes.

Divide the dough into 16 portions, roll each into a ball then flatten into 8 cm (3¼ inch) rounds. Place on the baking tray, brush with egg and sprinkle with sesame seeds. Cover and set aside for 10 minutes, or until puffed up. Bake for 12 minutes, or until golden.

Corn tortillas

preparation 15 minutes
cooking 20–25 minutes
makes 10

270 g (9½ oz/2 cups) masa harina (instant corn masa flour) plus extra, for dusting
¼ teaspoon salt

Put the masa harina and salt in a large bowl, add 330 ml (11¼ fl oz/1⅓ cups) lukewarm water and use your hands to mix together until well combined.

Sprinkle your work surface lightly with a little extra masa harina. Turn out the dough and knead for 3–5 minutes, until smooth and moist. If the dough seems a little dry, add a little water and if it seems too wet, add a little more masa harina.

Divide the dough into 10 equal portions and roll each into a ball. Cover with a slightly damp tea towel (dish towel). Cut up a medium to large snap-lock bag to make 2 squares that will cover the surface area of a 19 cm (7½ inch) diameter tortilla press (the corners can hang over the side).

Working with one ball of dough at a time, place a square of plastic on base of the tortilla press and put the ball in the centre. Cover with other square of plastic and close the press to flatten the dough. The tortilla should be about 16 cm (6¼ inches) in diameter. (Alternatively, if you don't have a tortilla press, you could flatten the balls, between plastic, using the base of a heavy casserole dish or pan. Use a rolling pin to roll flattened dough into 16 cm/6¼ inch rounds.)

Preheat a heavy-based frying pan (cast-iron is best for delivering consistent intense heat) over medium–high heat. Cook the tortilla for 30 seconds, then turn and cook for 1 minute. The tortilla should be very slightly puffed. Turn and cook for a final 30 seconds. The tortilla will be slightly charred.

Transfer the cooked tortilla to a tea towel and fold to enclose and keep warm. Repeat with the remaining balls of dough, pressing each tortilla as the previous one is cooking.

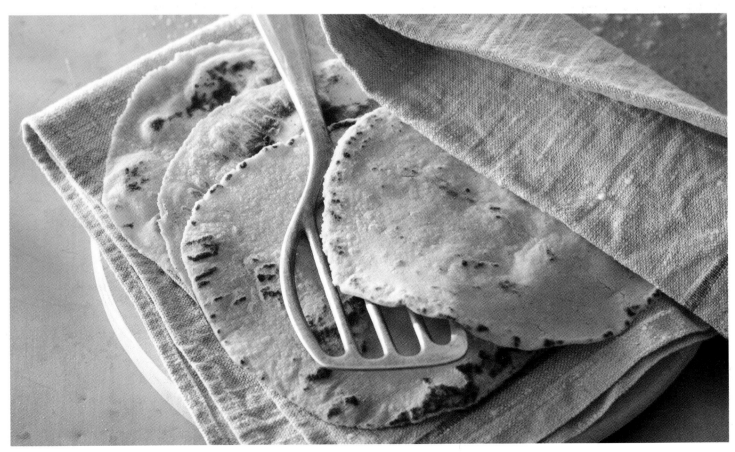

Corn Tortillas

Unleavened lavash

preparation 40 minutes + 1 hour refrigeration
cooking 35 minutes
makes 4

125 g (4½ oz/1 cup) plain (all-purpose) flour
½ teaspoon sugar
20 g (¾ oz) chilled butter, chopped
80 ml (2½ fl oz/⅓ cup) milk
sesame and poppy seeds, to sprinkle

Put the flour, sugar, butter and ½ teaspoon salt in a food processor. Process in short bursts until the butter is incorporated. With the machine running, gradually pour in the milk and process until the dough comes together — you may need to add an extra 1 tablespoon milk. Turn out onto a lightly floured surface and knead briefly until smooth. Wrap in plastic wrap and refrigerate for 1 hour.

Preheat the oven to 190°C (375°F/Gas 5). Lightly grease a large baking tray. Cut the dough into four pieces. Working with one piece at a time, roll until very thin, into a rough square shape measuring about 20 cm (8 inches) along the sides. Place the dough shapes on the tray, brush the tops lightly with water and sprinkle with the seeds. Roll a rolling pin lightly over the surface of the dough to press in the seeds. Bake for 6–8 minutes, or until golden brown and dry. Transfer to a wire rack until cool and crisp. Break into large pieces. Repeat the process with the remaining dough.

Turkish bread

preparation 30 minutes
cooking 30 minutes
makes 3 loaves

1 tablespoon dried yeast
½ teaspoon sugar
60 g (2¼ oz/½ cup) plain (all-purpose) flour
440 g (15½ oz/3½ cups) white strong flour
80 ml (2½ fl oz/⅓ cup) olive oil
1 egg, lightly beaten with 2 teaspoons water
nigella or sesame seeds, to sprinkle

Put the yeast, sugar and 125 ml (4 fl oz/½ cup) warm water in a small bowl and stir well. Add a little of the flour and mix to a paste. Leave in a warm, draught-free place for 10 minutes, or until bubbles appear on the surface. The mixture should be frothy and slightly increased in volume. If your yeast doesn't foam, it is dead, so you will have to discard it and start again.

Put the remaining flours and 1½ teaspoons salt in a large bowl and make a well in the centre. Add the yeast mixture, olive oil and 250 ml (9 fl oz/1 cup) warm water. Mix to a rough dough, then turn out onto a floured surface and knead for 5 minutes. Add minimal flour as the dough should remain damp and springy.

Shape the dough into a ball and place in a large oiled bowl. Cover with plastic wrap or a damp tea towel (dish towel) and leave in a warm place for 1 hour to triple in size. Punch down and divide into three. Knead each portion for 2 minutes and shape each into a ball. Cover with plastic wrap or a damp tea towel and leave for 10 minutes.

Roll each portion of dough into a rectangle 15 x 35 cm (6 x 14 inches). Cover with damp tea towels and leave in a warm place for 20 minutes. Indent all over the surface with your fingers, brush with the egg glaze and sprinkle with the seeds. Preheat the oven to 220°C (425°F/Gas 7).

For the best results, bake each loaf separately. Place a baking tray in the oven for a couple of minutes until hot, remove and sprinkle lightly with flour. Place one portion of dough on the hot tray and bake for 10–12 minutes, or until puffed and golden brown. Wrap in a clean tea towel to soften the crust and set aside to cool. Meanwhile, repeat baking the remaining portions of dough.

Puris

preparation 15 minutes + 50 minutes standing time
cooking 25 minutes
makes 18

375 g (13 oz/2½ cups) wholemeal (whole-wheat) flour
1 tablespoon ghee or oil
oil, for frying

Sift the wholemeal flour with a pinch of salt. Using your fingertips, rub in the ghee. Gradually add 250 ml (9 oz/1 cup) water to form a firm dough. Knead on a lightly floured surface until smooth. Cover with plastic wrap and set aside for 50 minutes.

Divide the dough into 18 portions and roll each into a 14 cm (5½ inch) circle. Heat 3 cm (1¼ inches) oil in a deep frying pan until moderately hot. Fry one puri at a time, spooning oil over until they puff up and swell. Cook on each side until golden brown. Drain on paper towel. Serve immediately.

Note *A puri is a traditional Indian bread, much like a deep-fried chapati, which puffs and swells as it cooks.*

Pitta bread

preparation 25 minutes + 1½–2 hours proving
cooking 15–20 minutes
makes 8

large pinch of sugar
310 ml (10¾ fl oz/1¼ cups) lukewarm water
7 g (⅛ oz/2 teaspoons) dried yeast
225 g (8 oz/1½ cups) plain (all-purpose) flour, plus extra, to dust
200 g (7 oz/1⅓ cups) plain (all-purpose) wholemeal (whole-wheat) flour, plus extra, for dusting
1½ tablespoons olive oil
1 teaspoon salt

Combine the sugar and 125 ml (4 fl oz/½ cup) of the lukewarm water in a large bowl, sprinkle over the yeast and set aside for 5–6 minutes or until foamy. Combine the flours in a bowl. Add the remaining lukewarm water and half the flour to the yeast mixture and use a wooden spoon to stir vigorously for 3–4 minutes or until the mixture is well combined and very elastic.

Cover bowl with plastic wrap and set aside for 10 minutes or until bubbly. Add the oil and salt and stir to combine, then gradually add the remaining flour, mixing well between each addition, until a soft, coarse dough forms. You may not need all the flour.

Turn out onto a lightly floured work surface and knead for 7–8 minutes or until smooth and elastic, adding a little extra flour if dough remains sticky. Put in a lightly oiled large bowl, turning to coat in oil. Cover bowl with plastic wrap and set aside in a warm, draught-free place for 1½–2 hours or until doubled in size.

Preheat the oven to 240°C (475°F/Gas 8) or to the maximum temperature. Knock back dough with just one punch to expel the air, then turn out onto a lightly floured work surface and divide into 8 equal portions. Working with one portion at a time, roll into a ball and then use a rolling pin to roll out to a round about 22 cm (8½ inches) in diameter. Place rounds on pieces of non-stick baking paper dusted with extra plain flour. Dust each round of dough with a little wholemeal flour, then cover with tea towels (dish towels).

Preheat a baking tray in the oven. Dust the tray with extra plain flour and place 2–3 rounds of dough on it, depending on size. Bake for 5 minutes or until puffed. Transfer to a baking tray or plate, stacking them as you go, and cover with a tea towel. Continue baking the breads, one tray at a time, until they are all baked.

Pitta bread

Chapattis

preparation 40 minutes
cooking 40 minutes
makes 20

310 g (11 oz/2½ cups) fine wholemeal (whole-wheat) flour
1 tablespoon oil
60 g (2¼ oz/½ cup) fine wholemeal (whole-wheat) flour, extra

Place the flour and 1 teaspoon salt in a large mixing bowl. Make a well in the centre. Add the oil and 250 ml (9 fl oz/ 1 cup) warm water all at once and use a wooden spoon, then your hands, to mix to a firm dough. Turn onto a lightly floured surface and knead for 15 minutes. Do not add the extra flour at this stage. Form dough into a smooth ball and place in a bowl. Cover with plastic wrap and set aside for at least 2 hours or overnight.

Divide the dough into 20 even-sized pieces. Form each piece into a smooth ball. With the aid of the extra flour, roll each ball into a thin, pancake-sized circle. Cover each chapatti with floured plastic wrap and leave to rest while rolling the remaining dough.

Heat a heavy-based frying pan until hot. Cook each chapatti for 1 minute, then turn and cook the other side for another minute. Adjust the heat so that the dough browns but does not burn. While the chapatti is cooking, press the edges with a folded tea towel (dish towel). This will help bubbles to form and make the chapatti lighter. Stack and wrap the cooked chapattis in a clean tea towel to keep them warm and soft. Serve immediately.

Parathas

preparation 30 minutes
cooking 20 minutes
makes 10

280 g (10 oz/2¼ cups) atta flour
40 g (1½ oz) ghee
extra melted ghee or oil, to brush and for pan-frying

Put the atta flour and a pinch of salt in a large bowl. Using your fingertips, rub in the ghee until fine and crumbly. Make a well in the centre and gradually add 185 ml (6 fl oz/¾ cup) cold water to form a firm dough.

Turn the dough out onto a well-floured surface and knead until smooth. Cover with plastic wrap and set aside for 40 minutes. Divide the dough into 10 equal portions. Roll each on a floured surface to form a 13 cm (5 inch) circle. Brush lightly with melted ghee. Cut from the centre of each round to the outer edge. Roll from one cut edge tightly to

form a cone shape, then press down on the pointed top (doing this forms the traditional flaky layers of the bread). Re-roll into a 13 cm (5 inch) circle. Cook one at a time in hot ghee or oil in a frying pan for about 1 minute each side until puffed and lightly browned on both sides. Drain on paper towel.

Naan

preparation 45 minutes + 1 hour proving
cooking 15 minutes
makes 6 naan

150 ml (5 fl oz) lukewarm milk
2 teaspoons caster (superfine) sugar
7 g (⅛ oz/2 teaspoons) dried yeast
450 g (1 lb/3 cups) plain (all-purpose) flour
1 teaspoon salt
1 teaspoon baking powder
2 tablespoons vegetable oil, plus extra, to grease
150 g (5½ oz) plain yoghurt
1 egg, lightly whisked

Combine the milk and sugar in a small bowl, sprinkle over the yeast and set aside for 5–6 minutes or until foamy.

Sift the flour, salt and baking powder into a large bowl. Add the yeast mixture, oil, yoghurt and egg. Stir with a wooden spoon to form a coarse dough.

Turn out onto a lightly floured work surface and knead for 10 minutes or until smooth and elastic. Shape into a ball and place in an oiled bowl, turning to coat in the oil. Cover the bowl with plastic wrap and set aside in a warm, draught-free place for 1 hour or until doubled in size.

Preheat the oven to 240°C (475°F/Gas 8). Preheat a large, heavy-based baking tray in the oven. If your oven has a separate grill (broiler), preheat that to high also.

Knock back the dough with just one punch to expel the air and divide it into 6 equal portions. Roll each portion into a ball, place on a lightly greased baking tray and cover with plastic wrap. Working with one ball at a time, use a rolling pin to roll out on a lightly floured work surface into a rough oval, about 25 cm (10 inches) long and 13 cm (5 inches) wide.

Working quickly, remove the hot baking tray from the oven and slap 2 naan bread onto it. Immediately place in the oven and bake for 3 minutes or until puffed. Transfer to a large tea towel (dish towel) to keep warm. Repeat to cook the remaining naan.

If your grill is not separate to the oven, change the oven setting to grill and preheat on the highest heat, or use the preheated separate grill. Grill (broil) each naan, about 10 cm (4 inches) from the heat, for 40–45 seconds each side, until lightly scorched.

index

Index

Published in 2012 by Murdoch Books Pty Limited

Murdoch Books Australia
Pier 8/9, 23 Hickson Road
Millers Point NSW 2000
Phone: +61 (0) 2 8220 2000
Fax: +61 (0) 2 8220 2558
www.murdochbooks.com.au

Murdoch Books UK Limited
Erico House, 6th Floor
93–99 Upper Richmond Road
Putney, London SW15 2TG
Phone: +44 (0) 20 8785 5995
Fax: +44 (0) 20 8785 5985
www.murdochbooks.co.uk

Publishing Director: Chris Rennie
Project Manager: Liz Malcolm
Cover Design: Adam Walker
Design: Susanne Geppert
Editor: Justine Harding
Index: Jo Rudd
Production: Alexandra Gonzalez

National Library of Australia Cataloguing-in-Publication Data:
The soup bible.
ISBN: 978-1-74266-721-8 (pbk.)
Includes index.
Subjects: Soups.
Cooking.
641.813

A catalogue record for this book is available from the British Library.

Printed by C&C Offset Pty Ltd. PRINTED IN CHINA